Oxford Studies in Lexicography and Lexicology

Series editors
Richard Bailey, Noel Osselton, and Gabriele Stein

Aspects of Semantic Opposition
in English

Aspects of Semantic Opposition in English

ARTHUR METTINGER

CLARENDON PRESS · OXFORD
1994

Oxford University Press, Walton Street, Oxford OX2 6DP
Oxford New York Toronto
Delhi Bombay Calcutta Madras Karachi
Kuala Lumpur Singapore Hong Kong Tokyo
Nairobi Dar es Salaam Cape Town
Melbourne Auckland Madrid
and associated companies in
Berlin Ibadan

Oxford is a trade mark of Oxford University Press

Published in the United States
by Oxford University Press Inc., New York

British Library Cataloguing in Publication Data
Data available

Library of Congress Cataloging in Publication Data
Aspects of semantic opposition in English / Arthur Mettinger.
(Oxford studies in lexicography and lexicology)
Includes bibliographical references and index.
1. English language—Semantics. 2. English language—Synonyms and
antonyms. I. Title. II. Series.
PE1585.M43 1994   401'.43—dc20   93-5372
ISBN 0-19-824269-7

1 3 5 7 9 10 8 6 4 2

Set by Hope Services (Abingdon) Ltd.
Printed in Great Britain on acid-free paper by
Bookcraft (Bath) Ltd., Midsomer Norton

Contents

Abbreviated Titles of Texts Cited
in Examples

For full bibliographical details, see the Bibliography at the end of the book.

ACP	A. Christie, *The adventure of the Christmas pudding and a selection of entrées*
AF	A. Christie, *After the funeral*
AHT	J. Listowel, *A Habsburg tragedy: Crown Prince Rudolf*
CP	D. Lodge, *Changing places: a tale of two campuses*
DAF	I. Fleming, *Diamonds are forever*
DON	A. Christie, *Death on the Nile*
DTA	N. Mitford, *Don't tell Alfred*
DW	A. Christie, *Dumb witness*
EEA	B. Cartland, *The private life of Elizabeth Empress of Austria*
EU	K. Amis, *Ending up*
HP	A. Christie, *Hallowe'en party*
LJ	K. Amis, *Lucky Jim*
LM	A. Christie, *The Listerdale mystery*
MAAS	A. Christie, *The mysterious affair at Styles*
MBT	A. Christie, *The mystery of the Blue Train*
MIE	A. Christie, *Murder is easy*
MMFC	A. Christie, *Miss Marple's final cases*
MOL	A. Christie, *The murder on the links*
MRA	A. Christie, *The murder of Roger Ackroyd*
NEM	A. Christie, *Nemesis*
NOM	A. Christie, *N or M?*
PEC	A. Christie, *Poirot's early cases*
PFR	A. Christie, *A pocket full of rye*
PI	A. Christie, *Poirot investigates*
POF	A. Christie, *Postern of fate*

Introduction

Yes, I cannot help still believing in two lovers who wished to get married, who were ready to take each other on for **better**, for **worse**, for **richer**, for **poorer**, in **sickness** and in **health**. She loved him and she would have taken him for **better** or for **worse**. As far as she had gone, she took him for **worse**. It brought about her death.

(NEM, 176, 177)

Binary semantic opposition, as exemplified above, has for a long time been regarded as an important means of structuring the vocabulary of natural languages and has therefore been receiving the due attention of linguists. The majority of studies concerning themselves with this topic are highly theoretical in nature, thus arriving deductively at classifications and subclassifications of binary semantic opposition into various types, without, however, considering an appropriate amount of data. The primary aim of this study is therefore to provide a treatment of binary meaning-relations obtaining between lexemes of the English language on a considerably enlarged empirical basis. For this purpose two corpora have been used: one is a collection of about 350 pairs of opposites as listed in the 1972 edition of *Roget's Thesaurus of English words and phrases*, whose meanings have been checked with Hornby's *Advanced learner's dictionary*. Their analysis in terms of semantic dimensions and semantic-feature relationships is given in Chapter 5; this is the first attempt at an analysis of this type comprising a larger number of opposites in English and will, hopefully, serve as a basis for discussion and further investigation in this field. In addition to this, a corpus of "opposites in context" has been assembled from forty-three (predominantly British) novels. This collection comprises more than 350 pairs of morphologically related and morphologically unrelated lexemes in a variety of contexts: morphologically related lexemes were, of

course, easier to find; the criterion for the inclusion of morphologically unrelated lexemes was their contiguous occurrence in
the investigated texts and, of course, my intuitive feeling that
they ought to be regarded as opposites in one way or the other.
The "opposites in context" corpus has, in fact, several important
functions:

(a) it has proved to be a valuable source of material for illus-
    trating, corroborating, or disproving theoretical assump-
    tions regarding semantic opposition;

(b) as the material contained in it is partially identical with the
    material analysed in Chapter 5 it has been possible to use
    it for the purpose of exemplification, which is particularly
    important with regard to gradability phenomena;

(c) 161 pairs of opposites contained in it have been used for a
    closed-set investigation and classification of syntagmatic
    relations (given in Chapter 2); and

(d) it has freed me from having to rely solely on dictionaries
    and introspection.

As to the theoretical framework within which binary semantic
opposition will be treated in this study, I must admit that I have
found it difficult to confine myself to one, narrowly limited
"model". As the main purpose of this study is to arrive at a
coherent description and explanation of a specific type of semantic relation obtaining between English lexemes, a descriptively
and explanatorily adequate framework had to be established
within which those tasks could be performed. It has turned out
that a basically structuralist semantic theory with a mentalistic
concept of meaning and a treatment of semantic relations as
properties of the language-system is most capable of achieving
this goal. Of course, generative grammar in its Standard Theory
version and Prototype semantics have also been considered,
although I have certainly been influenced more strongly by the
works of Coseriu, Geckeler, and Kastovsky, as well as by English
structuralist semanticists such as Lyons and Cruse. It is most
important to point out that in this study I have tried to give an
account of "antonymy" (in the wide sense of the term) along
strictly semantic lines, which entails that logical and pragmatic
factors have been regarded as having secondary importance.

Chapter 1 presents existing studies on the topic, both within linguistics proper and within related fields of studies, discusses the two senses in which the term "antonymy" is used, argues briefly against the treatment of semantic opposition in terms of logic or in terms of "polarity" (especially within one framework of transformational grammar), and then presents some basic ideas for the further treatment of semantic opposition in this study.

Chapter 2 is dedicated to opposites in texts (i.e. in language use), and is concerned especially with the distribution of pairs of opposites in contiguity, which inevitably leads to the question of when to treat a pair thus established as an instance of oppositeness of meaning on a systematic, semantic level, and when to treat such pairs as extralinguistically determined. This question is further discussed in Chapter 3.

Chapter 4 contains a presentation of various types of oppositeness of meaning, established on the most important semantic criterion, viz. scalarity. A differentiation will be made between "central" and "peripheral" oppositeness of meaning: the former will be the main topic of Chapter 4, and I will try to show that central oppositeness of meaning can be adequately handled in a model that operates with scalar semantic dimensions of various kinds.

Chapter 5 presents the analyses of the *Roget's Thesaurus* corpus according to the principles established in this study.

Chapter 6, finally, considers some remaining problems (questions of markedness, the alleged parallelism between phonological and semantic opposition) and briefly deals with the question whether the conclusions reached for central oppositeness of meaning in English might have parallels in other languages and could perhaps be regarded as linguistic universals.

1

"Antonymy": Scope and Delimitations

1.1 SOME REMARKS ON THE STATE OF THE ART

1.1.1 *Instead of a historical survey*

In studies such as the present one it is customary to give a critical survey of all the work that has been done so far in the respective field of research. To do so with regard to antonymy[1] would, however, lead to a monograph with a title like *Antonymy: the history of a term and a concept in philosophy, rhetoric,[2] logic, and linguistics, including lexicography, psycholinguistics, language acquisition, and text-linguistics* and clearly go beyond the scope of this book. Moreover, Gsell (1979) can be regarded as a valuable source of information on the treatment of antonymy up to the mid-seventies, with special emphasis on Romance studies; the chapter on 'Nichtstrukturelle Ansätze' (Gsell 1979, 24–34, with a discussion of works by Ch. Bally, C. K. Ogden, M. Peter, O. Ducháček, L. Guilbert, J. Pohl) is of special interest as it demonstrates some of the ideas "structuralist" semanticists such as Eugenio Coseriu and John Lyons drew upon when formulating their theories.[3] In line with the growing interest in linguistic semantics in the sixties and seventies antonymy has been given its place in handbooks on linguistics (e.g. Lyons 1968, 460 ff.), semantics proper (e.g. Leech 1974, Lyons 1977, Viehweger *et al.* 1977, Palmer 1981, Kastovsky 1982*b*, Cruse 1986),[4] and lexicology (e.g. Fomina 1978, Agricola and Agricola 1979, Hansen *et al.* 1982, H. Schmidt 1985, Lipka 1990), and a vast number of articles connected with the topic has been and is still being published. Unfortunately, Komissarov's (1957, 51) critical remark still holds true for many of them:

Normally a traditional definition is given, in which it is stated that antonyms are words with an opposite meaning, and then a number of words are cited which are, according to the author, antonyms. Apart from that, these lists normally contain words with completely different semantic characteristics. [translation A.M.]

In her discussion of antonymy and markedness Lehrer (1985) characterizes the situation as follows:

Standard treatments of antonymy regularly state that of a pair of antonyms, one member is marked while the other one is unmarked. Certain semantic and syntactic properties are predicated of the unmarked (or in some cases of the marked) member of the pair. A few examples are given, usually 20 or so, which bear out the predictions. (Lehrer 1985, 397)

There are, indeed, only a few studies of antonymy based on a larger collection of data, and the majority of them are concerned with French vocabulary. Thus, Gsell (1979) gives a word-class-differentiating typology of antonymous relations between approximately 1,900 French lexemes drawn from the 5,082 most frequent words of French as presented in Juilland *et al.*'s *Frequency dictionary of French words* (1970);[5] Nellessen (1982) arrives at a classification of antonymous verbs in Modern French into seven types, his basis of investigation being Busse and Dubost's *Französisches Verblexikon: die Konstruktion der Verben im Französischen* (1977).[6] Despite their undeniable merits both studies share a major drawback: they present results of analyses but not the analyses themselves, which means that the application of the criteria that were used in arriving at the aforementioned results remains in the dark—a drawback that this study will try to overcome (cf. Chapter 5).

The situation is even more deplorable with regard to the treatment of antonymy in English: Rusiecki (1985) is 'an attempt at presenting a unified approach to the semantics of gradable adjectives in English, in all their forms . . . and in all their uses' (Rusiecki 1985, xiii), done in set-theoretical terms, and based upon the University College London Survey of English Usage and on elicitation tests carried out by the author in London. Rusiecki's study, though containing some interesting theoretical points, seems not so much a description of the semantics of gradable adjectives in English but rather a characterization of the criteria a class of referents must meet in order to be referable to by a given gradable adjective. Nevertheless, the monograph is helpful because of the material it provides, especially for those who—like myself in Chapter 5 of this work—attempt an analysis of antonymous lexemes without contextualization.

Lehrer (1985) presents a sample of 17 questions concerning problems of markedness in connection with 158 pairs of antonymous English lexemes (adjectives, including past participles, and nouns) without, however, discussing them in greater detail. Still, Lehrer's list of gradable antonyms can be regarded as a further collection of material against which to check one's own data.[7]

In fact, Hundsnurscher's critical observation still holds true, at least as far as the empirical investigation of antonymy is concerned:

aber die bisherigen Arbeiten über Semantik kranken eben daran, dass sie dem methodischen Hauptproblem, nämlich den Materialmassen, aus dem Wege gehen: weder in der Phonologie noch in der Syntax sind solche Mengen an Material zu bewältigen und zu klassifizieren wie gerade in der Semantik.[8] (Hundsnurscher 1971, 26)

Studying antonymy in English empirically is, in a way, like fighting windmills: on the one hand it is extremely difficult to find "discovery procedures" for locating antonyms in English texts; on the other hand, if word-lists (as found in dictionaries of antonyms, for example) are taken as the basis of investigation important contextual information is missing. Moreover, it remains questionable whether the lists taken as the source contain all the relevant lexical material. Yet, despite Gsell's statement 'Es ist der deskriptiven Wortforschung grundsätzlich nicht möglich, auch bei einer noch so punktuellen Themenstellung, den gesamten Wortschatz einer natürlichen Sprache zu berücksichtigen, da dieser eine "offene Liste" darstellt'[9] (Gsell 1979, 96), I believe it is necessary to analyse and classify at least part of the vocabulary of a natural language (as is done in Chapter 5 of this study). Another, much more serious, methodological question is whether (and if so, how) to incorporate textual evidence into a study of antonymy in a natural language. Gsell, whose monograph can be regarded as the most comprehensive empirical treatment of antonymy so far, has decided against such a procedure for the following reasons:

Diese Erwägungen führen uns dazu . . . zu verzichten . . . auf den Versuch, ein Corpus von Originaltexten schriftlicher oder mündlicher Art als Materialgrundlage zu wählen, . . . nicht nur wegen der sicher überwindlichen Schwierigkeiten seiner Aufstellung bzw. Gewinnung, sondern vor allem, weil es einen geradezu unvorstellbaren Umfang haben müsste, sollte es einen wirklich repräsentativen Ausschnitt aus dem Gesamtwortschatz enthalten. Dazu kommt noch, dass der Hauptvorteil des Corpus, den untersuchten Wortschatz jeweils in authentischen Kontexten zu liefern, erst dann zum Tragen kommt, wenn für jedes Wort nicht nur einige wenige Umgebungen vorliegen, die durch die Zufälligkeiten der Textauswahl bestimmt sind, sondern so viele, dass einigermassen fundierte Aussagen über die Typizität der je einzelnen Verwendungsweise möglich wären.[10] (Gsell 1979, 97 f.)

This statement is probably true if the investigating linguist relies solely and absolutely on a collected corpus of (in most cases written) utterances. On the other hand, it seems necessary to check deductively established theories about linguistic phenomena against actual language data, and for that purpose a sample of antonyms in various contexts is indispensable. Moreover, such a collection of contextualized antonyms, incomplete as it may be, can and does make inductive generalizations possible that might otherwise be missed.[11]

1.1.2 Related studies

Before establishing reasons for the treatment of antonymy as a systemic linguistic phenomenon I would like to mention some studies dealing with antonymy from various other, related points of view, viz. psychology, language acquisition, naming and categorization, and, finally, philosophy and logic.[12]

For many years psychologists have been making use of the "semantic differential" proposed by Osgood *et al.* (1957):

The semantic differential is essentially a combination of **controlled association and scaling procedures**. We provide the subject with a **concept** to be differentiated and a **set of bipolar adjectival scales** against which to do it, his only task being to indicate, for each item (**pairing of a concept with a scale**), the direction of his association and its intensity on a seven-step scale. (Osgood *et al.* 1957, 20 [my emphasis])

The seven-step scale is established by combining each member of an antonymous adjective pair with 'the linguistic quantifiers "extremely," "quite," and "slightly," in both directions from a neutral "meaningless" origin' (Osgood *et al.* 1957, 327) in such a way that when a subject judges a concept like "father" against "happy"—"sad", "hard"—"soft", "slow"—"fast", etc. and arrives at a judgement for "father" as "slightly happy", "quite hard", "slightly fast", etc.,

each judgment represents a selection among a set of given alternatives and serves to localize the concept as a point in the semantic space. The larger the number of scales and the more representative the selection of these scales, the more validly does this point in the space represent the operational meaning of the concept. (Osgood *et al.* 1957, 26)

The actual "measurement of meaning" is a highly complex process, and what is measured is, in fact, the psychological aspect of meaning as one important variable of human behaviour, i.e.

those cognitive states of human language users which are necessary antecedent conditions for selective encoding of lexical signs and necessary subsequent conditions in selective decoding of lexical signs in messages. Within the general framework of learning theory, the meaning of a sign was identified as a representational mediation process—representational by virtue of comprising some portion of the total behavior elicited by the significate and mediating because this process, as a kind of self-stimulation, serves to elicit overt behaviors, both linguistic and non-linguistic, that are appropriate to the things signified. (Osgood *et al.* 1957, 318 f.)

Semantic measurement is intended to be applicable to 'attitude assessment, the study of personality traits and dynamisms . . . studies in psycholinguistics, in aesthetics, in advertising,[13] and in other mass communications' (Osgood *et al.* 1957, 329).

The fifty pairs of antonymous adjectives constituting bipolar scales (as listed in Osgood *et al.* 1957, 36) thus fulfil a merely auxiliary task, serving as triggers for psychological, associative reactions. The scales they establish are psychological ones, not semantic ones,[14] and are therefore of little interest to the semanticist who is basically interested in the meaning-relations holding between the members of such pairs of antonymous lexemes.

Of greater interest for our topic is the evidence of word-association tests. Clark states that '[i]f a stimulus [in a word association game] has a common "opposite" (an antonym), it will always elicit that opposite more often than anything else. These responses are the most frequent found anywhere in word associations' (Clark 1970, 275). These observations have led Clark to formulate the "minimal-contrast rule" which, based on the assumption that the surface structure realization of words can be assigned abstract deep structure characterizations consisting of hierarchically ordered features,[15] is proposed in the following form: '"Change the sign of one feature, beginning with the bottommost feature"'(Clark 1970, 276) and which, allowed to apply several times, is meant to account for *man* eliciting *woman* (by a change in the ultimate feature [+Male] to [−Male]) on the one hand and *boy* (by a change in the penultimate feature [+Adult] to [−Adult]) on the other hand.[16] The assumption of a "minimal contrast" obtaining between antonyms has been a basic tenet in linguistic research of antonymy in natural languages too. Cf.:

Opposites possess a unique fascination, and exhibit properties which may appear paradoxical. Take, for instance, the simultaneous closeness, and distance from one another, of opposites. The meanings of a pair of opposites are felt intuitively to be maximally separated . . . The closeness of opposites, on the other hand, manifests itself, for instance, in the fact that the members of a pair have almost identical distributions, that is to say, very similar possibilities of normal and abnormal occurrence . . . The paradox of simultaneous difference and similarity is partly resolved by the fact that opposites typically differ along only one dimension of meaning: in respect of all other features they are identical, hence their semantic closeness; along the dimension of difference, they occupy opposing poles, hence the feeling of difference. (Cruse 1986, 197)

Another field of research that must be mentioned in connection with antonymy is that of language acquisition,[17] which, though not directly relevant for a treatment of antonymy within the semantic framework adopted in this study, has been providing valuable additional information. Thus, Nelson and Benedict (1974) have shown for a group of thirty-three children (aged 3 years 10 months to 6 years 7 months) that there are apparently three ways in which children can code attributes or states of objects:

1. Absolute or categorial coding. In the case of adjectives used in this way, the entity is considered to either display or not display the property. There may be a true continuum with a· threshold above which the property is assigned and below which it is not, or there may be a specification that any degree of the presence of the quality indicates its assignment to that category. 'Striped,' 'furry,' 'round,' [*sic*] and 'red' are examples of this type.

2. Contrastive coding. For properties of this type, two poles at opposite ends of a continuum are involved and each is given a unique name. A middle ground exists between them which is neutral with respect to the antonymous quality. Common opposites such as 'happy'—'sad,' 'pretty'—'ugly,' and 'clean'—'dirty' belong to this type . . . They are dichotomous—each pole indicates the presence of a unique property, but one which represents an extreme along a common dimension such as affect or aesthetic quality. The two ends are therefore mutually exclusive in their application.

3. Relative coding. Adjectives such as 'big'—'little,' 'long'—'short,' 'thick'—'thin' . . . are abstractly characterized by two antonymous poles, as are the contrastive adjectives above, and each pole is given a unique lexical term. However, the *application* of these adjectives is always relative, not dichotomous. 'Big' and 'little', for example, are always relative, not only to each other but to the class of entities being considered. A comparison between two points along a scale is always involved when these terms are used. But the scale itself, as well as the location of the points, is relative to the perceptual array or to a stored class standard . . . (Nelson and Benedict 1974, 334 f.)

The study shows that contrastive terms and absolute terms are acquired more readily than relative terms but that, once acquired, 'greater difficulty of processing complexity is associated primarily with the comparative forms of the contrastive and absolute types. Relativity *per se* does not increase complexity' (Nelson and Benedict 1974, 341). These observations will become more important later in connection with the process of establishing semantic scales (cf. Chapter 4, where I will show that the differences between what Nelson and Benedict call "contrastive terms" and "relative terms" are due to different qualities of the scales involved). Another important observation is that contrastive terms—in contradistinction to relative ones—do not depend on internalized class norms or perceptual comparison. Cf.:

Thus relative terms such as 'long' and 'short' are learned as the expression of an apparent *relationship* between two objects. Contrastive terms like 'happy' and 'sad', however, are learned as the expression of a single *quality*, and to use the comparative form a comparison between two degrees of this quality must be made. This is apparently a more complex operation than the identification of either the categorical presence of a quality or the direction of a perceptually apparent relationship of size [better: length (A.M.)]. (Nelson and Benedict 1974, 341)

Experimental psycholinguistic studies, such as the ones on *near* vs. *far* (Colombo and Seymour 1983), *same* vs. *different* (Glucksberg *et al.* 1976), and especially on the acquisition of *front* vs. *back*, and *side* (Kuczaj II and Maratsos 1975) should not be overlooked, as their results contradict linguistic hypotheses on antonymy and markedness and thus prompt modifications of the respective theories. The fact, for example, that *front* and *back* are acquired simultaneously is accounted for in the following way:

More generally, at least two factors seem important for the acquisition of antonymic terms: the complexity of the meanings of each term and the complexity of the dimension along which they lie as opposites. The relative difficulty of each of these factors could lead to different acquisition outcomes. Where the dimension of opposition is relatively simple compared with the meaning of the individual terms, the oppositeness of the terms may be formulated by the child before he completely understands the meaning of either term, leading to the outcome found for *front* and *back* (which are indeed on a relatively simple dimension of opposition, on an axis through physical objects). When, in contrast, the continuum of opposition is complex relative to the individual meanings of the antonyms, an outcome such as noted by the [supporters of markedness theory] may ensue: the positive term is learned first and applied with some generality before the opposite negative term is acquired. (Kuczaj II and Maratsos 1975, 208)

In recent years yet another scientific context in which antonymy figures rather prominently has been established, viz. the study of conceptualization and categorization as domains of human cognition. In contradistinction to structural semantics[18] the aim of such studies is the investigation of 'the general character of conceptual structure in human cognition' (Talmy 1986, 2), based on the following assumption:

Die kognitiven Leistungen des Menschen, zu denen insbesondere die Beherrschung der natürlichen Sprache gehört, sind modular strukturiert, das heisst, sie beruhen auf dem Zusammenwirken verschiedener spezifischer Systeme und Subsysteme. Die verschiedenen Modalitäten der Wahrnehmung, die begriffliche Organisation der Erfahrung, die soziale Interaktion und die Sprache sind solche Systeme, die in sich wiederum modular strukturiert sind.[19] (Bierwisch *et al.* 1984, 490)

A group of German linguists has investigated spatial adjectives in German with special emphasis on 'cognitive operations organizing acts of comparison and conditions of spatial orientation'

(Bierwisch *et al.* 1984, 490);[20] Dirven and Taylor (1986) have concerned themselves with the conceptualization of vertical space in English, especially the concept of TALLNESS, its lexicalization, and resulting collocability phenomena; Bierwisch (1986) discusses *tall* vs. *short* with regard to their location on a conceptual scale of HEIGHT. Finally, Talmy (1986) discusses the relation of grammar to cognition,[21] stressing the assumption that a 'set of grammatically specified notions collectively constitutes the fundamental conceptual structuring system of language [such that] . . . grammar, broadly conceived, is the determinant of conceptual structure within one cognitive domain, language . . .' (Talmy 1986, 1 f.). The concepts and notions postulated by Talmy are regarded as being characteristic of language as a whole ("langage" in Saussurean terms) and thus universal. One such grammatically specified notion that may be regarded as pertinent to the study of antonymy is "axiality". Contrasting *He's slightly sick* vs. **He's slightly well* with *He's almost well* vs. *?He's almost sick* Talmy finds parallels with expressions specifying spatial relations (e.g. *at the border* corresponding to *well* and *past the border* corresponding to *sick*) and draws the following conclusions:

This behavior can be accounted for by positing that such adjectives, in referring to a more generic notional parameter, such as that of 'health', are not simply 'opposites' but, rather, presuppose a schematic axis that is structured and directed in a particular way. Each adjective, then, labels a different portion of that axis. The adjectives here seem in particular to presuppose a directed line bounded at one end: *well* refers to the end-point while *sick* refers to the remainder of the line, correlating greater magnitude with greater distance along the line. These are 'axial properties', or 'axiality', of the lexical items, i.e. the specific relations each has to a particular conceptual axis and to other lexical items with referents along the same axis. (Talmy 1986, 21)

The assumption of a conceptual axis could be a crucial point in the discussion of antonymy; unfortunately, however, the theoretical status of such an axis is far from clear: Talmy (1986) does not give empirical evidence to support his theoretical considerations so that the notion of "axiality" remains highly speculative at present.

This short survey of studies dealing with antonymy from various points of view has drawn attention to the most important questions that must be answered in order to arrive at a satisfactory account of antonymy phenomena in a natural language:

(a) In what way are antonyms similar, in what way are they different? How can this simultaneous similarity and difference be described in a systematic way?

(b) Are we justified in assuming that of a pair of antonymous lexemes one member is to be regarded as marked, while the other is unmarked?

(c) In what way is "axiality" involved, and what theoretical status should it be assigned?

(d) In what way are norms involved and, if they are, should they be regarded as part of the semantic structure of antonymous lexemes or should they rather be treated as pragmatic factors relevant in concrete utterance contexts?

Answers to these—and many other—questions will, of course, depend on the theoretical framework adopted by the investigating linguist. With regard to the scope of a linguistic investigation of matters concerning semantic opposition I will follow Lyons, who says:

We can leave to others to enquire whether the tendency to think in opposites, to categorize experience in terms of binary contrasts, is a universal human tendency which is but secondarily reflected in language, as cause producing effect, or whether it is the preexistence of a large number of opposed pairs of lexemes in our native language which causes us to dichotomize, or polarize our judgements and experiences. It is, however, a fact, of which the linguist must take cognizance, that binary opposition is one of the most important principles governing the structure of languages; and the most evident manifestation of this principle, as far as the vocabulary is concerned, is antonymy. (Lyons 1977, 271)

Before dealing with antonymy in the vocabulary of English it is, however, necessary to discuss briefly the scope of the term itself and its range of application in various theories of antonymy.

1.1.3 *The scope of the term "antonymy"*

In recent literature on semantics the term "antonymy" has been understood in at least two different ways:

In common parlance, and even in dictionaries of synonyms and antonyms, *antonymy* has a very broad meaning, sometimes equivalent to all types of opposition, including Aristotle's distinction between CONTRADICTORIES, in which the negation of one predication entails its contradictory, (*true—false* or *red—not red*) and CONTRARIES, in which the assertion of one predicate entails the denial of its contrary, but in which both contraries may be false, (eg. *red—green* or *big—small*). (Lehrer and Lehrer 1982, 483)

Thus, "antonymy" in this sense is also often referred to as 'Antonymie i.w.S.' (Geckeler 1980, 45; Kotschi 1974, 169 f.), '"antonymie" au sens large du terme' (Geckeler 1978, 183), or as 'acceptation large de l'antonymie' (Iliescu 1977, 164). "Antonimija" in Russian is almost exclusively used as a term referring to all kinds of opposition ("protivopostavlenie") in the lexicon (cf. Fomina 1978, 116 ff.; Novikov 1973*b*).[22] Leech (1974, 117) uses the terms "semantic contrast" and "types of opposition", Lyons takes "oppositeness of meaning" (Lyons 1977, 270) as a cover-term, although he points out:

The standard technical term for oppositeness of meaning between lexemes is antonymy. But this is hardly more precise in the usage of most authors than the word 'oppositeness' which it replaces, and dictionaries will classify as antonyms pairs of lexemes which, as we shall see later, are related in a variety of ways ('high' : 'low', 'buy' : 'sell', 'male' : 'female' , 'arrive' : 'depart, 'left' : 'right', 'front' : 'back', etc.). (Lyons 1977, 270 f.)

Gsell (1979) uses the term "Gegensatzrelationen" which, unfortunately, cannot be translated satisfactorily into English. For want of a better term I will use "semantic opposition" as a cover-term for both systemic and non-systemic (to be defined in Chapter 3) meaning-relations obtaining between English lexemes, thus freeing the term "oppositeness of meaning" for binary semantic opposition in the system of the English language.

The use of the term "antonymy" will be restricted to 'gradable opposites, such as "big" : "small", "high" : "low" etc.' (Lyons 1977, 279). This subcategory of semantic opposition has also been referred to as 'Antonymie i.e.S.' (Kotschi 1974, 193 ff.), 'Antithetika' (Geckeler 1980, 47), 'polar opposition' (Leech 1974, 108), 'l'antonymie contraire' (Iliescu 1977, 165), 'Antonymie (im eigentlichen Sinne)' (Agricola and Agricola 1979, 19). I will end my terminological *tour d'horizon* here, as enumerating terms without presenting the theoretical frameworks in which they appear seems a fruitless task. Rather, it seems advisable to present some basic characteristics of the most important theories of semantic opposition existing at the moment and to make clear which of them have been adopted for this work.

1.2 SEMANTIC OPPOSITION: TWO "AGAINSTS"

1.2.1 *Against definitions based on "logical" criteria*

In quite a number of treatments of semantic opposition a logical concept of "opposition" has been taken as the defining criterion both for the phenomenon as such and for further subclassification. Novikov (1973*a*, 260), for example, points out that 'logical opposition of various kinds within one essence (of quality, property, action, process, relation, etc.) makes up the semantic basis of antonymy' [translation A.M.]. The question whether semantic opposition is a manifestation or function of logical opposition has given rise to a number of discussions (e.g. Komissarov 1957, Isaev 1972, Martin 1973, Novikov 1973*a*, 17 ff., Novikov 1973*b*, Van Overbeke 1975, Henrici 1975, 24 ff., 187 ff., Nellessen 1982, 16 ff.) with as many arguments in favour of a logical treatment of semantic opposition as against it. The problem seems to be founded in the dichotomy of "language" vs. "thought" and, consequently, of "meaning (= Bedeutung)" vs. "concept (= Begriff)" dating back to Greek philosophy (cf. Di Cesare 1981, 25 f.). A treatment of semantic opposition as a phenomenon of language based on the assumption of structuralism that 'every language is a unique relational structure, or system, and that the units we identify, or postulate as theoretical constructs, in analysing the sentence of a particular language (sounds, words, meanings, etc.) derive both their essence and their existence from their relationships with other units in the same language-system' (Lyons 1977, 31 f.) should make as little recourse as possible to concepts and relations outside the domain of language. Cf.:

Es ist aber auch nicht möglich, . . . die Wortbedeutung mit dem Begriff gleichzusetzen, obwohl die Wortbedeutung das Ergebnis einer Verallgemeinerung ist. Zunächst ist einmal festzuhalten, dass es sich bei der Wortbedeutung um eine Kategorie der Linguistik, beim Begriff aber um eine Kategorie der Logik handelt . . .[23] (W. Schmidt 1963, 17)

I do not wish to postulate, of course, that logic[24] and linguistics are completely independent; yet it seems that opposition on the levels of reality and thought ('Gegensätze in Wirklichkeit und Denken': Agricola and Agricola 1979, 16) and semantic opposition ('Bedeutungsgegensätze': Agricola and Agricola 1979, 17) should be treated on different levels and not be mixed, as has been done much too frequently in previous studies.[25] It is interesting to note that more recent studies on semantic opposition tend to treat semantic properties and logical properties separately (cf. e.g. Iliescu 1977, Bierwisch *et al.* 1984, Cruse 1986, 252 ff.).

The situation is even more complicated in the case of sub-categories of semantic opposition. Novikov (1966, 80) distinguishes contrary concepts ("protivopoložnye ponjatija") from contradictory ones ("protivorečaščie ponjatija"), stressing that the former 'not only negate one another, but are characterized by a positive content; in contradistinction to the latter a third, middle, concept is always possible between them' (Novikov 1966, 80 [translation A.M.]), whereas contradictory concepts are characterized by a 'weakened, negative opposition ("protivopostavlenie")' (Novikov 1966, 80). In a later work by the same author (Novikov 1973*b*) the following types of semantic opposition (still apparently as a reflex of logical structures) are distinguished: contrary opposition (*young—old*), vectorial opposition (*go in—go out*), contradictory opposition (*married—unmarried*), and conversive opposition (*buy—sell*).

An interesting shift of bias from a logical basis to a semantic basis is observable in John Lyons's treatment of semantic opposition, especially with regard to the antonymy–complementarity distinction:

The first relation of 'oppositeness' to be discussed is that which holds between such pairs of words as *single : married, male : female*, etc. We will use the term *complementarity* for this, saying that *single* and *married*, or *male* and *female*, are complementaries. It is characteristic of such pairs of lexical items that the denial of the one implies the assertion of the other and the assertion of the one implies the denial of the other . . . Thus, *John isn't married* implies *John is single*; and *John is married* implies *John is not single*. In the case of those pairs for which we are reserving the term 'antonymy' (e.g. *good : bad, high : low*), only the second of these implications holds . . . *John is good* implies the denial of *John is bad*; but *John is not good* does not imply the assertion of *John is bad*. (Lyons 1968, 460 f.)

When discussing "antonymy" Lyons (1968, 463 ff.) states that antonyms are regularly gradable and then points out differences between explicit and implicit grading. A major change whose importance has not, perhaps, been sufficiently recognized by semanticists is Lyons's (1977) assumption that a distinction should be drawn between gradable and ungradable opposites:

Ungradable opposites, when they are employed as predicative expressions, divide the universe-of-discourse . . . into two complementary subsets. It follows from this, not only that the predication of either one of the pair implies the predication of the negation of the other, but also that the predication of the negation of either implies the predication of the other. For example, the proposition 'X is female' implies 'X is not male'; and 'X is not female' (provided that 'male' and 'female' are predicable of X) implies 'X is male'.

With gradable opposites, however, the situation is different. The predication of the one implies the predication of the negation of the other: the proposition 'X is hot' implies 'X is not cold'; and 'X is cold' implies 'X is not hot'. But 'X is not hot' does not generally imply 'X is cold' . . . (Lyons 1977, 271 f.)

A comparison of the two passages from Lyons (1968) and Lyons (1977) makes clear that in the later version syntactico-semantic criteria (i.e. gradability) are treated as being independent of logical criteria (i.e. propositions and their implications). What is more, Lyons (1977, 272) points out that the distinction between gradable and ungradable opposites should not be equated with the logical distinction of contradictories and contraries:

The distinction of contradictories and contraries corresponds to the distinction of ungradable and gradable lexemes within the class of opposites in a language, but it applies more widely; and the fact that gradable antonyms can generally be taken as contraries, rather than contradictories, is **a consequence of gradability, not its cause**. (Lyons 1977, 272 [my emphasis])

It thus follows that gradability is the basis on which to establish classifications of pairs of opposites in natural languages;[26] in fact, I shall go one step further and establish various types of semantic scales which can be shown to underly various types of semantic opposition.[27]

1.2.2   *Against "polarity"*

Another term that has often been mentioned in connection with
semantic opposition is "polarity". Below I will endeavour to show
that "polarity", in many of its senses,[28] is of little or no use for
the present study. The term will, therefore, be avoided.

Bierwisch (1967) tries—within the *Aspects*-framework of generative grammar—to establish universal semantic markers[29] for
German adjectives like *lang—kurz, breit—schmal, hoch—niedrig,
hell—dunkel, gut—schlecht, schön—hässlich*,[30] etc. Semantic markers,
according to Bierwisch, are connected with thought in that they
represent 'certain deep seated, innate properties of the human
organism and the perceptual apparatus, properties which determine
the way in which the universe is conceived, adapted, and worked
on' (Bierwisch 1967, 3). He points out 'the already known fact that
"polarity" plays an important role in the structure of adjectives'
(Bierwisch 1967, 6) and goes on to analyse each of the above-men-
tioned adjectives 'into a marker expressing the polarization, which
we will represent as (+Pol) and (–Pol), and a remainder R which
in turn consists of a set of markers that will be left unspecified for
the moment. We just note that in general R is identical for each
two adjectives that are paired [above]' (Bierwisch 1967, 7).

The assignment of (+Pol) is not arbitrary but "oriented" in
that only the (+Pol) marked member of a pair of antonymous
adjectives can be combined with *doppelt so, halb so, zehnmal so*,
etc., as representatives of a constituent *Deg(ree)*.[31] This does not,
however, hold true for adjectives of the *gut—schlecht* type:[32]

> Der Tisch ist doppelt so lang wie die Bank.
> * Der Tisch ist halb so kurz wie die Bank.
> Peter spielt doppelt so gut wie Klaus.
> Peter spielt halb so schlecht wie Klaus.
>
> (Bierwisch 1967, 8 f.)

Another important point in Bierwisch's argumentation in favour
of (Pol) is that only the (+Pol) marked members can be modified
by *M(easure) P(hrase)* as in *Der Zug ist 10 Wagen lang* vs. *Der
Zug ist zwei Wagen kurz*:

Only the (+Pol) marked elements of an antonymous pair of adjectives
can take an *MP*, and in this case the whole Adjectival does not indicate
one of the poles involved, but only the scale which is established by the

pair and a certain point within this scale. The orientation can be taken as 'neutralized'. (Bierwisch 1967, 9)

The assumption of a semantic marker (Pol) and the assignment of (+Pol) and (–Pol) is probably justified on formal grounds for a semantic theory that aims at describing not only the 'characterization of the lexical entries, i.e., the combination of the semantic markers within the words or morphemes' (Bierwisch 1967, 4), but also the rules determining the meanings of larger constituents on the basis of the word meanings and the syntactic structure of such constituents.[33] For a study of meaning-relations between lexemes, however, Bierwisch's concept of polarity is too general and too vague. If we look at what semantic properties are represented by (+/–Pol) for the adjectives in question, we can identify at least three of them:

(*a*) 'for measurable adjectives (+Pol) is that of the increasing number of units' (Bierwisch 1967, 11);

(*b*) for a pair like *lang—kurz* in *Die Zigarette ist lang* vs. *Die Zigarette ist kurz* the adjectives refer to a presupposed average (norm) and '(+Pol) and (–Pol) indicate that the modified objects are placed at the one or the other half (or end) of the scale relative to the average point' (Bierwisch 1967, 12);

(*c*) for pairs like *gut—schlecht, schön—hässlich* Bierwisch suggests assuming scales that are not divided into two parts by an average point, but contain the norm as one of their end points such that '(+Pol) here means: meeting this norm (or near to it), (–Pol) means: missing the norm (or far from it)' (Bierwisch 1967, 12).

The semantic phenomena Bierwisch tries to deal with in terms of (+/-Pol), on closer inspection, turn out to be consequences of various types of underlying semantic scales: with regard to the (+Pol) marked member of an adjective pair taking *MP*s Teller points out:

this is only the case for adjective pairs which determine a scale of measurement which admits of only positive measure from a zero point. For any adjective pair which determines a scale which admits of positive or negative measure from a zero point, the applicability of measure phrases is symmetric. Thus:

4 hours early
4 hours late

(Teller 1969, 200)

Adjectives of the *gut—schlecht, schön—hässlich* type seem to allow *Deg*-modifications for both members (*doppelt so gut, halb so gut, doppelt so schlecht, halb so schlecht*), which clearly contradicts Bierwisch's assumption of the combinability of only the (+Pol) member with a constituent *Deg* and thus makes the (+Pol)/(–Pol) distinction rather problematic. Apart from this, I can see no reason why (+Pol) in these cases should be interpreted as "meeting the norm" and (–Pol) as "missing the norm". It seems more appropriate to assume an underlying scale that differs from the one constituted by the *lang—kurz* type; I will assume such a scale in Chapter 4 of this study.

In treatments of semantic opposition in non-generative frameworks the terms "polarity" and "polar opposition" are usually equivalent to "antonymy" as defined in 1.1.3 (e.g. Leech 1974, 108 ff.).[34]

Viehweger *et al.* (1977) use "polarity" as a cover-term for antonymy, complementarity, and converseness (Viehweger *et al.* 1977, 337 ff.), regarding polarity as a direct reflection of extralinguistic reality:

Paradigmatische Polarität erweist sich als symmetrische Relation zweier Sememe, die sich gegenseitig widersprechen im Sinne von alternativen Aussagen, die sich gegenseitig als Gegensätze bedingen. Sie entspricht damit der allgemeinen Definition von Polarität, nach der die gegensätzliche Natur zweier Pole und die Tatsache, dass die Existenz des einen die des anderen voraussetzt, die Polarität determinieren . . . Polare Sememe spiegeln damit objektive Gegensätze der Realität wider, sie sind Abbilder aussersprachlicher Gegebenheiten: "schnell"—"langsam"; "anfang"—"ende"; "sprechen"—"schweigen"; "verheiratet"—"ledig". Es gibt jedoch nicht immer eindeutige Gegensätze, vielmehr können auch mehrere Pole für ein Ausgangssemem vorliegen, ja, jeder Unterschied kann, sofern eine sinnvolle Bezugsebene denkbar ist, als Gegensatz aufgefasst werden. So ist aus der objektiven Anordnung räumlicher Festlegungen (Himmelsrichtungen) oder aus der Abfolge zeitlicher Kategorien (Jahreszeiten, "vergangenheit"—"gegenwart"—"zukunft") eine Abstufung der Gegensätzlichkeit interpretierbar, aber sie erscheint semantisch kaum tragfähig, da als Voraussetzung für Polarität immer nur das Verhältnis zwischen zwei Partnern zu gelten hat.[35] (Viehweger *et al.* 1977, 336)

The above definition of polarity highlights one basic problem that is crucial to a coherent description of semantic opposition, viz. the relationship of extralinguistic reality, meaning, and language use. I will briefly elaborate below on the concept of meaning adopted in this study and then attempt to show that there must be a strict separation between the treatment of phenomena pertaining to the levels of extralinguistic reality, meaning, and language use.

1.3 ADVERSATIVITY, OPPOSITENESS OF MEANING, AND CONTRAST

"Meaning"[36] in this study is understood as pertaining to the language-system, i.e. Saussure's "langue" (cf. Lipka 1990, 41 f.). Such a concept of meaning is in accordance with what Lyons (1977, 231) has called the 'central thesis of structuralism':

that every language is a unique relational structure, or system, and that the units we identify, or postulate as theoretical constructs . . . derive both their essence and their existence from their relationships with other units in the same language-system. (Lyons 1977, 231 f.)

"Structure" in this context must be understood as 'structure in an analytical respect, as the structuring of the content-level by means of functional lexical oppositions. The analysis of lexical meanings leads to the decomposition of the contents into smaller elements, i.e. into meaning-differentiating features' (Coseriu and Geckeler 1974, 114).

With regard to the vocabulary, or lexicon, of a given language, a linguistic sign is defined negatively in that it differs formally and semantically from other linguistic signs of that language. Yet, the linguistic sign as an entity comprising form and content (meaning) is also defined positively in that it refers to an object, property, or relation of the extralinguistic reality.[37] This has led to the important distinction of meaning ("Bedeutung") vs. designation ("Bezeichnung") and referent ("Bezeichnetes").[38] Thus Coseriu points out:

Im Prinzip sind nur die Bedeutungsbeziehungen strukturierbar, aber nicht die Bezeichnungsbeziehungen. Die konkrete Bezeichnung (eines bestimmten Objektes) ist ein Faktum der "Rede", während die Bedeutung zur "Sprache" . . . gehört. Daher sind die Bedeutungsbeziehungen (vom Standpunkt der Synchronie aus) konstant, während die konkreten Bezeichnungsbeziehungen inkonstant (variabel) sind.[39] (Coseriu 1970a, 44)

This can be illustrated by the following example:

(1) . . . and saw the face of the woman who had sagged back against the cushions . . . Death had come to **Adele Fortescue** suddenly and swiftly . . .
  'Well?' demanded Inspector Neele impatiently . . . The doctor looked at him with slight curiosity.
  'You're taking this hard. Any special reason?'
  'She was cast as a **murderess**,' said Neele.
  'And she turns out to be a **victim**. Hm. You'll have to think again, won't you?' (*PFR*, 74)

(*a*) The words *Adele Fortescue, murderess,* and *victim* are used in text (1) to designate one person, the "referent", in a (fictitious) extralinguistic world; in this case three linguistic expressions have the same designation, yet the meanings of *murderess* and *victim* are not the same. In text (2) the designation vs. meaning contrast is even more evident:

(2) Now, for example, the stewardess lays before him **a meal of ambiguous designation** (could be **lunch**, could be **dinner**, who knows or cares four miles above the turning globe) but tempting: smoked salmon, . . . (*CP*, 22)

(*b*) *Murderess* and *victim* in (1) designate, or label, items of extralinguistic reality: we know that there are people, men and women, who deliberately kill other people, and that there are people who are murdered by fellow human beings, and we know that the relation between them is basically an antagonistic one. The term "adversativity" will henceforth be used for 'Gegensätze in Wirklichkeit und Denken' (Agricola and Agricola 1979, 16). "Oppositeness of meaning", on the other hand, is the term I will use for systemic relations obtaining between the meanings of two linguistic signs.[40] The task of this study, therefore, is a description of oppositeness of meaning (as a special type of Coseriu's "Bedeutungsbeziehungen"), not of adversativity.

Adversativity is, of course, reflected in language use. Cf.:

(3) 'It is as well you are in France,' said Van Aldin. 'We are made of sterner stuff in the States. **Business** comes before **pleasure** there.' (*MBT*, 131)

(4) She drew out from her handbag the letter she had received that morning from Lady Tamplin. Katherine was no fool. She understood the *nuances* of that letter as well as anybody and the reason of Lady Tamplin's show of affection towards a long-forgotten cousin was not lost upon her. It was for **profit** and not for **pleasure** that Lady Tamplin was so anxious for the company of her dear cousin. (*MBT*, 51 f.)

Business and *pleasure* in (3) as well as *profit* and *pleasure* in (4) express adversativity, but an analysis of the meaning of these lexical items shows that they cannot be regarded as instances of oppositeness of meaning on the level of the language system, as is the case with *pleasure—pain* in

(5) Philip lay face down on the floor while Melanie walked up and down his back in her bare feet. The experience was an exquisite mixture of **pleasure** and **pain**. (*CP*, 100)

The pairs *business—pleasure* and *profit—pleasure* I will term "non-systemic opposites"; *pleasure—pain* I will call "systemic opposites", and criteria for delimiting the two groups will be given in Chapter 3.

(*c*) Semantic opposition on the level of "parole" will be referred to as "contrast"; when talking about individual lexical items exhibiting such a contrastive relationship, I will refer to them as "opposites".

The following diagram schema illustrates the relationship between the three levels involved and the phenomena to be discussed:

Extralinguistic reality/thinking	Adversativity
Linguistic system	Systemic semantic opposition
	Non-systemic semantic opposition
Speech/parole	Contrast

Notes to Chapter 1

1. At this point, the term "antonymy" (in its broad sense) is used because it is still the most current term referring to the phenomenon of opposition in the lexicon of a natural language; its scope will, however, be discussed and restricted in 1.1.3.
2. Cf. Kalverkämper (1980, 156, esp. n. 4) for further literature on this topic.

3. A thorough discussion of these works at this point would be somewhat redundant, as Gsell's comprehensive presentation leaves little room for further extension; I will return to the monographs and papers mentioned in Gsell (1979, 24–59 ('Zum Stand der Forschung')) whenever it is necessitated by the discussion of phenomena connected with antonymy. Another recommendable survey and discussion of work on antonymy can be found in Nellessen (1982, 20–32); Geckeler (1980) gives valuable information on the history of the treatment of antonymy in (mostly French) dictionaries.

4. Prototype theory, one of the latest developments in the field of semantics (Blutner 1985 and especially Taylor 1989 can be recommended as good introductory surveys) has not made antonymy one of its topics; rather, prototype theory is concerned with establishing principles of mental categorization (cf. Leuninger 1986) and the establishing of "prototypes" that determine appropriate word-use. Cf. e.g. Verschueren's (1981, 332) remark: 'Briefly, for each lexicalized category human cognition contains a prototypical example (which does not have to be an actual member of the category itself, but which is a kind of "mental image"), which is used as a yardstick to decide whether a particular object can or cannot be **referred to by means of the lexical item in question** [my emphasis].' In a just comparison Lipka (1986*a*) juxtaposes prototype theory and semantic feature theory, pleading for an integrated view, as 'semantic features and prototype theory do not represent true alternatives' (Lipka 1986*a*, 92). It is interesting to note, perhaps, that Lipka, in enumerating semantic phenomena that prototype theory is incapable of dealing with, mentions 'deictics (*come/go*), relational words (like *precede, love, height, father*) and syntagmatic relations . . . in general' (Lipka 1986*a*, 92). It can, I think, be assumed that prototype theory (at least in its present stage) is incapable of handling antonymy, which, as will be shown later, requires mechanisms capable of handling "relational words".

   There are, however, studies on conceptualization and human categorization that seem to have taken prototype theory proper as a starting-point but have then apparently directed themselves towards studying the "grammaticalization/lexicalization" of conceptual structure in natural languages; these studies do, I think, represent a more psychologically oriented trend in semantics and should not be subsumed under "prototype semantics"; for their discussion see 1.1.2.

5. Cf. Gsell (1979, 95–104) for further considerations with regard to aims and objectives of his empirical work; one important point of criticism is mentioned by Geckeler (1981*c*, 420 f.): 'Was Gsells

Arbeit nicht leistete und natürlich auch nicht leisten konnte, waren ähnlich wie für das Französische durchgeführte Analysen in den anderen drei romanischen Sprachen [Italian, Romanian, and Spanish (A.M.)]; die kontrastiven Beobachtungen bleiben zu pauschal und sind auch nicht überprüfbar . . . ['What has not been and of course could not have been achieved in Gsell's book was analyses of Italian, Romanian, and Spanish analogous with the ones performed of French; his contrastive observations remain too vague and cannot be tested either . . .'].

6. Cf. Nellessen (1982, 108–10) for methodological considerations.

7. This list is given as appendix II (Lehrer 1985, 425–8), which might mean that we may expect a more thorough and extensive discussion of gradable antonyms by Lehrer in the future. Cerutti (1957) has not been included in the discussion of the treatment of antonymy in English because it is based on an older concept of "Sinn und Gegensinn", viz. cases like Latin *hospes*, which means either "host" or "guest". Cf. also Gsell (1979, 3 f.).

8. 'one of the major shortcomings of works in semantics up to now has been their avoidance of the most important methodological problem, viz. the enormous amount of data: neither phonology nor syntax has to deal with and classify such an enormous quantity of data.'

9. 'Even if the object of investigation is narrowed down considerably, descriptive lexical studies will find it basically impossible to take into account the entire vocabulary of a natural language, as it represents an "open list".'

10. 'On the basis of these considerations we have refrained from trying to use a corpus of written or oral texts as the basis of investigatgion, . . . not only because of the certainly surmountable difficulties in collecting such data, but particularly because such a collection would be of practically unimaginable size if it were to contain a really representative selection of the entire vocabulary. Though one of the major advantages of a corpus lies in the fact that it gives the vocabulary under scrutiny in authentic contexts, this advantage will be effective only if every word is contained in not just a few contexts which have been determined fortuitously by the choice of the texts, but in such a multitude of contexts that fairly well-founded statements on the typicality of individual instances are possible.'

11. A list of the texts that have been investigated and from which the contextualized examples in this study have been taken can be found at the end of the Bibliography; the abbreviated forms of their titles used in references are listed on pp. vii–viii.

12. The list of works discussed in this subsection is by no means

exhaustive; as most of the work done in related fields of study is not directly relevant for the treatment of antonymy in a strictly linguistic framework (as done in this study) I have confined myself to the discussion of some prototypical papers for illustrative purposes. For the role of antonymy in semiotics, see e.g. Eco (1985*a*, esp. 97 f., 169–75; 1985*b*, esp. 79–132); antonymy and lexicography is treated in Fomina (1978, 127 f.), Gsell (1979, 195 ff.), Agricola and Agricola (1979), Agricola (1982; 1983), Schippan (1983, 102 f.), Miller (1984, 81), H. Schmidt (1985, 57–61), and many others.

13. Schertzer (1981), discussing scaling adjectives used in marketing research along affective, cognitive, and conative attitude scales, is in a way comparable to Osgood *et al.* (1957) (though their book is not mentioned in Schertzer's bibliography!); for further references on the application of the semantic differential see Gsell (1979, 198 n. 271).

14. In contradistinction to psychological, associative scales, semantic scales (as will be shown in greater detail in Ch. 4) are established on the basis of gradability phenomena observable in actual language-use. Whereas Osgood *et al.* (1957) assume the same seven-step scale for, e.g., "beautiful"—"ugly", "yellow"—"blue", "clean"—"dirty", a semantic analysis must show why *extremely beautiful, quite beautiful, ?slightly beautiful* and *slightly ugly, quite ugly, extremely ugly* are possible, whereas *slightly clean, quite yellow,* or *extremely blue* sound odd. (It will be shown that the oddity results from the kind of semantic scale involved, which is different for the three adjectival pairs discussed here.)

15. I have used the term "feature" here without further specification because Clark (1970) does not make clear which features in a deep structure feature list he regards as syntactic and which as semantic. This is, however, crucial to the concept of the feature [Polarity] which is a characteristic feature of "polar" adjectives and responsible for the elicitation of an adjective's antonym. Bierwisch (1967), who is referred to by Clark in connection with [Polarity], regards (+Pol) and (–Pol) as semantic markers expressing polarization (Bierwisch 1967, 7). "Polarity" will be dealt with in greater detail in 1.2.

16. Clark (1970, 276 f.) also postulates a 'marking rule' as a particularization of the 'minimal contrast rule', which I do not, however, wish to discuss here. The problem of markedness will be discussed in Ch. 6.

17. For more information see Clark (1974), Clark and Clark (1977), Evans (1983); see also Lazerson (1977) and Mills (1984) for the acquisition of colour-terms.

18. For a summary of the aims and tasks of structural semantics see Kastovsky (1982*b*, 66 f.).

19. 'Man's cognitive achievements, especially the mastering of a natural language, are structured in a modular fashion, i.e. they are based on the cooperation of various specific systems and subsystems. Such systems, which in turn exhibit an internal modular structure, are represented by the various modalities of perception, the conceptual organization of experience, social interaction, and language.'

20. Bierwisch *et al.* (1984) is the most comprehensive study within this framework. It is divided into several sections, each of them dealing with one particular aspect of spatial adjectives. In 'Basic assumptions' (Bierwisch *et al.* 1984, 490–7) Bierwisch defines structural and processual aspects of the language system: 'Die Struktur des Gegenstandsbereiches, in den die Dimensionsadjektive einzuordnen sind, lässt sich damit für das Sprachsystem wie folgt zusammenfassen: Ein System UG von Prinzipien und Parametern — die **Universalgrammatik** — bestimmt den Rahmen möglicher, das heisst unter normalen Bedingungen **erwerbbarer Grammatiken** G. Eine Grammatik G ist ein komplexes System von Regeln und Bedingungen, das eine **Klasse von Strukturrepräsentationen** SR determiniert. Eine Repräsentation SR **strukturiert den aktualen internen Zustand**, der dem Verstehen (oder Produzieren) einer sprachlichen Äusserung zugrunde liegt. Sie bestimmt die auf der Sprachkenntnis beruhenden Eigenschaften der Äusserung. Die Erzeugung und Verarbeitung einer Repräsentation SR entsprechend den Regeln von G geschieht durch einen **komplexen Prozessmechanismus** P, der die verschiedenen, am Produzieren, Verstehen, Bewerten, Behalten, Wiedererkennen von sprachlichen Äusserungen beteiligten Prozesse realisiert' ['With regard to the language-system we can summarize the structure of the subject-matter to which dimensional adjectives belong as follows: a system UG of principles and parameters—**the universal grammar**— determines the frame of possible grammars G, i.e. **grammars that can be acquired in normal circumstances**. A grammar G is a complex system of rules and conditions determining a **class of structural representations** SR. Such a representation SR **structures the actual internal state** underlying the understanding (or producing) of a linguistic utterance. It determines the characteristics of the utterance which are based on linguistic knowledge. The production and the processing of a representation SR in accordance with the rules of G is performed by a **complex process mechanism** P which realizes the various processes taking part in producing, understanding, assessing, retaining, and recognizing

linguistic utterances'] (Bierwisch *et al.* 1984, 491 [my emphasis]).
Complementary to, and independent of, such a linguistic system
Bierwisch assumes a "conceptual system" C which 'determiniert
die mentale Repräsentation dessen, was durch sprachliche
Äusserungen wiedergegeben wird, was ihre Bedeutung im Sinn des
begrifflich strukturierten Umweltbezuges ausmacht' ['determines
the mental representation of what is rendered by linguistic utterances, what makes up their meaning as conceptually structured
relations with their surroundings'] (Bierwisch *et al.* 1984, 492).
Mediating between G and C is the "semantic representation".
Bierwisch then presents a classification of adjectives on the basis of
gradability phenomena (Bierwisch *et al.* 1984, 495 ff.), distinguish-
ing—among other types—between quantitative and evaluative
adjectives (a distinction that will be of some importance for my
discussion of antonymous lexemes in Ch. 4). Bierwisch and
Zimmermann (Bierwisch *et al.* 1984, 497–9) discuss some syntactic properties of spatial adjectives; most relevant for the present
study is Bierwisch's discussion of the semantics of gradation
(Bierwisch *et al.* 1984, 500–5), where various scale-models are
introduced. Lang (Bierwisch *et al.* 1984, 505–12) presents considerations on the concept SPATIALITY and opts for the priority of the
conceptual system in the description of the semantic representation
of spatial adjectives; Dölling discusses logical properties of spatial
adjectives (Bierwisch *et al.* 1984, 664–70); Goede assesses various
theories of the acquisition of "grösser" and "mehr" (Bierwisch *et
al.* 1984, 670–5); Blutner deals with a model of the comprehension
of comparative sentences (Bierwisch *et al.* 1984, 676–80); the
study is concluded by a summary (Bierwisch *et al.* 1984, 680–4).

   Though the study's aims go far beyond those of my own, some
of the considerations and suggestions proposed by Bierwisch and
his collaborators will be shown to tally with the results of my
analyses. I will not, however, deal with the "modularity of mind"
issue (see Taylor 1989, 16 ff.).

21. Cf. Langacker (1987, 1): 'In the theory of *cognitive grammar*,
     meaning is equated with conceptualization, and semantic structure
     is held to embody conventional *imagery* (i.e. it reflects the ability of
     speakers to shape and construe a conceived situation in alternate
     ways).' For basic principles and further literature on cognitive
     grammar see Langacker (1983*a*, *b*; 1987) as well as Rudzka-Ostyn
     (1988).

22. See Fomina (1978, 128–30) for a sample of various definitions of
     "antonym" in Soviet linguistics.

23. 'Neither is it possible . . . to equate word-meaning and concept,
     although word-meaning must be regarded as the result of a gener-

alization process. It is important to point out that word-meaning is a linguistic category whereas the concept is a category from the field of logic . . .'

24. In fact, Schmidt assumes a universal validity of logic; cf.: 'Die Wörter besitzen als lexikalische Einheiten entsprechend den besonderen historischen Entwicklungsbedingungen der einzelnen Sprachen jeweils eine gewisse qualitative Eigenständigkeit, während die Begriffe als wichtigste Form des Denkens allgemeingültigen Charakter haben. Es gibt zwar verschiedene Formen und Möglichkeiten des sprachlichen Ausdrucks der Gedanken, aber die Formen der gedanklichen Widerspiegelung der Welt sind für alle Menschen gleich; es gibt verschiedene Sprachen in der Welt, aber nur eine Logik' ['Words as lexical units possess a certain amount of qualitative independence (according to the specific historic development of individual languages), while concepts as the most important form of thought have general validity. Though there are various forms and possibilities of expressing thoughts through language, there seem to be the same forms of mental reflection of the world for everybody; the world has various languages, but only one logic'] (W. Schmidt 1963, 17 f.).

25. Cf. e.g. Palmer (1981, 83), who speaks of relations of semantic opposition as being of a 'semi-logical' kind. See also Gsell (1979, 20 ff.) for a brief discussion of 'Gegensatzrelationen in der Logik' and their (ir)relevance for a description of semantic opposition.

26. Marsh-Stefanovska (1982, 3) points out that '[t]he laws of logic alone are found wanting in grouping adjectival opposites, since, although most are either contradictories or contraries by logical tests, the contraries include a far wider range of concepts which are not normally considered opposites, e.g. *horse : cow, green : yellow*'. Although she arrives at the conclusion that 'gradability should be the essential criterion in grouping opposites and that logical tests are secondary from this viewpoint' (Marsh-Stefanovska 1982, 3 f.) the distinction between contradictories and contraries still plays an important role in her work.

27. See Ch. 4.

28. I will not discuss so-called "polarity-sensitive" words, i.e. 'items . . . occurring only in affirmative or only in negative contexts' (Borkin 1971, 53) in this context. Baker (1970) discusses the behaviour of polarity restrictions and polarity reversal in counterfactual constructions; Borkin (1971) describes the distribution of positive and negative polarity items in questions (linking this distribution to affirmative and negative assumptions on the part of the speaker and to the type of question containing polarity-sensitive items); Fauconnier (1975) attempts to relate the behaviour of

polarity-sensitive phrases to an 'independent scale principle' (Fauconnier 1975, 188), taking into account logical structures, context, and pragmatic scales.

29. For an excellent survey of "semantische Merkmale" (in various semantic theories) see Sprengel (1980). For the treatment of semantic opposition in generative grammar see also Katz (1972, 157 ff.), and Davis's (1973) criticism of the semantic theory advanced by Katz; Bierwisch (1969) discusses antonymy and negation without, however, mentioning (Pol) as a semantic marker.

30. The English equivalents of the German adjectives behave in the same way, so I have decided to quote the original examples used by Bierwisch (1967).

31. In this context Teller (1969, 199) points out: 'What then is the relation of the phrases "twice as" and "half as" to such antonymous pairs of adjectives? We seem to use "twice as thin" or "half as thin" when we are concerned with objects which are thin compared to the average of objects in their class. If this is the case we should use "twice (half) as thick" for comparatively thick items; . . . If this regularity for "thick" and "thin" is a real one, it would be surprising if the same did not hold for other adjectives of measurement. Indeed, we *do* use "half (twice) as slow" if we are talking about things which move very slowly, such as turtles, snails (which are slow for animals), or cars in a traffic jam (which are slow for cars). We can say that one newborn infant is twice as young as another. And though it may be indiscreet, it is linguistically perfectly appropriate to describe Jane's mini-skirt as twice as short as Mary's.' We will come back to Teller's statement later in connection with the discussion of meaning vs. reference.

32. Unfortunately, Bierwisch (1967) does not elaborate further on this type of adjective. Hundsnurscher (1971), who took over the principle of (Polarity) from Bierwisch (1967), states that "wertende Adjektive" like *schön* and *gut* are characterized by (Pol) and must be interpreted relatively; cf.: 'Wenn jemand sagt . . . *Dieses Mädchen ist schön*[,] so stellt er damit nicht ein an der objektiven Realität überprüfbares Merkmal fest, . . . sondern er stuft das Mädchen auf seiner ästhetischen Wertskala ein; . . . In der ästhetischen Wertskala von X (= Sprecher) rangiert dieses Mädchen "oben". Das Zustandekommen dieser Wertskala ist ein kulturpsychologisches Problem, das ausserhalb der Semantik liegt' ['If somebody says . . . *This girl is beautiful* he does not declare a feature that can be checked against objective reality but places the girl on his aesthetic scale of values; . . . in X's (the speaker's) scale of values this girl ranges "up". How this scale of values is established is

a problem of cultural psychology and thus outside the realm of semantics'] (Hundsnurscher 1971, 109)

In her review of Hundsnurscher (1971), Wierzbicka (1974) regards "polarity" as a highly dubious semantic marker: 'Mr. Hundsnurscher introduces it without much conviction, admitting that it "gives only general and formal information". But a semantic element which gives only "formal information" is a *contradictio in adiecto*. The marker "polarity" has been introduced [. . . as] an attempt to formalize the traditional concept of antonymity. The attempt is misconceived, for it is based on the fallacious idea that the semantic relation between the members of s.c. [so-called] antonymical pairs is a constant' (Wierzbicka 1974, 107). See also Nellessen (1982, 30 f.).

33. Here we touch upon the distinction between synthetic and analytic approaches towards the description of natural languages (cf. Kastovsky 1982*b*, 13, 16 f.). For this study I have adopted Geckeler's view that 'the first task of structural semantics is to build up a paradigmatic type of semantics, i.e. word semantics, and that **any attempt to work seriously on combinatorial semantics,** i.e. sentence semantics or even text semantics, **must turn out to be premature unless linguists have first established a solid basis of word semantics . . .'** (Geckeler 1981*a*, 381 [my emphasis]).

34. For technical reasons I will not deal with "positive and negative polarity" as used by Lyons (1977, 275 f.) and with "logical polarity", "quantity polarity", "evaluative polarity", and "normality polarity" as introduced by Cruse (1976; 1979; 1980; 1986) and Marsh-Stefanovska (1982) at this point. It seems more appropriate to argue against these concepts when I discuss oppositeness of meaning in detail.

35. 'Paradigmatic polarity is a symmetrical relation between two sememes contradicting each other as alternative predications that constitute one another as oppositions. Thus it is in accordance with the general definition of polarity, which determines this phenomenon by the oppositional nature of two poles and by the fact that the existence of one pole presupposes the existence of its counterpart . . . Polar sememes thus mirror objective oppositions of reality, they are representations of extralinguistic facts: "fast"— "slow"; "beginning"—"end"; "talk"—"be silent"; "married"— "single". Oppositions are, however, not always unambiguous: there may be several poles to one sememe. In fact, any difference can be regarded as an opposition provided an appropriate frame of reference can be thought of. Thus, on the basis of the objective arrangement of spatial determination (cardinal points) or the

sequence of temporal categories (seasons, "past"—"present"—
"future") one might infer a gradience of oppositeness, which, however, seems hardly tenable semantically, as a relationship between
two partners has been postulated as the prerequisite of polarity.'

36.   For a short summary of various theories of meaning see e.g. Lyons
(1981, 30 f.); for the concept of meaning as 'abstract reflection of
a piece of the objective world' see Komissarov (1957, 49); for
an explanation of meaning as 'bewusstseinsmässiges Abbild der
Realität' see Hansen *et al.* (1982, 14 f.), also Kastovsky (1982*b*,
47 f.) for an evaluation of this type of definition.

37.   Cf. Kastovsky (1982*b*, 24 f.).

38.   For Frege's (1892) classic example see Lyons (1977, 197 ff.); for
Husserl's *der Sieger von Jena—der Besiegte von Waterloo*, referring
to the "referent" Napoleon I, see Coseriu and Geckeler (1974,
147); a brief survey of the history of the "meaning"—"designation" contrast and subsequent terminological difficulties can be
found in Kastovsky (1982*b*, 24 f.).

39.   'In principle only meaning-relations can be analysed from the
structural point of view, not relations between designations. The
concrete designation (of a specific object) is a matter of "speech",
whereas meaning pertains to "language". Therefore, meaning-relations are (synchronically) constant, while concrete relations
between designations are not constant (variable).'

40.   For practical reasons the term "oppositeness of meaning" is
restricted to binary semantic opposition, as this is the topic of this
study; binary vs. multiple semantic opposition will be discussed in
Ch. 3.

2

Contrast

2.1 INTRODUCTION

Oppositeness of meaning, as has been shown in the previous chapter, has often been regarded as an important principle structuring the vocabulary of a natural language. In a way, however, the phenomenon as such has always been treated as simply existing, with hardly any consideration as to the actualization and textual function of semantic opposition on the level of language-use (parole).[1] It is not difficult to see the reason for avoiding such an enterprise: establishing opposites on the expression plane presupposes knowing that the meaning of lexeme A and the meaning of lexeme B can/do enter a relation of oppositeness on the content plane, and meaning-relations on the content plane are accessible only via generalizations on the expression plane—which means that the investigator is trapped in a vicious circle. Nevertheless, with a certain amount of "pretheoretical" knowledge it is possible to 'identify units by virtue of their potentiality of occurrence in certain syntagms' (Lyons 1977, 241), i.e. it can be shown that opposites show a tendency to appear more often and more regularly in some syntagmas than they do in others. The basis for such a procedure is Saussure's distinction of paradigmatic vs. syntagmatic relations:

Words as used in discourse, strung together one after another, enter into relations based on the linear character of languages . . . Outside the context of discourse, words having something in common are associated together in the memory . . . This kind of connexion between words is of quite a different order. It is not based on linear sequence. It is a connexion in the brain . . . We shall call these *associative relations* [= paradigmatic relations]. Syntagmatic relations hold *in praesentia*. They hold between two or more terms co-present in a sequence. Associative relations, on the contrary, hold *in absentia*. They hold between terms constituting a mnemonic group. (Saussure 1916/1983, 121 f.)

A similar train of thought was pursued by Sîrbu (1979), who suggested that any paradigmatic manifestation should have its reflex on the syntagmatic level, i.e.:

(a) dans divers types de constructions grammaticales où l'on emploie les termes d'un couple antonymique,
(b) dans les classes sémantiques de mots avec lesquelles ils se combinent,
(c) dans les structures syntaxiques les plus caractéristiques où ils apparaissent.

Autrement dit, par l'analyse syntagmatique on arrive à établir les lois de l'emploi des antonymes dans le discours, à relever ce qu'il y a de typique dans le contexte donné, pour deux mots opposés du point de vue sémantique, selon un ou plusieurs traits sémantiques distinctifs.[2] (Sîrbu 1979, 166 f.)

In view of the material I have investigated, Sîrbu's suggestions are decidedly too optimistic, as they suggest an isomorphism between the levels of content and expression, which, however, does not exist. Apart from that, any expression that is used in a given syntagma can be used meaningfully only on the basis of its semantic content,[3] so that it is virtually impossible to establish a pair of opposites X and Y solely on the basis of their syntagmatic distribution. Though the notion "syntagmatic opposition" has been given much emphasis by some Soviet linguists (Novikov 1973*a*, *b*; Fomina 1978, 119 ff.; Kočergan 1981), they still acknowledge that meaning is of primary importance:

Systemic syntagmatic and paradigmatic parameters of a word depend (on the synchronic plane) on its denotative meaning, and not the other way round, as is sometimes maintained in linguistic literature. In other words, the syntagmatics and paradigmatics of a word are transponents of its denotative meaning. Starting from this proposition, we can make use of the syntagmatic and paradigmatic parameters of a word for the definition of the semantics of [this] word, its semic make-up. (Kočergan 1981, 33 f. [translation A.M.])

Examples (1) and (2) are cases in point:

(1) . . . and girls, girls of every shape and size and description, girls with long straight hair to their waists, girls in plaits, girls in curls, girls in **short** skirts, girls in **long** skirts, girls in jeans, girls in flared trousers, girls in Bermuda shorts, girls without bras, girls very probably without panties, girls **white**,

brown, yellow, black, girls in kaftans, saris, skinny sweaters, bloomers, shifts, muu-muus, granny-gowns, combat jackets, sandals, sneakers, boots, Persian slippers, bare feet, girls with beads, flowers, slave bangles, ankle bracelets, earrings, straw boaters, coolie hats, sombreros, Castro caps, girls **fat** and **thin, short** and **tall, clean** and **dirty,** girls with **big breasts** and girls with **flat chests** . . . (*CP*, 194)

(2) In Morris Zapp's view, the root of all critical error was a naive confusion of **literature** with **life. Life** was **transparent, literature opaque. Life** was an **open, literature** a **closed** system. **Life** was composed of **things, literature** of **words.** (*CP*, 47)

Paradigmatic commutation[4] is observable in *girls in short skirts* vs. *girls in long skirts, girls fat and thin, short and tall, clean and dirty*; the juxtaposition of opposites is here used in an inclusive sense, i.e. by enumerating girls of opposite qualities the author stresses the presence of girls of 'every shape and size and description' (*CP*, 194).

In passage (2) *literature* is juxtaposed with *life*, and this juxtaposition is further stressed by an obvious syntactic parallelism rendering the opposites *life* vs. *literature*,[5] *transparent* vs. *opaque*, *open* vs. *closed*, *things* vs. *words*. Probably no native speaker of English would doubt that *transparent* and *opaque*, *open* and *closed* are stored as opposites in the vocabulary and do not depend for their interpretation on contextual information; *life* and *literature*, *things* and *words*, on the other hand, can be used contrastively and interpreted accordingly only in specific (mostly extralinguistically determined) contexts.[6]

Texts like those in (1) and (2) raise two questions:

(*a*) are there any contextual/syntagmatic environments favouring the application of opposites; and, if there are, what are their characteristics?

(*b*) do the opposites used in such contextual/syntagmatic environments share the same status with regard to the linguistic system of English; and, if they do not, what is the basis on which to distinguish various groups?

Problem (*a*) will be the concern of the remainder of this chapter, question (*b*) will be answered in Chapter 3.

2.2 OPPOSITES IN CONTEXT: BASIC ASSUMPTIONS

2.2.1 *General remarks*

The idea of taking syntagmatic contrast as the starting-point for an investigation of sense-relations stems from two different sources: the notion of "antonymic context" ("antonimičeskij kontekst", with "antonimičeskij" being used in the wide sense of the term) in Soviet linguistics, and the question whether any transfer could be made from Gauger's (1972) suggestion of establishing "synonymische Kontexte" (Gauger 1972, 65 ff., 87–119; further developed in Schreyer 1976). Incidentally, each of these two sources exhibits a different bias, thus mirroring the formal aspect (the establishing of "syntactic frames") and the functional aspect (the establishing of "textual functions" of opposites in different syntagmas), respectively.

2.2.2 *Syntactic frames*

In his book on oppositeness of meaning in Russian Novikov (1973*a*) stresses the importance of the syntagmatic, paradigmatic, and pragmatic aspects of analysis. Thus, from a syntagmatic point of view opposites[7] are defined as 'words which are characterized [by the fact that] they can often be found in specific contexts, in which one of their typical textual functions[8] (confrontation, comparison, conjunction, and others) is realized' (Novikov 1973*a*, 95). It must be emphasized, however, that the term "context" is used by Novikov in the sense of 'characteristic syntactic contexts (formulae)' (Novikov 1973*a*, 96) to denote 'syntagmatic opposition' (Novikov 1973*b*, 57), which, in turn, pertains to the level of parole; cf.:

Words with opposite meanings can be used in speech ["reč'"] in various ways, although their most characteristic and most frequent application is their recurrence in text[s] in specific constructions (formal contexts) which are characterized by contiguous arrangement of the antonyms [opposites]. (Novikov 1973*b*, 57 [translation A.M.])

The same equation of syntagmatic opposition and 'antonymic contrast' (Kočergan 1981, 37), which is defined on the basis of the regularity of contiguous application of words on the syntagmatic level (Kočergan 1981, 36), has led to the proclamation of syntagmatic opposition as a 'basic linguistic index of the affiliation of words to antonyms [opposites] (the more contexts of juxtaposition of words there are, the more reasons there are to regard these words as antonyms [opposites]), and the basis for their classification' (Kočergan 1981, 37 [translation A.M.]). Such a firm belief in the power of syntagmatic opposition is hardly tenable; I therefore suggest the following: the most important observation that can be borne out by facts is that opposites in texts are in many cases characterized by contiguous arrangement (as shown in 2.3) and can thus be isolated for analysis. Cf.:

(3) Other men, he gathered, met each new dawn with a refreshed mind and heart, full of optimism and resolution; or else they moved sluggishly through the first hour of the day in a state of blessed numbedness, incapable of any thought at all, **pleasant** or **unpleasant**. (*TBMIFD*, 7)

(4) He begged her to marry him, but she refused . . . He followed her back to London, and they resumed the relationship, now as **mistress** and **keeper**. (*TBMIFD*, 141)

(5) Philip Swallow had been **made** and **unmade** by the system in precisely the same way. (*CP*, 16)

(6) And there are three types of story, the story that ends **happily**, the story that ends **unhappily**, and the story that ends **neither happily nor unhappily**, or, in other words, doesn't really end at all. (*CP*, 87)

(7) Miss Wade runs straight into my arms. And at that moment the game changes. It's no longer **attack** but **defence**. (*SDM*, 183)

(8) Poirot nodded. 'Yes, she is dead,' he said. 'Someone has turned the **comedy** into a **tragedy**.' (*ACP*, 43)

(9) His own papers were works of art on which he laboured with loving care for many hours, tinkering and polishing, weighing every word, deftly manipulating *eithers* and *ors*, judiciously balancing **difficult** questions on **popular** authors with **easy** questions on **obscure** ones, . . . (*CP*, 17 f.)

(10) Certainly the soldiers often looked as if they would like to throw down their arms and join the protesting students,

especially when the girl supporters of the Garden taunted them by stripping to the waist and opposing bare breasts to their bayonets, a juxtaposition of **hardware** and **software** that the photographers of *Euphoric Times* found irresistible. (*CP*, 172)

The second important observation is that contrast in texts, as indicated by the contiguous arrangement of opposites (as in (3) to (10) above), is further characterized by the favoured placement of such opposites X and Y in a syntactically definable environment. On the basis of a corpus of 161 pairs of opposites in context the following "syntactic frames" could be established for English:[9]

Frame A: X *and* Y

(11) It's a large industrial city, with the usual **advantages and disadvantages**. (*CP*, 81)

Frame B: *neither* X *nor* Y

(12) . . . she was a rather mediocre child, **neither stupid nor** particularly **intellectual**. (*HP*, 68)

(13) The children involved seem **neither old enough nor young enough** for it to fall into any special class. A psychological crime is indicated. (*HP*, 67)

Frame C: X *or* Y; *whether* X *or* Y; *either* X *or* Y

(14) At the moment the situation is that we Catholics expend most of our moral energy on **keeping or breaking** the Church's teaching on birth control . . . (*TBMIFD*, 63)

(15) Her neck and arms were her usual shade of summer tan for the country—**whether naturally or artificially** produced it was impossible to tell. (*TAT*, 17)

(16) Neighbours are so important in the country. One has **either** to be **rude or friendly**; one can't, as in London, just keep people as amiable acquaintances. (*SC*, 69)

Frame D: X *or* (= "and") Y

(17) Other men, he gathered, met each new dawn with a refreshed mind and heart, full of optimism and resolution; or else they moved sluggishly through the first hour

of the day in a state of blessed numbedness, incapable of any thought at all, **pleasant or unpleasant**. (*TBMIFD*, 7)

Frame E1: *not* X, (*but*) Y

(18) Mr. Renauld wrote this letter. Without blotting it, he re-read it carefully. Then, **not on impulse, but deliberately**, he added those last words, and blotted the sheet. (*MOL*, 13)

Frame E2: X, *not* Y

(19) . . . and his advice is that after a shock of any kind, the trouble must be **faced, not avoided**. (*SC*, 72)

E1 and E2 have been established as one frame because of the negation of one member (X or Y) of the pair.

Frame F: X *rather than* Y; X-*er than* Y; Y-*er than* X

(20) 'And after that,' said Tuppence, 'everyone forgot about her.'
'I'm afraid so,' said Miss Packard. 'It's sad, isn't it? But it's **the usual rather than the unusual** thing to happen.' (*POMT*, 34)

(21) It was one more argument to support his theory that **nice** things are **nicer than nasty** ones. (*LJ*, 140)

(22) Your left hand little finger is **short** but your right hand one is **much longer**. (*TZ*, 66)

Frame G: X *turns* (*in*)*to/becomes* Y

(23) Poirot nodded. 'Yes, she is dead,' he said. 'Someone has **turn**ed the **comedy into a tragedy**.' (*ACP*, 43)

Frame H: *from* X *to* Y

(24) Near to it were placed a number of suitcases, ranged neatly in order of size **from large to small**. (*TBF*, 7)

Frame I: X,Y (connectorless placement)

(25) 'The truth is,' said George, 'that one very seldom looks properly at anyone. That's why one gets such wildly differing accounts of a person from different witnesses in court. You'd be surprised. A man is often described as

Contrast

> tall—short; thin—stout; fair—dark; dressed in a **dark—light** suit; and so on.' (*AF*, 150)

A specific subtype of Frame I should be added, which can best be described as a morpho-syntactic variant of connectorlessly conjoined opposites X and Y. This subgroup is made up of verb-pairs with one member denoting the reversal of the activity denoted by the other member. As a rule, verb X is unprefixed, whereas verb Y is morphologically characterized by a prefix carrying a reversative meaning:

> (26) Strange flowers, red poinsettias rising proudly from a dusty garden . . . **Packing, unpacking**—where next? (*TATF*, 36)

In an investigation of 161 pairs of opposites in twenty English novels, which will be presented in 2.3, 61.5 per cent of opposites were syntactically assignable to Frames A to I. It must be admitted, however, that such a formal characterization of opposites in texts, though certainly helpful for further analysis of the meaning and relations of opposites on the level of the language-system, is impracticable without an intuitive knowledge on the part of the investigator[10] as to which words in the text denote something that is felt to be a case of adversativity[11] in a speech-community's world.

2.2.3 *Textual functions*

2.2.3.1 *General remarks*

What was called "syntactic environment" (in 2.2.2), on closer inspection, turns out to represent two significantly different types: either X and Y are elements of a coordinate structure, which 'is made up of a *connector* and two or more *conjuncts* it links' (Lang 1984, 20) and where the connector can sometimes appear as zero (cf. Frame I), or X and Y are lexically (Frames G, H; partly Frame F) or morpho-lexically (Frame F) connected. Thus we can observe a structural cline from completely coordinate structures at the one end via (regular) lexically/morpho-lexically conjoined conjuncts to structurally unrelated opposites at the other end. The assumption of such a structural scale explains why Frames A, B, C, D, E, and I exhibit the formal and semantic properties pertinent to coordination[12] as a particular structural relation,[13] why there are no structural grounds on which to establish the opposites in (27) to (32), and why Frames F, G, and H are difficult to locate on such a structural scale.

2.2.3.2 *Cohesion*

Before continuing the discussion of the pairs of opposites established on the basis of the structural criteria in 2.2.2 it seems necessary to give a brief sketch of those 38.5 per cent of the 161 pairs of opposites that were not allocated a place in Frames A to I:[14]

(27) 'Oh, Mr. Cade, what an **adventurous** life you must have led!'

'Very **peaceful**, I assure you.'

But it was clear that the lady did not believe him. (*TH*, 10)

(28) She shook her head. 'He's a **bad** loser.'

'But you, Mademoiselle, are a **good** loser.' (*DON*, 214)

(29) '. . . You've got to **break down** and destroy before you can **build up**.' (*DON*, 78)

(30) Its title—'Sanitation in Victorian Fiction'—seemed modest enough; but . . . the **absence** of reference to sanitation was as significant as the **presence** of the same, and his work thus embraced the entire corpus of Victorian fiction. (*TBMIFD*, 40)

(31) 'I can't make that child out,' said Mrs. Allerton. 'She varies so. One day she's **friendly**; the next day, she's positively **rude**.' (*DON*, 79)

(32) 'The police are blockheads,' he said sweepingly. 'What have they looked for in Ellis's room? Evidences of his **guilt**. We shall look for evidences of his **innocence**—an entirely different thing.' (*TAT*, 72)

In (27) to (32) it is the context that stresses the contrast constituted by the juxtaposition of X and Y. In the field of text-linguistics these cases have been described as instances of "cohesion",[15] which is defined as part of the text-forming component in the linguistic system. It is the means whereby elements that are structurally unrelated to one another are linked together, through the dependence of one on the other for its interpretation. The resources that make up the cohesive potential are part of the total meaning potential of the language, having a kind of catalytic function in the sense that, without cohesion, the remainder of the semantic system cannot be effectively activated at all. (Halliday and Hasan 1976, 27 f.)

Cases like (27) to (32) could be regarded as cases of "lexical cohesion", i.e. 'the cohesive effect achieved by the selection of vocabulary' (Halliday and Hasan 1976, 274), or, to be more precise, as instances of 'the most problematical part of lexical cohesion, cohesion that is achieved through the association of lexical items that regularly co-occur' (Halliday and Hasan 1976, 284), i.e. "collocation". According to Halliday and Hasan (1976, 285 ff.) the cohesive force of lexical items in collocation is not primarily a matter of systematic semantic relationship between them, but rather a matter of typical association of one item with the other because of their tendency to occur in similar environments. Yet this tendency to co-occur can, I think, be accounted for in a majority of cases only on the basis of the meaning of the lexical items in question. Thus, cohesion can explain the reader's awareness that, in texts (31) and (31')

(31) 'I can't make that child out,' said Mrs. Allerton. 'She varies so. One day she's **friendly**; the next day, she's positively **rude**.' (*DON*, 79)

(31') 'I can't make that child out,' said Mrs. Allerton. 'She varies so. One day she's **friendly**; the next day, she's positively **gracious**.'

rude and *gracious* depend on *friendly* for their interpretation, yet, cohesion as a concept devised for describing semantic relations between sentences presupposes knowledge of semantic relations between lexical items that are elements of these sentences.[16] This is also (implicitly) acknowledged by Halliday and Hasan:

When analysing a text in respect of lexical cohesion, the most important thing is to use common sense, combined with the knowledge that we have, as speakers of a language, of the nature and structure of its vocabulary. (Halliday and Hasan 1976, 290)

Thus, for the discovery of opposites in texts, the role played by lexical cohesion is comparable to that played by syntactic frames: by giving prominence to the (more or less) contiguous arrangement of opposites it facilitates the process of finding and interpreting them, but it must be regarded as the effect and not the cause of specific meaning-relations between X and Y.

2.2.3.3 *Coordination*

As has already been pointed out, opposites appear as constituents of coordinate structures in frames A, B, C, D, E, and I, more precisely as conjuncts linked by a connector (*and, neither . . . nor, or, either . . . or, not . . . but*; zero, etc.). The occurrence of opposites in coordinate structures entails that they meet the requirements of conjuncts[17] in such structures; these requirements have been convincingly established in an interesting study by Lang (1984). In the following I will enumerate the most important criteria for conjuncthood pertinent to a description of opposites in such frames:

(*a*) ' . . . conjoining is a fundamentally semantic-cognitive process, a mental technique. A semantically oriented approach is thus only plausible' (Lang 1984, 18).

(*b*) 'In a simple sentence such as *I need a book*, the meaning of *book* (disregarding grammatical relations) reduces to what is contained in its lexical entry, i.e. to a relatively small set of conceptual elements arranged in such a way as to leave room for a wide range of additional specifications to be filled in somehow from the context in which *book* occurs. If, however, *book* enters a coordinate structure as a conjunct, and hence occurs in the linguistic context of other conjuncts, then the semantic interpretation of *book* will be richer than the one specified in the lexicon in that conjuncts exemplify a certain common integrator. Being exemplifications they represent more than themselves because they stand for typical elements of the set defined by their respective common integrator' (Lang 1984, 29).

(*c*) 'The closer the conjunct meanings are conceptually related to each other,
—the closer to them is also the common integrator they exemplify . . .
—the more naturally its deduction will proceed along the nodes and branches of the conceptual hierarchy,
—the less factual knowledge and/or situational information is needed to perform the deduction' (Lang 1984, 28).

The concept of "common integrator", which will be helpful in a further classification and analysis of opposites, is defined as follows: Lang regards the connectors as having an "operational meaning", i.e. 'the language-bound capability of triggering a certain sequence of mental operations' (Lang 1984, 69) on the conjunct-meanings. As a result of these operations, Lang maintains, two things are established:

(i) a "common integrator" (CI) is set up, i.e. a conceptual entity which encompasses the conjunct-meanings in that the entities represented therein are deemed to be exemplifications of this CI,

(ii) within the domain defined by the CI, the entities represented in the conjunct-meanings [CMs] are brought into a specific relationship with each other according to the particular meaning of the connector (Lang 1984, 71).

Establishing CIs is a complex process (cf. Lang 1984, 73 ff.), and it is important to point out that the CI relies also on '[o]perations supplying contextual information or providing evaluations and frames of reference from general knowledge of the world, from belief-systems etc.' (Lang 1984, 72).[18]

In 2.3 I have tried to establish several types of "approximative information content" on the basis of the conjunct-meanings CM(X), CM(Y) and the operational connector-meanings as established in Lang (1984, 77 ff.) with regard to the CI:

(A) simultaneous validity of CM(X) and CM(Y); cumulative establishment of CI:

    (33) Johnson was always well up in **arrivals and departures**.

(B) confrontation of CM(X) and CM(Y) within CI; strongly context-dependent:

    (34) I always thought that everyone knew the **difference between right and wrong**.

(C) choice between CM(X) and CM(Y) within CI:

    (35) Neighbours are so important in the country. One has **either to be rude or friendly**.

(D) correction[19] of NEG CM(X) to CM(Y); alternatives within CI are usually given for reasons of emphasis:

    (36) At dinner . . . Henrietta was put next to David, and

from the end of the table Lucy's delicate eyebrows telegraphed **not a command** . . . **but an appeal**.

Retrospective correction, i.e. the correction of CM(X) to NEG CM(Y), has been included here as D'.

Such types of information content are but a tentative systematization of the text-constituting function of opposites in coordinate constructions, which should, however, allow further generalizations as to the semantic make-up of pairs of opposites.

2.2.3.4 *Lexically/morpho-lexically connected conjuncts*

For the sake of completeness the text-constituting function of the opposites in Frames F, G, and H must be discussed. These frames, as has been mentioned, are difficult to locate on a structural scale: on the one hand, their members appear in specific structural frames (like conjuncts), yet are not connected by connectors with an operative meaning; on the other hand, in comparison with cases of lexical cohesion they exhibit a higher degree of contiguity and semantic connectedness. Two types of information content must be added to types (A) to (D):

(E) comparison: CM(X) is compared with CM(Y) with regard to CI:

(37) Her lips were dry, and **hard rather than soft**.

(F) mutation: CM(X) is mutated into CM(Y) within CI:

(38) **Love turns to hate** more easily than you think, Mr. Strange.

2.3   OPPOSITES IN CONTEXT: CORPUS

2.3.1 *Introduction*

This section contains the results of an investigation of 20 English novels published between 1920 and 1979 (listed as section 1 of 'Corpus of investigated texts' in the Bibliography) with regard to the occurrence of opposites as instances of contrast on the level of parole. The corpus presented here is a corpus of types, i.e. of the 161 pairs of opposites each was considered only once. What should be regarded as a pair of opposites in the process of data-collecting was determined by my pre-theoretical knowledge of

what opposites are and by the contiguous occurrence of such
opposites in the investigated texts. This principle was also maintained for such pairs where one member can be regarded as the
result of word-formation processes.

From a formal point of view it can be said that 61.5 per cent
(99 pairs) appear in syntactic frames as established in 2.2.2; 38.5
per cent (62 pairs) appear without such syntactic frames.

As to the interpretation of the function of such pairs of opposites with regard to a message conveyed in a text, it must be
admitted that such an interpretation can be made systematically
only on the basis of opposites appearing in syntactic frames. This
allows them to be treated along the lines suggested in 2.2.3.3 as
instances of syntactically/lexically/morpho-lexically coordinate
structures, although that sometimes means stretching a point.

This investigation has been intended as a first attempt at showing that contrast is a phenomenon showing greater regularity than
has hitherto been assumed; moreover, establishing contrast on the
level of speech is a valuable heuristic device enabling the investigator to look for significant generalizations on the level of the language-system. It is important to stress once again that within this
study the established frames are heuristic in nature, not criterial.
They have been considered as pertaining above all to the level of
parole, which explains why they apparently attract opposites of
heterogeneous status with regard to the level of langue; this problem will be discussed in greater detail in Chapter 3.

2.3.2   *Opposites in syntactic frames*

The following list contains all pairs of opposites occurring in syntactic frames in the corpus, arranged according to syntactic
frames. The pairs of opposites are given in the first column, the
number in parentheses indicating the number of each pair in the
index contained in Appendix A. In the second column each pair
of opposites is quoted within its context (sometimes slightly
abbreviated for reasons of space). The "textual function" allotted
to each pair along the lines established in 2.2.3.3 and 2.2.3.4 is
given in the last column, a question mark indicating that the
assignment of a textual function was impossible or extremely
dubious, and that this is a case to be discussed in the course of
the work.

FRAME A: X *and* Y

Major textual functions:
(A) Simultaneous validity of X, Y
(B) Confrontation

ARRIVAL—DEPARTURE (6)	Johnson was always well up in arrivals and departures.	(A)
BLACK AND WHITE (17*a*)	. . . set down in black and white.	(?)[20]
BLACK-AND-WHITE (17*b*)	. . . chic in a severe black-and-white kind of way.	(?)[20]
BODY—SOUL (18)	Veronica would have swallowed him body and soul.	(A)[20]
CAUSE—EFFECT (24)	. . . a clear case of cause and effect	(A)
CONVENIENCE— INCONVENIENCE (30)	. . . giving statements as to . . . conveniences and inconveniences of her employment	(A)
FORMER—PRESENT (54)	. . . his former and his present wife	(B)
HIGH—LOW (70)	. . . search high and low	(A)[20]
HOT—COLD (72)	. . . hot and cold water	(A)
IN—OUT (76)	she went in and out of the house	(A)
LIFE—DEATH (86)	. . . life and death are the affair of the good God	(A)
NEW—OLD (103)	The new wife and the old wife making friends is quite disgusting in my mind.	(B)
NOW—THEN (106)	. . . seeking to differentiate between what she knew now and what she had known then.	(B)
OBEDIENCE—DISOBEDIENCE (107)	. . . illustrating in him that . . . inseparable mixture of real . . . obedience and covert . . . disobedience	(A)
REALITY—ILLUSION (126)	. . . if you can only make up your mind what is reality and what is illusion.	(B)
RIGHT—WRONG (129)	I always thought that everyone knew the difference between right and wrong.	(B)
SANITY—INSANITY (134)	. . . you and I represent opposite points of view. One might almost call them sanity and insanity.	(B)
SAY—DO (136)	. . . say one thing and do another	(B)[21]

SILENT—LOQUACIOUS (142)	Poirot was alternately silent and loquacious.	(B)
SUPPLY—DEMAND (155)	Supply and demand complemented each other and all was well.	(A)
UP—DOWN (158)	He looked Poirot up and down . . .	(A)

FRAME A': X, *at the same time* Y

Major textual function:
  (A) Simultaneous validity of X, Y

EMBARRASSED—THRILLED (30)	Cornelia was the prey of conflicting emotions. She was deeply embarrassed but at the same time pleasurably thrilled.	(A)[21]
LIKE—DISLIKE (88)	It is always difficult to know if you like anyone beautiful. You like beauty to look at, at the same time you dislike beauty almost on principle.	(A)
SIMPLICITY—COMPLEXITY (144)	I was puzzled by the simplicity and at the same time the complexity.	(A)

Frame B: *neither* X *nor* Y

Major textual function:
  (A) Simultaneous validity (rather: non-validity) of X, Y

OLD—YOUNG (109)	The children . . . seem neither old enough nor young enough for it . . .	(A)
SHORT—TALL (141)	'. . . Anyway, I do, don't I, Shorty? . . .'. The man Bernard Bastable had spoken to was not short. Nor was he tall enough for the name to be appropriate as an irony.	(A)
STUPID—INTELLECTUAL (154)	. . . a rather mediocre child, neither stupid nor particularly intellectual	(A)

FRAME C: X *or* Y; *whether* X *or* Y; *either* X *or* Y

Major textual function:
  (C) Choice (exclusive)

BELIEF—DISBELIEF (14)	It didn't seem the kind of theory to which belief or disbelief could be attached.	(C)
EXERCISE—RESTRAIN (46)	You could have exercised this charm or you could have restrained it.	(C)
FAT—THIN (52)	Is he deafer or blinder or fatter or thinner?	(C)
FORTUNATE—UNFORTUNATE (55)	Whether that is fortunate or unfortunate, I cannot at the moment decide.	(C)
GLAD—SORRY (59)	She glanced up quickly as if she'd been expecting to be asked this, but he couldn't tell whether she was glad or sorry when it came.	(C)
GUILTY—INNOCENT (63)	. . . a speculation as to whether the prisoner had been guilty or as innocent as the court had pronounced him to be.	(C)
HANG—DROWN (64)	Do you think the old saying is true—about you're born to be hanged or born to be drowned?	(C)[21]
HAPPY—UNHAPPY (66)	. . . how things were going with her. Whether she was happy or unhappy.	(C)
HEAD—HEEL (68)	. . . we don't know whether we're on our heads or our heels	(C)[21]
HEAVY—LIGHT (69)	Was the pile of underclothes . . . heavy or light?	(C)
INSULT—COMPLIMENT (78)	. . . I can't make up my mind about . . . whether it is an insult or a compliment to be considered a potential murderess.	(C)
NATURAL—ARTIFICIAL (101)	. . . her usual shade of summer tan for the country—whether naturally or artificially produced it was impossible to tell.	(C)

RUDE—FRIENDLY (131)	Neighbours are so important in the country. One has either to be rude or friendly;	(C)
SIMPLE—COMPLEX (143)	. . . either this crime was very simple . . . or else it was extremely complex.	(C)
SMALL—BIG (146)	. . . all those things. They might have had small significance or a big one.	(C)
STRENGTH—WEAKNESS (153)	I never knew whether it was strength or weakness that took me away from Veronica,	(C)

FRAME D: X *or* (= "and") Y

Major textual function:

   (A) Simultaneous validity of X,Y (weak disjunction; non-exclusive; indicators in italics)

EVIL—GOOD (43)	She would hear . . . *all* about the house, who had lived there, who had been of evil or good repute in the neighbourhood . . .	(A)
EXPECTED—UNEXPECTED (47)	Marigold was off now . . . : off, that is, not in *any* expected or un-expected direction, just *somewhere*.	(A)
HAPPINESS—UNHAPPINESS (65)	. . . George's *state of mind*, his happiness or unhappiness, had become . . . perfectly indifferent to him.	(A)
HONOURABLE—DISHONOURABLE (71)	. . . she was at this moment a mother . . . willing to defend her young by *any* means, honourable or dishonourable.	(A)
LEAVE—RETURN (83)	As *always when* leaving or return-ing, she paused . . .	(A)
LOSE—GAIN (94)	. . . my watch is right. It's a perfect time-keeper. It *never* loses or gains.	(A)
MORE—LESS (99)	. . . his wife more or less knew about the affair.	(?)[20]
REAL—SUPPOSED (125)	. . . it could hardly have been due to *any* personal merit, real or supposed, . . .	(A)

SOON(ER)—LATE(R) (149)	You will have to know, of course, . . . sooner or later . . .	(?)[20]

FRAME E1: *not* X, (*but*) Y
Major textual functions:
  (B) Confrontation
  (D) Correction (Substitution)

CHANCE—DESIGN (25)	It could not be chance that Simon Doyle had a bottle of red ink in his pocket. No, it must be design.	(D)
COMMAND—APPEAL (28)	At dinner . . . Henrietta was put next to David, and from the end of the table Lucy's delicate eyebrows telegraphed not a command . . . but an appeal.	(D)
FACT—IDEA (50)	This isn't facts. Just an idea. And it's impossible, anyway.	(D)
GENERAL—PARTICULAR (58)	Was she capable of murder? . . . Capable not of murder in general, but of one particular individual murder.	(D)
IMPULSE—HABIT (75)	' . . . I much prefer men who propose on impulse.' 'Like me?' 'It's not an impulse with you, Bill. It's habit.'	(D)
INFANT—GROWN-UP (77)	He had that infant paralysis, . . . , though . . . it isn't infants as suffer from it. It's grown-ups.	(D)
KILL OFF—KEEP ALIVE (81)	A nerve specialist doesn't kill off many of his patients. He keeps 'em alive and makes his income out of them.	(D)
LISTEN—LOOK (90)	She was not listening to the conversation, she was only looking.	(D)[21]
LUXURY—NECESSITY (96)	Children aren't a luxury, they're a necessity.	(D)
ORDINARY—EXTRAORDINARY (111)	'I'm not an ordinary person,' said Anthony in a shocked tone. 'I'm very extraordinary'	(D)

PROBABILITY—POSSIBILITY (119)	His words were a denial not of probability, but of possibility.	(D)[21]
REAL—ARTIFICIAL (124)	I remember Ada had an evening-dress . . . Mauvy-blue and she had pink rosebuds on it . . . They weren't real, of course. Artificial.	(D)
SAFE—DANGEROUS (133)	. . . look after yourself, Rosaleen. Life isn't safe, remember—it's dangerous, damned dangerous . . .	(D)
SLEEPY—AWAKE (145)	She herself did not feel in the least sleepy. *On the contrary* she felt wide awake and slightly excited.	(B)
SOOTHE—ENRAGE (150)	Occasional words came from Lewis . . . But they seemed not to soothe, but *on the contrary* to enrage the young man still further.	(B)

FRAME E2: X, *not* Y

Major textual function:
(D') Retrospective correction (Emphasis)

ASK—ANSWER (8)	But I found he was not communicative. Even when I asked where we were going, he would not answer.	(?)
ASSIST—HINDER (9)	I wish to assist a love-affair—not to hinder it.	(D')
CONSTRUCTIVE— DESTRUCTIVE (29)	Anything that mitigates suffering is worth while—and anything that's constructive and not destructive	(D')
FACE—AVOID (49)	. . . and his advice is that after a shock of any kind, the trouble must be faced, not avoided.	(D')
FORWARD—BACK (56)	It does no good to go over and over a thing in your mind. Look forward—not back.	(D')
LISTENER—TALKER (91)	Lord Caterham has commented on the fact that when it is a question of the first editions . . . he is always the listener, never the talker.	(D')

LORD—LAW (93)	. . . he might have left him to die. The same thing before the Lord, but not the same thing before the law.	(D')[21]
MURDER—SUICIDE (100)	You had no suspicions at the time of Mr. Barton's death that it might be murder, not suicide?	(D')[21]
NECESSITY—CHOICE (102)	So all he did was pass the time . . . No brain-work . . . before luncheon: nothing but a long sojourn—from necessity, not choice—on the lavatory . . .	(D')
PRECISE—VAGUE (117)	Grace Lamble was a most precise woman, not at all vague or absent-minded . . .	(D')
SATISFIED—DISSATISFIED (135)	'You were satisfied with him as an employee?' 'I would rather describe it as not dissatisfied. He had his points . . .'	(?)
STATEMENT—QUESTION (151)	She added, 'You're fond of him.' It was a statement, not a question.	(D')
TOMORROW—YESTERDAY (156)	You've got your life to live and most of that is in front of you now. Think of tomorrow, not of yesterday.	(D')[21]
WIN—LOSE (160)	. . . and we can win the war . . . but only if we don't lose it first.	(D')

FRAME F: X *rather than* Y; X-*er than* Y; Y-*er than* X
Major textual function:
(E) Comparison

HARD—SOFT (67)	. . . her lips were dry, and hard rather than soft.	(E)
INHUMAN—HUMAN (73)	. . . we are up against . . . a touch, shall we say, of madness? Not there originally, but cultivated. A seed that took root and grows fast. And now perhaps has taken charge, inspiring an inhuman rather than a human attitude to life.	(E)

NICE—NASTY (104)	It was one more argument to support his theory that nice things are nicer than nasty ones.	(E)
PROCURE—GIVE (120)	Miss Bligh's conversation was of a less melodramatic and juicy nature than that of Mrs. Copleigh, and was concerned more with the procuring of information, than of giving it.	(E)
SHORT—LONG (140)	Your left hand little finger is short but your right hand one is much longer.	(E)
USUAL—UNUSUAL (159)	. . . it's the usual rather than the unusual thing to happen . . .	(E)

FRAME G: X *turns (in)to/becomes* Y

Major textual function:
  (F) Mutation

ENEMY—FRIEND (40)	We want to turn some of our enemies into friends—those that are worth while.	(F)
LOVE—HATE (95)	Love turns to hate more easily than you think, Mr. Strange.	(F)
UNSELFISH—SELFISH (137)	. . . you were born unselfish but have become more selfish as time goes on.	(F)

FRAME H: *from* X *to* Y

Major textual function:
  (A) Cumulative validity of X, Y

LARGE—SMALL (82)	Near to it were placed a number of suitcases, ranged neatly in order from large to small.	(A)

Frame I: X, Y (unconjoined placement)

Major textual functions:
  (A) Cumulative validity
  (B) Confrontation

LIGHT—SHADE (87)	It is a duel between us . . . He is in the light, I in the shade.	(B)

SMILE—SIGH (147)	He half-smiled, half-sighed.	(A)
UGLY—PRETTY (157)	Au-pair girls—they're a part of daily life. Ugly ones, pretty ones . . .	(A)

FRAME I': X, Y (Y = "UNDO" X)

Major textual function:
(G) Reversal (of activity)

CLENCH—UNCLENCH (26)	Bertrand clenched his fist; then . . . unclenched it again.	(G)
DISAPPEAR—REAPPEAR (37)	. . . cried Poirot, disappearing into his bedroom, and reappearing with a hat.	(G)[22]
ENTANGLE—DISENTANGLE (41)	He had . . . got entangled with the local tobacconist's daughter—been disentangled and sent off to Africa . . .	(G)
MAKE—UNMAKE (98)	. . . history had been made and unmade at informal weekend-parties at Chimneys.	(G)[22]
PACK—UNPACK (113)	Packing, unpacking—where next?	(G)
PARCEL UP—DEPARCEL (114)	. . . the expertise of a man accustomed to handle the parcelling up and deparcelling of all different-sized works of art.	(G)[22]
STEADY—UNSTEADY (152)	[Her husband] steadied his nerves with brandy . . . Or unsteadied them, some would say.	(G) (?)

2.3.3 *Opposites without syntactic frames*[23]

2.3.3.1 *Morphologically unrelated pairs of opposites (N=43)*

adventurous—peaceful	cold—hot
alive—dead	crazy about—tired of[27]
amateur—professional	dead—alive
angular—round	death—life
bad—good	early—late
bad-tempered—sweet-tempered	everything—nothing
before—afterwards	excitement—apathy[28]
break down—build up	exciting—dull
broad—angular[24, 25]	false—true
buyer—seller	friendly—rude
cat—mouse[26]	going up—going down

good—bad
guilt—innocence
hard—soft
justice—mercy[29]
leisured—working[30]
lie—speak the truth
mad—sane
nice—sinister
outgoing—ingoing
polite—rude
positive—negative

present—past
prosecution—defence
public—private
reap—sow[31]
remembrance—oblivion
rough—smooth
sad—gay
senior—junior
severe—lenient
wits—looks[32]

2.3.3.2 *Morphologically related pairs of opposites (N=15)*

artistic—inartistic
attractive—unattractive
believe—disbelieve
businesslike—unbusinesslike
correct—incorrect
delicate—indelicate
dependent—independent
expression—non-expression

imaginative—unimaginative
interesting—uninteresting
likely—unlikely
logical—illogical
official—unofficial
ordinary—extraordinary
social—anti-social[33]

Notes to Chapter 2

1. Some studies are based on dictionaries of antonyms (Gsell 1979, Nellessen 1982), others (like Tottie 1980) work with a text corpus, yet investigate relatively motivated, i.e. morphologically related members of pairs of opposites, which are easy to find in texts; Marsh-Stefanovska (1982) relies on her intuition as a native speaker of English.

2. '(a) in different types of grammatical constructions where one employs the terms of an antonymic pair,
   (b) in the semantic classes of the words they combine with,
   (c) in the most characteristic syntactic structures where they appear.
   In other words, by means of syntactic analysis one manages to establish the laws for the use of antonyms in speech, to find out what is typical in a given context for two words opposed from the semantic point of view, according to one or more differentiating semantic features.'

3. Cf. Henrici (1975, 184) for a discussion of the paradigmatic dimension, especially of what has been called "wortsemantischer Ansatz".

4. For a brief summary of the most important characteristics of syntagmatic and paradigmatic relations see Kastovsky (1982*b*, 21 f.).

5. In a German weekly I found an interesting parallel to the English *life—literature* example: 'Hunderttausende haben hierzulande Erica Jong gelesen und kultisch über ihre Vision vom Spontanfick (mit einem wortlosen Mitpassagier im Eisenbahntunnel) diskutiert. Aber wenn's draufankommt [*sic*], ist Literatur halt kühner als das Leben' ['In this country hundreds of thousands have read Erica Jong and it has been a popular fashion to discuss her vision of a spontaneous fuck (with a silent co-passenger in the railway tunnel). But when it comes to putting it into practice, literature is more daring than life'] (*Stern* 1986/14, 97).

6. For an explanation of this see Ch. 3.

7. Novikov (1973*a*, *b*) uses the term "antonym" in its broad sense; in a description of the parole-level I prefer to speak of "opposites" (for reasons given in Ch. 1) and have thus replaced the term "antonym" as used by Novikov by "opposite" whenever it applies to phenomena of speech/parole.

8. The term "meaning", which would be the literal translation of Russian "značenie" as used by Novikov (1973*a*, *b*), is definitely misleading here. I have therefore replaced it by "textual function", thus probably rendering Novikov's intention more appropriately.

9. I have introduced the term "syntactic frame" to refer to the observable, analysable position of opposites in a linear sequence of words (mostly conjunctions), thus freeing the term "context" as used by Novikov (1973*a*, *b*) from its reference to syntagmatic contrast; for the sense of "context" as used in the present work see 2.2.3.

10. As to the scope of applicability of "syntactic frames" Novikov (1973*a*, 100) points out: 'the analysis of opposition [Russ. "protivopoložnost'"] in the lexicon starts out with an intuitive selection of phrases containing such oppositions. A multitude of such phrases is reduced to a limited number of typical [Russ. "tipovye"] sentences' [translation A.M.].

11. For a discussion of adversativity vs. oppositeness of meaning see also Ch. 3.

12. "Coordination" is here used in Lang's sense as '*the underlying principle* which is manifested in a variety of *coordinate structures*' (Lang 1984, 14).

13. Cf. Halliday and Hasan (1976, 233 ff.) as to the status of *and* and *or*.

14. In examples (27) to (32) I have avoided morphologically related pairs of opposites, as such pairs are easy to establish on formal grounds. These special formal properties, viz. the easily identifiable affix, require a special treatment (see Chs. 4 and 6).

15. For a brief survey see e.g. Beaugrande and Dressler (1981, ch. 4); their treatment of "Junktion" (Beaugrande and Dressler 1981, 76 ff.) must be kept apart from Halliday and Hasan's (1976, 226 ff.) concept of "conjunction"; my remarks on cohesion in this paragraph are based on Halliday and Hasan (1976); as for their concept of "structure", see Halliday and Hasan (1976, 6 ff.).

16. An interesting parallel from the field of synonymy should not remain unmentioned, as it also stresses the primacy of the systematicity of semantic relations. When discussing synonymity as a parole phenomenon Gauger (1972, 57 ff.) establishes the term "synonymische Kontexte" (Gauger 1972, 65 ff.) as denoting a manifestation of what has been called '"bewusstes" Sprechen' (Gauger 1972, 58), i.e. in such synonymic contexts 'the speaker is conscious of *how* he can say what he wishes to convey. Awareness of the choices open to him implies awareness of his linguistic competence. Such a speaker will therefore notice the differences between potential synonyms' (Schreyer 1976, 6). Examples of such "synonymic contexts" would be:

    "Also Gundermanns. Gut. Und dann vielleicht Oberförsters. Das älteste Kind hat freilich die Masern, und die Frau, das heißt die Gemahlin (und Gemahlin ist eigentlich auch noch nicht das rechte Wort), die erwartet wieder" ['Let's agree on the Gundermanns. Good. And then maybe the senior forester and his wife. Their oldest child is down with the measles, though, and the *wife*, that is the *spouse* (and spouse is not really the right word either), is expecting again'] (Th. Fontane, Der Stechlin, 1. Kapitel).

    "Sie war wirklich nur noch ein Bündel von Knochen und Haut, und ihr Kopf wurde zum Schädel" ['Really she was nothing but skin and bones, and her *head* was turning into a *skull*'] (J.Maass, Der Fall Gouffé, S.61). (Gauger 1972, 87)

17. 'Coordinate structures—in the presence, latent or actual, of connectors—consist of two or more conjuncts whose syntactic format can range from the category *Sentence* via a number of different major constituents, down to parts of lexical items. It follows that a conjunct meaning is a specific part of a sentence meaning according to the syntactic format it encompasses' (Lang 1984, 30).

18. For a discussion of the concept "common integrator" in comparison to related concepts see Lang (1984, ch. 5); a discussion and definition of the similarities and differences of "common integrator" and "semantic dimension" will be given in Chs. 3 and 6.

19. 'The meaning of (*not —*) *but* contains the instructions:
    (1) "*Take* the entities represented in CM1, CM2 with regard to

CF *as not simultaneously valid* within the domain defined by CI (although they are alternatives within this domain)";

    (2) "*Select* as valid the entity represented in CM2";

    (3) "In your cognitive system *replace* the entity represented in CM1 by that in CM2'" (Lang 1984, 79).

20. These are cases where the meaning of the construction is no longer deducible from the meanings of X, Y, and the connector; they must, therefore, be treated as lexicalized constructions (idioms, irreversible binomials; cf. Ch. 3).

21. These cases are of special interest as they illustrate a sort of "foregrounding" function of Contrast: X and Y are either members of sets of multiple oppositeness on the level of the language-system or represent instances of Adversativity; see also Ch. 3.

22. I have included these pairs in Frame I' despite the presence of a connector because they represent a separate group of opposites and should, therefore, be grouped together despite their (purely formally established) appearances in other syntactic frames.

23. I have decided against a more extensive presentation of opposites without syntactic frames in this work. It would seem that lexical cohesion can be achieved primarily with the help of systemic opposites, i.e. lexemes whose meanings are in a relation of oppositeness on the level of the language-system, whereas the syntactic frames, according to the material investigated, attract a wider variety of opposites, both systemic and non-systemic, binary and non-binary. Corroboration of such a hypothesis would, however, require the investigation of a considerable amount of empirical data as well as psycholinguistic testing.

24. Many of the pairs labelled as opposites in 2.3.3 will be regarded as uncontroversial by speakers of English. There are, however, several cases (listed in nn. 25–33 below) whose status is not quite clear. They have been included in the sample as instances of Contrast on intuitive grounds; their semantic properties will be discussed in greater detail in Ch. 3.

25. Elspeth McKay was as unlike her brother, . . . , as she could be in every way. Where he was **broad**, she was **angular**. (*HP*, 51)

26. Battle said nothing—but he waited—waited like an elderly father **cat**—for a **mouse** to come out of the hole he was watching. (*TZ*, 138)

27. 'You leave your wife, come bull-headed after me, get your wife to give you a divorce. **Crazy about** me one minute, **tired of** me the next . . .' (*TZ*, 105)

28. He seemed to be labouring under a mixture of **excitement** interlarded with great spaces of complete **apathy** when he sunk in a coma. (*SC*, 26)

29. Too much **mercy** . . . often resulted in further crimes which were fatal to innocent victims who need not have been victims if **justice** had been put first and **mercy** second. (*HP*, 114)
30. Lucy, Henry, Edward . . . they were all divided from her by an impassable gulf—the gulf that separates the **leisured** from the **working**. (*TH*, 110)
31. Nevile was obstinate. He would insist on bringing these two together—and now he is **reaping** what he has **sown**! (*TZ*, 62)
32. ' . . . I should very much like to know how he manages to live as he does.'

    'By his **wits**,' suggested Mary.

    'One might pardon that. I rather fancy he lives by his **looks** . . .' (*TZ*, 36)
33. Mrs Drake . . . concealed almost entirely . . . a feeling of vigorously suppressed annoyance at the position in which she found herself as the hostess at a **social** occasion at which something as **anti-social** as murder had occurred. (*HP*, 39)

3

Semantic Opposition: Systemic versus Non-Systemic

3.1 INTRODUCTION

Among the pairs of opposites established on the basis of syntagmatic contrast in 2.3 we find, among others, the following cases:

(1) He'd been madly in love with Veronica but it wouldn't have done. Veronica would have swallowed him **body and soul**. (*TH*, 25)

(2) I wish she would explain it to me, he thought wrily, gazing into another mirror, I'm damned if I can make **head or tail** of it. (*CP*, 170)

(3) Do you think the old saying is true—about you're **born to be hanged or born to be drowned**? (*HP*, 87)

(4) It was indeed, he thought, a perfect marriage of **Nature and Civilization**, this view, where one might take in at a glance the consummation of man's technological skill and the finest splendours of the natural world. (*CP*, 56)

(5) Unable to decide on the relative accuracy of the **oral and rectal** methods of taking her temperature, Barbara had decided to employ both. (*TBMIFD*, 10)

(6) Caroline dissented. She said that if the man was a hairdresser, he would have **wavy hair, not straight**. All hairdressers did. (*MRA*, 19)

(7) She drew out from her handbag the letter she had received that morning from Lady Tamplin. Katherine was no fool. She understood the *nuances* of that letter as well as anybody and the reason of Lady Tamplin's show of affection towards a long-forgotten cousin was not lost upon her. It was **for profit and not for pleasure** that Lady Tamplin was so anxious for the company of her dear cousin. (*MBT*, 51 f.)

The question that arises in this context is: should pairs like *body—soul, head—tail, hang—drown, nature—civilization, oral—rectal, wavy—straight,* and *profit—pleasure* be treated on a par with *love—hate, like—dislike, broad—narrow, pleasure—pain?* The answer to this question depends on the concept of semantic opposition adopted by the investigating linguist. The following definition represents a rather broad view of the matter and is a typical example of a lexicographer's point of view:

Ein grosser Teil des Lexembestandes, soweit es sich nämlich um Wortschatzeinheiten mit kontrastfähigen Bedeutungen handelt, ist in das Sybsystem [*sic*] der Oppositionsrelationen eingegliedert. Der Begriff der Opposition ist . . . recht weit zu fassen, um alle von den Sprechern als starke Differenz oder als Kontrast verstandenen Lexempaarungen an extremen Positionen unter einem gemeinsamen Hyperonym einbeziehen und darstellen zu können, die Ausdruck eines logischen (kontradiktorischen bzw. konträren) oder eines dialektischen (realen) Gegensatzes sind.[1] (Agricola 1983, 14)

Semanticists who adhere to the (theoretically well-founded[2]) assumption that the vocabulary of a natural language is 'at least on the semantic level . . . organized according to uniform principles' (Kastovsky 1981*a*, 431) and who try to investigate these uniform structural principles would regard Agricola's definition as being too vague and, in fact, blurring the distinction between relatively stable, context-independent meaning-relations anchored in the semantic structure of a given language (i.e. in the language-system) and strongly context-dependent instances of contrast.[3] The following discussion will show that cases of the former type (in the following referred to as "systemic semantic opposition") can be handled adequately along strictly semantic lines, whereas the treatment of "non-systemic semantic opposition" requires recourse to encyclopaedic and pragmatic knowledge.

3.2 SYSTEMIC SEMANTIC OPPOSITION

3.2.1 *Archisememes, dimensions, and features*

A semantic analysis of the contrasting pairs of lexemes[4] in (8) to (11) must be able to show their simultaneous similarities and dissimilarities:

(8) Near to it were placed a number of suitcases, ranged neatly in order of size from **large** to **small**. (*TBF*, 7)

(9) Whether there had been **much** or **little** money in the house at the time of her death was a debatable point. None had been found. (*LM*, 70)

(10) Mrs. Milray turned out to be almost ludicrously unlike her daughter. Where Miss Milray was **hard**, she was **soft**, where Miss Milray was angular, she was round. (*TAT*, 161)

(11) The two of us dance as one person; the tango is not **male** and **female**, but their union as a couple. (*Time*, 4 Nov. 1985, 56)

The theoretical framework that seems best suited for a treatment of systemic semantic opposition is a modified version of a sub-part of the semantic theory[5] advanced by Coseriu (e.g. in Coseriu 1964; 1967; 1970a; 1970b; 1973; 1975; Coseriu and Geckeler 1974; 1981) and further developed by Geckeler (e.g. in Geckeler 1978; 1979; 1981a) and Kastovsky (e.g. Kastovsky 1981a; 1982b;[6] 1982c). Meaning-relations of the type exemplified in (8) to (11) will be examined in the broader context of Coseriu's definition of the lexical field:

Ein Wortfeld ist in struktureller Hinsicht ein lexikalisches Paradigma, das durch die Aufteilung eines lexikalischen Inhaltskontinuums unter verschiedene in der Sprache als Wörter gegebene Einheiten entsteht, die durch einfache inhaltsunterscheidende Züge in unmittelbarer Opposition zueinander stehen. So ist z.B. die Reihe *jung—neu—alt* im Deutschen ein Wortfeld. Ein Wortfeld kann aber auch in einem anderen Wortfeld höheren Niveaus eingeschlossen sein. Jede in der Sprache als einfaches Wort gegebene Einheit ist inhaltlich ein Lexem. Eine Einheit, die dem ganzen Inhalt eines Wortfeldes entspricht, ist ein Archilexem.[7] (Coseriu 1967, 294)

This concept of the lexical field[8] is characterized negatively in that lexical fields do not represent scientific classifications of extralinguistic reality, are not "thing-spheres" of an objective kind, and must not be equated with fields of associations or with conceptual fields (Geckeler 1981a, 393 f.).

In contradistinction to Lyons (1977, 271 ff.), who defines "sense-relations" in terms of implications holding between sentences,[9] Coseriu treats semantic opposition in analogy to phonological opposition.[10] Cf.:

The distinctive features of phonology result from immediate paradigmatic oppositions between phonemes. Such oppositions presuppose not only differences between the terms involved, but also a common basis, i.e. something that these terms have in common, because functional differences (distinctive features) can only be established against the background of a common basis. (Kastovsky 1982*c*, 31 f.)

In fact, two different interpretations of "common basis" must be distinguished in this context: one is the interpretation of "common basis" as "basis of comparison" which is a necessary prerequisite for systemic opposition in general:

Ein Gegensatz (eine Opposition) setzt nicht nur solche Eigenschaften voraus, durch welche sich die Oppositionsglieder voneinander unterscheiden, sondern auch solche Eigenschaften, die beiden Oppositionsgliedern gemeinsam sind. Solche Eigenschaften können als "Vergleichsgrundlage" bezeichnet werden. Zwei Dinge, die gar keine Vergleichsgrundlage, d.i. keine einzige gemeinsame Eigenschaft besitzen (z.B. ein Tintenfass und die Willensfreiheit) bilden keinen Gegensatz.[11] (Trubetzkoy 1939/1958, 60 f.)

With regard to systemic semantic opposition, the task of acting as the basis of comparison is performed by the "archisememe/ archilexeme". Thus, for a pair like *boy* and *girl* the common semantic denominator is the archilexeme CHILD[12] (cf. Kastovsky 1981*a*, 436 f.; 1982*c*, 34); *kick, punch, slap, bash, smack, pound* all involve the archilexeme HIT (cf. Lipka 1980, 103 f.; Kastovsky 1981*a*, 441 f.). The archisememe/archilexeme as the basis of comparison can account for the similarities in the elements opposed to each other.

The other interpretation of "common basis" is connected with the dissimilarities in the elements contrasted with each other, i.e. "common basis" refers to the opposition as such and states with regard to which property/quality the meanings of lexical items are opposed to each other: *boy* and *girl* differ with regard to SEX; *kick, punch,* and *slap* are different with regard to INSTRUMENT; *bash, smack, pound,* etc. can be differentiated according to the category MANNER (cf. Kastovsky 1981*a*, 441 f.). Thus, there is a common basis against which immediate paradigmatic oppositions are established; this common basis is called "semantic dimension"[13] and is defined as follows:

La configuration des champs lexicaux, c'est-à-dire la façon dont les lexèmes sont agencés à l'intérieur de ces paradigmes, dépend en premier lieu du nombre des "dimensions sémantiques" qui y fonctionnent (et de la façon dont celles-ci y sont combinées les unes avec les autres) et en second lieu des types formels des oppositions établies par rapport à ces dimensions. . . . Une *dimension*, c'est le point de vue ou critère d'une opposition donnée quelconque, c'est-à-dire, dans le cas d'une opposition lexématique, la propriété sémantique visée par cette opposition: le contenu par rapport auquel elle s'établit et qui, du reste, n'existe — dans la langue respective — qu'en vertu, précisément, du fait qu'une opposition s'y rapporte, qu'il est le support implicite d'une distinction fonctionnelle.[14] (Coseriu 1975, 35)

It is essential to make a clear distinction between the notions "archisememe/archilexeme" and "dimension":[15]

La dimension, ce n'est pas non plus ce qui est commun aux termes d'une opposition (la "base de comparaison"): **c'est ce qui est commun aux différences entre ces termes, c'est-à-dire à leurs traits distinctifs.**[16] (Coseriu 1975, 36 [bold emphasis mine])

This distinction must also be captured in the labels given to archisememes/archilexemes[17] and dimensions: this is quite obvious in the *boy—girl* case with the archilexeme CHILD and the semantic dimension SEX (or rather GENDER in order to avoid unwanted connotations), i.e. both the archisememe and the semantic dimension can be designated by different, intuitively convincing metalinguistic terms. Adjectival opposites such as *large—small* in (8) as well as *male—female* in (11), however, cause greater problems, because 'very often, at least at the lowest hierarchical level, archisememes and semantic dimensions coincide' (Kastovsky 1982c, 35; cf. also Kastovsky 1982b, 90). This last statement, however, requires a slight modification: unquestionably, *large* and *small* constitute the dimension SIZE, *male* and *female* operate over the dimension GENDER, and one might assume that the archisememes should also be SIZE and GENDER, respectively, so that archisememe and semantic dimension would coincide. Yet, as the lexical field has been defined as consisting of lexemes which 'among themselves subdivide a larger area of meaning' (Kastovsky 1981a, 437) and which 'must belong to the

same part of speech, because otherwise they could not enter into
minimal oppositions with each other' (Kastovsky 1981*a*, 437),
the archisememe for *large—small* must be labelled HAVING SIZE;
analogously, the archisememe for *male—female* is HAVING GENDER.

In this study I will thus assume contrasting pairs of lexemes to
be instances of systemic semantic opposition if they constitute
semantic micro-fields (cf. Kastovsky 1981*a*, 437 f.), if they can
be traced back to an archisememe that fulfils the task of acting as
basis of comparison, and if they differ with regard to one semantic dimension which acts as a basis for the differences between
them. With regard to the archisememe, systemic opposites are
co-hyponyms: *boy* and *girl*, differing along the semantic dimension GENDER, constitute a semantic micro-field with CHILD func-
tioning as the archi-unit. The relation between archi-unit and
hyponym is a hierarchical, exclusively binary one (cf. Kastovsky
1982*c*, 35; Viehweger *et al.* 1977, 326 ff.), whereas systemic
semantic opposition must be regarded as a non-hierarchical
semantic relation between 'the co-hyponyms of a given archise-
meme/archilexeme [that] can be either binary or multiple'
(Kastovsky 1982*c*, 35).[18]

For a systematic description of oppositeness of meaning (this
is the term I will use for designating systemic semantic opposition obtaining between a pair of co-hyponyms) in the lexicon of
a given natural language it is the semantic dimensions and
semantic features that are the decisive factors. Both concepts are
strongly interdependent, as semantic dimensions result from the
immediate paradigmatic oppositions obtaining between the meanings of lexical items and are themselves in turn specified by the
semantic features:[19]

Semantic features thus characterize the internal semantic structure of an
individual lexical item and at the same time specify the meaning relations existing between lexical items, e.g. hyponymy, antonymy, complementarity, converseness, etc. (Kastovsky 1982*c*, 33 f.)

In Chapter 4 the nature of semantic dimensions and semantic
features characterizing systemic opposites will be discussed in
greater detail, and it will be shown how these notions can be successfully incorporated into the analysis and explanation of non-
hierarchical paradigmatic opposition.

3.2.2 *The sememic basis*

Another point that must be briefly discussed in this context is whether a description of oppositeness of meaning should result in a typology of lexical units in terms of actual sense-relations or whether it should primarily characterize the meaning-side of linguistic signs and point out more abstract, system-inherent semantic properties. The former point of view will be called the "lexemic approach", the latter I will call the "sememic approach".

The problem becomes apparent whenever we come across cases such as (12) and (13):

(12) The children involved seem neither **old** enough nor **young** enough for it to fall into any special class. A psychological crime is indicated. (*HP*, 67)

(13) The **new** wife and the **old** wife making friends is quite disgusting in my mind. (*TZ*, 34)

Adherents of the lexemic or 'dictionary approach' (Lehrer 1974, 8) would regard *old* either as an instance of polysemy, i.e. 'der Polysemie des Ausgangswortes, wobei dann den einzelnen Inhaltsvarianten des polysemischen Wortes jeweils ein verschiedenes Antonym zugeordnet wird'[20] (Geckeler 1980, 56), or as a case of homonymy, i.e. 'es handelt sich dabei um die Auflösung des lexikalischen Ausgangselements in Homophone[21] mit nachfolgender Zuordnung jeweils eines Antonyms zu jedem Homophon'[22] (Geckeler 1980, 57). There is, of course, a lot of disagreement among linguists as to when to assume a case of homonymy and when to assume a case of polysemy. Thus, Lyons (1977, 554 ff.) favours the polysemy approach,[23] Hansen *et al.* (1982, 199) regard *hot* as a polysemous lexical item, in one of its senses contrasting with *cold* ("of relatively low temperature"), in its other sense contrasting with *mild* ("not sharp or strong in taste or flavour").

Hundsnurscher (1971, 104), on the other hand, suggests a treatment of the following cases as instances of homonymy/homophony: *alt-1* vs. *jung*, *alt-2* vs. *neu*, *falsch-1* vs. *richtig*, *falsch-2* vs. *aufrichtig*, etc., yet regards *child* as a polysemous lexeme (cf. Hundsnurscher 1971, 36), whereas Lipka (1986*b*, 136) differentiates between the homonyms *child-1* ("nichterwachsener Mensch") and *child-2* ("Kind von").

It is, in fact, questionable whether the homonymy–polysemy distinction is really relevant for a systematic treatment of oppositeness of meaning; cf.:

Im übrigen ist dieses Problem für eine strukturelle Semantik von untergeordneter Bedeutung, da es hier primär um **Bedeutungsoppositionen** geht, unabhängig davon, ob nun diese verschiedenen Bedeutungen einem oder mehreren Lexemen zugeordnet werden, solange feststeht, dass es sich um verschiedene Bedeutungen handelt.[24] (Kastovsky 1982*b*, 122 [my emphasis])

The basic tenet of the sememic approach is thus the following assumption:

toute opposition sémantique s'établit entre les sémèmes (plan de contenu) et pas entre les lexèmes (plan de l'expression). Il s'en suit que si le signifié d'un lexème (L) présente plusieurs sémèmes . . . , chaque sémème peut entrer en relation d'opposition avec n'importe quel sémème et ceci indifféremment du lexème par lequel le sémème donné est réalisé sur le plan de l'expression.[25] (Iliescu 1977, 155)

On the content plane "old" and "young" in (12) are opposites along the semantic dimension AGE, "old" and "new" in (13) operate along a semantic dimension that could be labelled TIME OF EXISTENCE. A sememe-based[26] treatment of oppositeness of meaning is thus capable of handling cases like *good—bad* vs. *good—evil* by showing that they operate along different semantic dimensions, viz. QUALITY and MORAL QUALITY, respectively. Cf.:

(14) She shook her head. 'He's a **bad** loser.'
      'But you, Mademoiselle, are a **good** loser.' (*DON*, 214)

      ' . . . But I do think things come in—waves.'
      'Waves?'
      'Waves of **bad** luck and **good** luck . . .' (*MIE*, 76)

(15) Morris Zapp experiences a rush of missionary zeal to the head. He will do a good deed, instruct this innocent in the difference between **good** and **evil**, talk her out of her wicked intent. (*CP*, 33)

      She would hear, she was sure, all about the house by the bridge, who had lived there, who had been of **evil** or **good** repute in the neighbourhood, what scandals there were and other such likely topics. (*POMT*, 76)

Apart from that, the sememe-based treatment can show that near-synonyms such as *infant* and *child* on the basis of their identical denotative meaning share a common semantic dimension if opposed to *grown-up*:

(16) He had that infant paralysis, as they call it, though as often as not it isn't **infants** as suffer from it. It's **grown-ups**. Men and women too. (*HP*, 120)

(17) Just for a moment he felt the rôles reversed. The doctor's smile had been that of a **grown-up** amused by the cleverness of a **child**. (*MIE*, 69)

Yet another reason for preferring the sememe-based approach over the lexeme-based one is that it shows clearly the different semantic make-up of *man* if opposed to *woman* and of *man* when used as the archilexeme of the lexical field of which both *man* and *woman* are elements (cf. Lipka 1986*b*, 132 f.)—a problem that I will discuss in Chapter 6 in connection with the marked/unmarked distinction.

3.3 NON-SYSTEMIC SEMANTIC OPPOSITION

Contrast on the level of parole can, as has been pointed out in Chapter 2, also be expressed by pairs of lexical items whose meanings, when investigated in relation to each other, do not satisfy the criteria established for oppositeness of meaning in 3.2.1. Such cases have been referred to as 'fakultative Gegenwortpaare' (Agricola and Agricola 1979, 20) or as instances of 'konventionelle oder fakultative Kontrastsetzung' (Agricola 1983, 15).[27] Their interpretation as the linguistic realisation of adversativity requires encyclopaedic and/or pragmatic knowledge; furthermore, a 'gemeinsame Einordnungsinstanz' (Schippan 1983, 101) is necessary. In contradistinction to systemic opposites, where the archisememe acts as the basis of comparison, non-systemic opposites display a wide variety of possible common bases:

(18) 'Mind you, I don't think Rex would have actually murdered MacKenzie, but he might have left him to die. The same thing before the **Lord**, but not the same thing before the **law**. If he did, retribution's caught up with him . . .' (*PFR*, 111)

(19) Too much **mercy** . . . often resulted in further crimes which were fatal to innocent victims who need not have been victims if **justice** had been put first and **mercy** second. (*HP*, 114)

(20) And not only were they [= the prostitutes] beautiful, but also unexpectedly wholesome . . ., so that one might almost suppose that they did it for **love** rather than for **money** . . . (*CP*, 113)

(21) ' . . . I should very much like to know how he manages to live as he does.'
'By his **wits**,' suggested Mary.
'One might pardon that. I rather fancy he lives by his **looks** . . .' (*TZ*, 36)

In examples (18) to (21) the interpretability of the bold-faced lexemes as instances of a relation of contrast is founded mainly on the situational context; in (22) to (29) more profound, wider extralinguistic or encyclopaedic knowledge is a necessary prerequisite for their acceptance as what I will call "encyclopaedic opposites":

(22) Battle said nothing—but he waited—waited like an elderly father **cat**—for a **mouse** to come out of the hole he was watching. (*TZ*, 138)
' . . . Why, I was only in the room about three minutes before the lady came up, and then you were sitting here the whole time, as you always do, like a **cat** watching a **mouse**.' (*PI*, 116)

(23) Lucy, Henry, Edward . . . they were all divided from her by an impassable gulf—the gulf that separates the **leisured** from the **working**. (*TH*, 110)

(24) **Scholarship** and **domesticity** were opposed worlds, whose common frontier was marked by the Museum railings. (*TBMIFD*, 96)

(25) 'It's a special form of scholarly neurosis,' said Camel. 'He's no longer able to distinguish between **life** and **literature**.' (*TBMIFD*, 56)

(26) Edward wondered whether the Marchesa Bianca would have made an excellent wife. Somehow, he doubted it . . .

No, Bianca was **Romance**, and this was **real life**. He and Maud would be very happy together. She had so much common sense . . . (*LM*, 82)

(27) 'H'm,' said George. 'It will be one of those marriages made in **Heaven** and approved on **earth** . . .' (*LM*, 63)

(28) It was indeed, he thought, a perfect marriage of **Nature** and **Civilization**, this view, where one might take in at a glance the consummation of man's technological skill and the finest splendours of the natural world. (*CP*, 56)

(29) Jane amused herself by taking stock of her immediate neighbours. In each case she managed to find something wrong—fair eyelashes instead of dark, eyes more grey than blue, fair hair that owed its fairness to **art** and not to **Nature**, interesting variations in noses . . . (*LM*, 106)

In the majority of cases non-systemic opposites in texts appear in the syntactic frames established in Chapter 2 of this study. It is possible, therefore, to regard them as conjuncts in coordinate structures and to establish their common integrator, which fulfils the task of acting as the basis of comparison. In contradistinction to archisememes, which are established on intralinguistic, functional grounds, common integrators, as has been pointed out by Lang (1984, 74 ff.), take recourse to various sorts of pragmatic information as well and can therefore act as "gemeinsame Einordnungsinstanz" for non-systemic opposites.

Examples (30) to (32) illustrate cases of collocationally fixed opposites that are almost terminological in nature (cf. also Gsell 1979, 61):

(30) Caroline dissented. She said that if the man was a hair-dresser, he would have **wavy** hair, not **straight**. All hair-dressers did. (*MRA*, 19)

(31) Unable to decide on the relative accuracy of the **oral** and **rectal** methods of taking her temperature, Barbara had decided to employ both. (*TBMIFD*, 10)

(32) 'Seriously,' he said, 'this **venial** sin–**mortal** sin business is old hat.' (*TBMIFD*, 64)

Debit—credit in (33) and *theory—practice* in (34) are probably encyclopaedic opposites, too, but with a strong terminological tinge:

(33) 'How lovely. You are kind. I do love money! I'll keep beautiful accounts of our expenses—all **debit** and **credit**, and
the balance on the right side, and a red line drawn sideways
with the totals the same at the bottom . . .' (*TSA*, 37)

(34) But to people like Ralph Paton, turning over a new leaf is
easier in **theory** than in **practice**. (*MRA*, 191)

Luke laughed.
  'Oh, no, with me it's **theory**—not **practice**.'
  'No, I do not think you are the stuff of which murder-
ers are made.' (*MIE*, 66)

Sometimes non-systemic opposites are established along connota-
tive components of meaning and can be described in terms of
inferential features as suggested by Lipka (1985):

(35) She drew out from her handbag the letter she had received
that morning from Lady Tamplin. Katherine was no fool.
She understood the *nuances* of that letter as well as anybody and the reason of Lady Tamplin's show of affection
towards a long-forgotten cousin was not lost upon her. It
was for **profit** and not for **pleasure** that Lady Tamplin
was so anxious for the company of her dear cousin.
(*MBT*, 51 f.)

(36) 'It is as well you are in France,' said Van Aldin. 'We are
made of sterner stuff in the States. **Business** comes before
pleasure there.' (*MBT*, 131)

The treatment of *murder*, *suicide*, and *accident* in (37) causes
some problems. On the one hand, *murder* and *suicide* can be
treated as an instance of oppositeness of meaning along the
dimension AGENT, but *accident* is somehow less specific in meaning and cannot be treated on a par with *murder* and *suicide*. On
the other hand, in the texts given in (37) all three lexemes sub-
categorize violent deaths. It seems that on the level of parole a
lexeme can be contrasted with both a systemic opposite (*suicide*
vs. *murder*) and a non-systemic one (*suicide* vs. *accident*):

(37) 'But you don't think her death was **a natural one**?'
  'No.'
  'You don't believe it was an **accident**?' . . .
  'You don't think it was **suicide**?'

'Emphatically not.'

'Then,' said Luke gently, 'you *do* think that it was **murder**?' (*MIE*, 105)

'No, as I say, I inclined to the view that it was a case of **murder**, not **suicide**, but I realized that I had not a shadow of proof in support of my theory . . .' (*PI*, 46)

He thinks every death that takes place here must necessarily be a case of foul play fraught with grave political significance . . . You've no idea the fuss he made. I've been hearing about it from Tredwell. Tested everything imaginable for fingerprints. And of course they only found the dead man's own. The clearest case imaginable— though whether it was **suicide** or **accident** is another matter. (*SDM*, 28)

Examples (38) to (41) illustrate cases of "pseudo-binarity", i.e. two members of a set of multiple opposites are contrasted:

(38) Sitting quietly, her eyes half closed, she was nevertheless scrutinising everyone in the room with close attention. She was not **listening** to the conversation, she was only **looking**. (*POMT*, 163)

(39) 'It's all very well,' I said, my anger rising, 'but you've made a perfect fool of me! From **beginning** to **end**! . . .' (*PI*, 31)

(40) The **present** is nearly always rooted in the **past**. (*HP*, 142)

(41) You've got your life to live and most of that is in front of you now. Think of **tomorrow**, not of **yesterday**. (*TZ*, 95)

Adjectives denoting TEMPERATURE and COLOUR have traditionally been regarded as instances of multiple semantic opposition along the respective semantic dimensions (cf. e.g. Kastovsky 1982*b*, 138). It seems, however, that *hot* and *cold*, as well as *black* and *white*, are contrasted more often than other members of the sets: the former are used in (42) with a terminological tinge, the latter are used in (43) to denote the highest degree of adversativity:

(42) Mrs. Neele had never discovered the pleasures of electric irons, slow combustion stoves, airing cupboards, **hot** and

cold water from taps, and the switching on of light by a
mere flick of a finger. (*PFR*, 21)

Hot and **cold** shivers chased themselves up and down his
spine. He had the sense of being caught in a terrible
dilemma. (*LM*, 167)

(43) She'll lie for him, swear **black's white** for him and everything else. (*HP*, 30)

'. . . Ah, by the way, this Miss Lawson, is she the kind
that might conceivably lose her head under cross-examina-
tion in court?'
Charles and Theresa exchanged glances.
'I should say,' said Charles, 'that a really bullying KC
could make her say **black** was **white**!' (*DW*, 105)

This section has presented only a brief survey of problems
connected with establishing and describing non-systemic semantic opposition,[28] as this is not the main objective of this study. It
might be noted that non-systemic semantic opposition has not
attracted the attention of many structural semanticists. It would,
however, be a profitable field of research for any kind of conceptual approach towards the study of meaning-relations.

Notes to Chapter 3

1. 'A large part of the vocabulary pertains to the subsystem of relations
   of opposition, which can, of course, concern only lexical units with
   meanings that can enter relations of contrast. The concept of opposition . . . must be defined in a rather broad sense in order to be able
   to accommodate under a joint hyperonym all pairs of lexemes in
   extreme positions which have been interpreted by speakers as strong
   difference or contrast and which thus express either a logical (contradictory or contrary) or a dialectic (real) opposition.'
2. See e.g. Bahr (1974; repr. 1985), Kotschi (1974, 73 ff.), Viehweger
   et al. (1977, 83 ff., 99 ff.), Lyons (1977, 230 ff.), Coseriu and
   Geckeler (1981, 19 ff.), Kastovsky (1981*a*; 1982*b*, 66 ff. (especially
   for further literature on this topic)), Hansen *et al.* (1982, 220 ff.),
   Lipka (1990, 130 ff.).
3. Cf. 1.3 above; Nellessen (1982, 37 f.) gives the following reasons
   against a treatment of semantic opposition based on parole phenomena: 'Erstens ist die Zahl der möglichen Redebedeutungen bei vielen
   Wörtern nahezu unbegrenzt, so dass es schon aus quantitativen

Erwägungen nicht ratsam erscheint, diese Bedeutungsebene zu analysieren . . . Zweitens ist es gerade ein Phänomen der Rede, Wörter oder Begriffe einander gegenüberzustellen, die man—für sich genommen — nicht für Gegensätze halten würde. . . . Ein solcher die Redebedeutungen zugrundelegender Antonymie-Begriff würde also erstens dem intuitiven Vorverständnis von Bedeutungsgegensätzen widersprechen und zweitens nur auf die Analyse von konkreten Texten anwendbar sein.' ['First, for many words the number of potential parole meanings has almost no limit, so that in view of quantitative considerations it does not seem to be a good idea to analyse this meaning-level . . . Second, it is a typical phenomenon of speech to contrast words or concepts which would not be regarded as opposites if looked at in isolation. . . . A concept of antonymy taking parole meaning as basis would thus contradict our intuitive preliminary concept of meaning-oppositions and would be applicable to the analysis of individual texts only.']

4. The use of the term "lexeme" in this context indicates that the field of investigation is the language-system; lexemes are, in general, regarded as 'Einheiten des Sprachsystems, Wörter hingegen [als] ihre konkrete Realisierung auf der Ebene der Rede' ['entities of the language-system, whereas words are regarded as their concrete realization on the level of speech'] (Kastovsky 1982*b*, 74 f.). Marchand (1969, 1) defines the word as 'the smallest independent, indivisible, and meaningful unit of speech [!], susceptible of transposition in sentences'. The lexeme, on the other hand, can be defined in the following way: 'Lexeme sind Entitäten einer relativ stabilen Zuordnung von Laut- und Bedeutungsstrukturen. Sie vereinigen in sich sowohl denotativ-semantische und nichtdenotativ-semantische als auch morphologisch-syntaktische und phonologische Eigenschaften, und sie spielen eine entscheidende Rolle in den Beziehungen zwischen Syntax und Semantik' ['Lexemes are entities with a relatively stable combination of sound- and meaning-structures. They combine denotative-semantic and non-denotative-semantic as well as morpho-syntactic and phonological properties, and they play an important role in the relations between syntax and semantics'] (Karl 1983, 25). An integrated (lexicographically biased) definition is given by Bahr (1974; repr. 1985, 165): 'Das Wort hat auf jeder Sprachebene, als Lexem und als Wortform, einen Ausdrucksbereich und einen Inhaltsbereich. Der Ausdrucksbereich bleibt im folgenden unberücksichtigt. Der Inhaltsbereich eines Lexems wird durch eine Bedeutung oder durch ein Gefüge mehrerer Bedeutungen gebildet. Jede Bedeutung kann modifiziert sein. Wortbedeutungen und Wortbedeutungsmodifikationen sind immer Bedeutungen und Modifikationen des Lexems. Der Inhalt einer Wortform als der Aktualisierung des Lexems in der Rede

ist nicht identisch mit der oder einer Bedeutung des betreffenden Lexems, er ist vielmehr eine Funktion der Lexembedeutung.' ['On each linguistic level, both as a lexeme and as a word-form, the word has an area of expression and an area of content. In the following we will not take the area of expression into account. The area of content of a lexeme is made up of one meaning or a structure of several meanings. Every meaning can be modified. Word meanings and modifications of word meanings are always meanings and modifications of the lexeme. The content of a word-form as the actu- alization of a lexeme in speech is not identical with the meaning or one of the meanings of that lexeme; rather, it is a function of the meaning of the lexeme.']

5. What I present here is a rather eclectic selection of various important semantic concepts introduced and/or elaborated by Coseriu. This choice has been motivated by the empirical goals of this study. The lexical field, in particular, is treated only marginally, as I am not interested in establishing various lexical fields but rather in establish- ing meaning-relations characterizing pairs of members of lexical fields; thus, the lexical field only serves as the overall frame of refer- ence. See also Lehrer (1974), Lipka (1980), Strauss (1986); Verschueren (1981) criticizes the structuralist concept of the lexical field and advances an alternative, conceptual approach; Ziegler (1984; 1986) and Leiss (1986) have engaged in an interesting (though sometimes futile) debate on the nature of lexical fields.

6. An excellent survey of Coseriu's theoretical concept of lexical struc- tures (lexical fields, semantic features, and semantic dimensions), together with a comparison of Coseriu's assumptions with other lin- guists' views on these matters (including, of course, Kastovsky's), is found in Kastovsky (1982b, 80 ff.).

7. 'From the structural point of view a "lexical field" is a lexical para- digm which comes into existence by the division of a continuum of lexical content into various units existing as words in a language and standing in immediate opposition to each other by simple meaning- differentiating features. Thus, for example, the series *young—new— old* in German constitutes a lexical field. One lexical field can be included in another, higher-level one. From the point of view of con- tent any linguistic unit that exists as a simple word in a language is a "lexeme". A unit that corresponds to the entire content of a lexical field is an "archilexeme".'

8. Similar definitions are given by Coseriu (1970a, 49 f.; 1970b, 166 f.; 1973, 54 f.), but with one important modification concerning the archilexeme: 'Dem Gesamtinhalt eines Wortfeldes entspricht ein Archilexem, das durch ein Lexem realisiert sein kann . . . , aber nicht notwendigerweise eine lexemische Entsprechung haben muss' ['The

entire content of a lexical field is represented by an archilexeme, which can be realized as a lexeme . . . but need not necessarily have a lexemic realization'] (Coseriu 1973, 54). Apparently Coseriu uses the term "lexeme" in two senses: on the one hand, the term refers to the content-level only ('Die lexikalische Inhaltseinheit, die im sprachlichen System ausgedrückt ist und einen Teil eines Wortfeldes besetzt, wird als Lexem bezeichnet' ['The lexical unit of content which is expressed in the linguistic system and covers part of a lexical field is called a "lexeme"'] (Coseriu 1973, 54)); on the other hand, it refers to "vocabulary words" comprising form and content, in which use Coseriu sometimes refers to it by using the term "word", cf.: 'Nur für die Lexeme [= content-level] ist die Existenz eines entsprechenden Wortes [= expression + content; yet ≠ "Wort" in the sense given in n. 4 above!] erforderlich, während Archilexeme nicht immer durch Wörter bezeichnet werden' ['Only lexemes [= content-level] require the existence of a corresponding word [= expression + content; yet ≠ "word" in the sense given in n. 4 above!], while archilexemes are not always referred to by words'] (Coseriu 1973, 55).

9. Gsell (1979, 35 ff.) presents a valuable comparison of the treatment of semantic opposition (within the framework of lexical fields of different persuasions) by Lyons and Coseriu. It must be borne in mind, however, that Gsell does not include Lyons (1977); thus, some of his observations must be viewed with caution.

10. 'Die Analogie dieses Wortfeldmodells zur Phonologie bezieht sich nicht nur darauf, dass nach ihm der Wortinhalt gleich dem Phonem in distinktive Züge zerlegt werden kann, sondern erstreckt sich auch auf eine Anzahl weiterer Aspekte, deren für uns wichtigster in der Übertragbarkeit der verschiedenen von Trubetzkoy aufgestellten Oppositionstypen auf die Verhältnisse im Wortfeld besteht' ['This model of the lexical field is analogous to phonology not only in that it regards the content of words as analysable into distinctive features (like the phoneme) but also with regard to a number of other aspects, the most important of which is the transferability of the types of opposition established by Trubetzkoy to the situation in the lexical field'] (Gsell 1979, 41). This mainly concerns Trubetzkoy's (1939/1958, 67) distinction between privative, gradual, and equipollent opposition. I will relegate a discussion of their applicability to the description of systemic semantic opposition (as suggested by Coseriu) to Ch. 6 (i.e. after the presentation of the analyses performed in this study).

11. 'An opposition has two important prerequisites: properties with regard to which the members of the opposition differ from each other, and properties which both members of the opposition have in

common. These latter properties can be called "basis of comparison". Two things that have no basis of comparison, i.e. do not
share any common property (such as an inkpot and free will, for
example), do not form an opposition.'

12. The use of small capitals indicates the metalinguistic status of
archisememes/archilexemes, semantic dimensions, and semantic features. 'The metalinguistic use of lexical items as designations of
semantic features [as well as of semantic dimensions and archise-
memes] must . . . not be confused with the object-linguistic meaning of these designations, although there is, without any doubt, an
inherent relationship between these two levels, the nature of which
is, however, far from clear' (Kastovsky 1982c, 32). Cf. also n. 13
below.

13. Verschueren (1981, 327) points out that '[t]he meaning of each
word covers a relatively small *conceptual area* which is part of a
wider *conceptual field*. The collection of words which together cover
a complete conceptual field is called a *semantic field*, a *lexical field* or
lexical domain. Within such a lexical field the size of the conceptual
area associated with a particular word is determined by the size of
the conceptual areas of the surrounding words.' In this context it is
important to emphasize the fact that in this study semantic dimensions are established on the basis of intralinguistic, functional criteria, not on the basis of considerations of human perception and
conceptualization of the world. We are thus dealing with metalinguistic constructs. To my knowledge there is not enough conclusive
evidence to allow an identification of semantic dimensions with
mental concepts. It must be admitted, of course, that the results of
semantic analyses (cf. Ch. 5) often suggest such an identification,
yet it would be dangerous to draw hasty conclusions before more
evidence is available.

The task I am performing in this study should be understood as
"model-building" where 'models can be very different from the original, yet still embody some of its essential features . . . Models, then,
are not necessarily scaled-down replicas, but more usually simplified
versions of what they represent. But they may be different from the
thing they are modelling in another way also: they are likely to be
guesses rather than copies' (Aitchison 1987, 29).

14. 'The configuration of lexical fields, that is to say the way in which
the lexemes are arranged in these paradigms, depends in the first
place on the number of "semantic dimensions" operating there (and
on the way they are combined with each other) and in the second
place on the formal types of the oppositions established with regard
to these dimensions. . . . A *dimension* is the viewpoint or criterion of
any given opposition, which in the case of a lexemic opposition is to

be interpreted as the semantic property established by this opposition: the content with regard to which this opposition establishes itself and which apart from that exists in the respective language only because of the fact, to be precise, that an opposition refers to it, that it is the implicit support of a functional distinction.'

15. In his structural analysis of kinship vocabulary Lounsbury (1964) first introduced the term "dimension", which was then taken over and adapted by Geckeler and Coseriu (see Coseriu and Geckeler 1974, 150). Lounsbury regards a kinship vocabulary as constituting a paradigm which he defines as 'any set of linguistic forms wherein: (a) the meaning of every form has a feature in common with the meanings of all other forms of the set' (Lounsbury 1964/1978, 165); the common feature is called 'root meaning' (Lounsbury 1964/1978, 165) and corresponds to the archisememe/archilexeme. The second condition for the paradigm is that '(b) the meaning of every form differs from that of every other form of the set by one or more additional features . . . The variable features define the SEMANTIC DIMENSIONS of the paradigm' (Lounsbury 1964/1978, 165). The third parameter that is involved in Lounsbury's structural analysis is the "feature": 'A feature is an ultimate term of characterization in a set of descriptive terms appropriate for the analysis of a particular given paradigm. A dimension is thus an "opposition", and the features of a dimension are the terms of the opposition' (Lounsbury 1964/1978, 165).

16. 'The dimension is not what is common to the terms of an opposition either (the "basis of comparison"): **it is what is common to the *differences* between these terms, i.e. to their distinctive features**.'

17. Kastovsky (1981*a*, 437) points out that '[t]he semantic features shared by all lexemes of a field, i.e. their intersection, represent the meaning of the field, which is called an "archisememe". This in turn may but need not be represented by a lexeme, which then functions as the name of the lexical field, as an "archilexeme".' In 3.2.2 I will argue in favour of a treatment of systemic semantic opposition on a strictly sememic basis so that the question whether an abstract, metalinguistic archisememe has a lexical expression or not becomes irrelevant. (Cf. also Kastovsky's (1982*c*, 34f.) discussion of the treatment of hyponymy in Lyons (1968) and Lyons (1977), which also deals with the problem of whether an archi-unit must have a corresponding lexical expression.)

18. Multiple non-hierarchical semantic relations between co-hyponyms have not been investigated in this study. Such non-binary oppositions also operate on the basis of archisememes, semantic dimensions, and semantic features, but 'they involve more than two terms'

(Leech 1974, 107). For a brief summary of Leech (1974, 107 ff., 114 ff.) and Lyons (1977, 287 ff.) see Kastovsky (1982*b*, 138 f.). Hansen *et al.* (1982, 215 f.) treat non-binary relations of the type *poodle—collie—pekinese—pug* etc. as cases of "Heteronymie". Cruse (1986) introduces some new terms within the field of what he calls 'lexical configurations' (Cruse 1986, 112 ff.): among "non-branching hierarchies" (Cruse 1986, 181 ff.) he distinguishes between "chains" (e.g. *birth, childhood, adolescence, adulthood, old age, death; beginning, middle, end*), whose members exhibit pure linear ordering (Cruse 1986, 189), and "helices", which have 'a hybrid linear/cyclical ordering' (Cruse 1986, 189 f.). Helices exhibit 'the typical characteristics of chains, with a first item, a last item, and a unique ordering between them' (Cruse 1986, 189), but 'the relation "— stands immediately between — and —" organizes these terms into an apparently cyclical structure' (Cruse 1986, 190). Examples of helices are sequences like *Monday, Tuesday, . . . Sunday; January, February, . . . December;* the colour terms *red, orange, yellow, green, blue, purple;* the names of the seasons, etc.

Apart from that, Cruse singles out ordered sets whose 'constituent lexical units relate to different values of some variable underlying property' (Cruse 1986, 192). Among them, he distinguishes between "rank-terms", which operate on a discontinuous scale (e.g. military ranks) and are non-gradable, "degree-terms", which operate on a continuous scale, yet are non-gradable (e.g. examination assessments), and "grade-terms", which, like degree-terms, operate on a continuous scale, yet are gradable (e.g. adjectives denoting temperature, size, etc.) (cf. Cruse 1986, 192 ff.).

19. It is not possible to discuss the notion "feature" and all its implications in this study. Suffice it to say that I will use the term "semantic feature" in the sense used in Kastovsky (1982*b*, 81 ff.), i.e. "semantisches Merkmal", or "sème" as used by Martin (1973, 75 f.). See also Lipka (1980, 111 f.; 1990, 107 ff.), Sprengel (1980, 149 ff.), Lyons (1977, 317 ff. in connection with Kastovsky (1982*c*, 41 ff.)); for arguments against semantic features (and in favour of "atomic predicates") see Starosta (1982); reasons for the exclusion of "classeme" are given by Kastovsky (1982*b*, 86 ff.). See also Taylor (1989, 23 ff.).

20. 'the polysemy of the word that is taken as the starting point, whereby each of the meaning-variants of the polysemous word is matched with a different antonym'.

21. "Homophony" is one subtype of homonymy (cf. Lipka 1986*b*, 129). For a discussion of "homonymy" vs. "polysemy" see e.g. Lehrer (1974, 8 ff.), Lyons (1977, 550 ff.), Hansen *et al.* (1982, 197 ff.), Kastovsky (1982*b*, 121 ff.), Lipka (1986*b*).

Gsell (1979, 76 ff.) discusses the problem in connection with what he calls "mehrseitige Gegensätze"; Cruse (1986), who adopts a "contextual approach" in defining word-meanings (cf. Cruse 1986, 16 ff.), rejects both polysemy and homonymy:

It is commonplace to describe a lexeme which has a number of senses as *polysemous* (or as manifesting the property of *polysemy*), and a lexical form which realises lexical units belonging to more than one lexeme as *homonymous*. These terms, especially *polysemous* and *polysemy*, although innocuous if used circumspectly, are not entirely ideal for our purposes, because they carry with them a view of lexical meaning in which there is a tendency to regard the lexeme as the primary semantic unit, and the different lexical units as 'merely variants'. Our approach, however, focusses on the individual lexical unit as the primary operational semantic unit, and consigns the lexeme to a secondary position. (Cruse 1986, 80)

A very interesting contribution in this context is G. D. Schmidt's (1982) discussion of the polysemy of elementary linguistic signs ("elementare Sprachzeichen"). After evaluating both the monosemic and the polysemic linguistic sign-models he arrives at the conclusion:

Es gibt . . . eine Reihe von Ungereimtheiten, die das etablierte polyseme Sprachzeichenmodell sehr in Frage stellt. Das entscheidende Argument bleibt jedoch die Feststellung, dass das sog. "elementare Sprachzeichen" — solange es polysem ist — gar nicht als Element des Wortschatzes (Sprachzeicheninventars) fungieren kann, sondern hierfür in kleinere, durchaus selbständige, monoseme Einheiten aufgeteilt werden muss . . . Die Eigenschaften polysem und elementar schliessen sich hier gegenseitig aus. Damit ist keineswegs die Existenz der Polysemie in Frage gestellt. Polysemie gibt es. Doch sie gehört nur zu jener aus der Rezeptionspraxis hervorgegangenen Einheit höherer Stufe, in der eine Reihe von (stets monosemen) Sprachzeichen unter ihrem gemeinsamen Signifikanten assoziativ zusammengefasst ist. [There are a number of absurdities that call into question the established polysemous model of the linguistic sign. And yet, the most important argument . . . is the statement that the so-called "elementary linguistic sign"—as long as it is polysemous—cannot function as an element of the vocabulary (inventory of linguistic signs) but must for that purpose be divided into smaller, independent, monosemic entities . . . Polysemous and elementary are mutually exclusive characteristics in this context. This is not to question the existence of polysemy. Polysemy exists. It does, however, belong to that higher-level entity derived from the practice of reception, which is characterized by the fact that a number of (always monosemous) linguistic signs have been associatively united under their joint significant.] (G. D. Schmidt 1982, 10 f.)

22. 'in which case the lexical element that is taken as the starting-point is split into homophones, whereby each homophone is matched with an antonym'.

23. Cf. Lyons (1977, 553 f.):

> There are two possible ways of circumventing, rather than solving, the problem of drawing a sharp line between polysemy and homonymy in the analysis of a particular language-system: one is to maximize homonymy by associating a separate lexeme with every distinct meaning; . . . if we adopt [this] approach, . . . , we will end up with many more lexical entries than are recognized in the standard dictionaries of the language we are describing. This is not in itself a very damaging criticism. But many of these entries will duplicate the phonological and grammatical information that is contained in other entries . . . The equally radical alternative is to maximize polysemy. This will have the effect of producing a lexicon with far fewer entries than are to be found in our standard dictionaries. But there is little doubt that, on methodological grounds, if for no other reason, it is preferable.

Lipka (1986*b*, 137 f.) points out:

> Grundsätzlich gilt nach meiner Auffassung, dass es ein vorsichtigeres Verfahren ist, zwei oder mehr homonyme Lexeme anzunehmen, als sich für ein polysemes Lexem zu entscheiden. . . . Wir können also zum Schluss feststellen, dass Homonymie und Polysemie nicht absolute Gegensätze sind. Sie stellen vielmehr die Endpunkte einer Skala, eines Kontinuums dar, das von völlig verschiedener Bedeutung zweier Lexeme mit gleicher Form bis ˋ zur unzweifelhaft grossen Übereinstimmung verschiedener Bedeutungen eines Lexems reicht. [I think that basically it is a more prudent procedure to assume two or more homonymous lexemes than to decide on one polysemous lexeme. . . . In the end we can state that homonymy and polysemy are not absolute opposites. Rather, they represent end-points on a scale (a continuum) stretching from the completely different meanings of two lexemes with the same form to the undoubtedly large overlap of the various meanings of one lexeme.]

Both quotations make it clear that the lexeme (i.e. the combination of form and meaning) is taken as the entity relevant for the description of the lexicon. Apart from that, they illustrate that the choice of the lexemic approach over the sememic one is primarily determined by the objectives of the studies undertaken by the investigating linguist. Both approaches can, of course, be combined, as illustrated by Leech (1974, 97, 248).

24. 'After all, this problem is of minor importance for structural semantics, as it is interested primarily in **meaning-oppositions**. As long as it is clear that different meanings are involved it is immaterial whether these different meanings are attached to one or several lexemes.'

25. 'any semantic opposition is established between sememes (level of content) and not between lexemes (level of expression). It thus follows that if the signifié of a lexeme (L) contains several sememes . . . each sememe can enter into a relation of opposition with any other sememe independently of the lexeme by which the given sememe is realized on the level of expression.'

26. See also Martin (1973), Kotschi (1974, 86 ff.), Viehweger *et al.* (1977, 330 ff.), Kastovsky (1982*b*, 123 f.), Lipka (1986*b*, 136).

27. See also Fomina (1978, 117, 124), Schippan (1983, 97), H. Schmidt (1985, 60); Geckeler (1981*b*, 77) refers to the cases discussed here as "kontextuelle Antonyme". As to the treatment of terminologies see also the respective chapters in Coseriu (1970*a*).

28. Non-systemic and systemic opposites (binary and multiple) are also often found in what is commonly called "idiomatic expressions", if a broad definition of "idiom" as 'a complex expression whose meaning cannot be derived from the meanings of its elements' (Weinreich 1969, 26) is taken. Examples (1) to (3) in this chapter are cases in point.

Idioms and all the problems connected with their definition, description, etc. are not dealt with in this study. For discussions of terminological problems in this area see Fleischer (1982*b*, 8 ff.); an overview of the treatment of idioms, especially English ones, in different grammatical frameworks is given in Makkai (1972, 22–58); further references can be found in Kastovsky (1982*b*, 287) and Lipka (1990, 94 ff.). For the treatment of cases like *black-and-white* see Gläser (1986, 86); cases like *heads or tails, the long and short of it* (Gläser 1986, 75), *bread and water, flesh and blood* (Gläser 1986, 79), *sooner or later* (Gläser 1986, 97) belong to the group of idiomatic expressions too. Furthermore, opposites are often found as members of irreversible binomial idioms (see Makkai 1972, 155 ff., 314 ff.).

4

Oppositeness of Meaning: Basic Assumptions

4.1 INTRODUCTION

In this chapter pairs of systemic opposites, i.e. those that constitute semantic micro-fields, share the same archisememe, and differ along one semantic dimension, will be looked at in greater detail.[1] I do not, however, wish to establish a typology of systemic opposites; the main objective of the remainder of this study is to describe and explain the semantic relations obtaining between the members of a pair of systemic opposites in terms of semantic dimensions and semantic features, or rather, feature-relations. In doing this, I have found it advisable to confine myself to the study of cases of complementarity (*male—female, existence—inexistence, affirm—negate*), antonymy (*heavy—light, beautiful—ugly, curiosity—incuriosity, love—hate*), and gradable complementarity (*certain—uncertain, content—discontent, innocent—guilty, sound—silence*), not only because the majority of opposites found in the *Roget's Thesaurus* corpus belong to these groups,[2] but also because these types of opposites can be regarded as prototypical instances of systemic semantic opposition. Apart from this, antonymy, complementarity, and gradable complementarity share one common criterion, viz. gradability, which can, as will be shown presently, serve as the point of departure for the investigation of the semantic properties characterizing pairs of antonyms, complementaries, and gradable complementaries. I will therefore concentrate on this group of "central oppositeness of meaning"; the discussion of basic assumptions concerning central oppositeness of meaning in this chapter depends on, and is supplemented by, the analyses given in Chapter 5.

"Peripheral oppositeness of meaning" (converseness, directional opposition) will be treated only marginally, not only because of the small number of instances in the *Thesaurus* corpus but also because peripheral opposites have already been investigated in greater detail[3] and thus leave little room for further analysis.

4.2 CENTRAL OPPOSITENESS OF MEANING

4.2.1 *Gradability and scalarity*[4]

Grading is characteristically defined as the application of an ordered set of criteria in order to arrive at an ordered classification exhibiting 'degrees of rank, merit, intensity, etc.' or 'a scale or series of degrees in rank, merit, intensity, or difference from some particular type' (*OED*). It is not enough simply to apply an unordered set of criteria to a grading situation. This will merely result in classification. (Gnutzmann 1975, 421)

In contradistinction to Gnutzmann (1975, 421), who regards gradability as a phenomenon belonging primarily to the province of semantics, I will use the term "gradability" to denote syntactically observable phenomena such as the insertability of gradable adjectives into syntactic frames of the *more . . . than/less . . . than* type, superlative or equative constructions, and exclamatory sentences, and their combinability with intensifiers; the term "scalarity" will be used to denote the semantic properties accounting for the syntactic behaviour of the respective lexical items. "Scalarity" is thus not directly observable, but must be inferred from, for example, collocability with degree adverbs.[5] In his discussion of adjective comparison Bolinger (1967) points out that the notion of "scales" pertains to the area of meaning; Bierwisch (1967, 10 f.) assumes scales, as do Van Overbeke (1975), Cruse (1976, 291 f.; 1980; 1986, 205, 211 ff.), Seuren (1978, 342 ff.), Lehrer and Lehrer (1982), Rusiecki (1985, 5 ff.), Lehrer (1985)—to name but a few.[6] The point of departure for the analysis of oppositeness of meaning in this study is thus the assumption that semantic dimensions can be interpreted in terms of scalarity, and that the members of a pair of systemic opposites can be defined in terms of semantic features representing values or ranges of values along the respective scales.

4.2.2   *The nature of semantic features*

In view of the relational character of systemic semantic opposites
it is necessary to assume variable relational features (let us call
them feature x and feature y) that specify the meanings of two
lexemes A and B along a semantic dimension. Thus, for a pair
like *big* and *small* a specification in terms of such features would
give a specification of *big* as "x SIZE" and *small* as "y SIZE". Such
features exhibit the following characteristics:

- (*a*) they are relational with regard to the semantic dimension
  involved: *big* ("x SIZE") and *small* ("y SIZE"), *important* ("x
  IMPORTANCE") and *unimportant* ("y IMPORTANCE"), *innocent*
  ("x GUILT") and *guilty* ("y GUILT") relate to the common
  semantic dimensions SIZE, IMPORTANCE, and GUILT, respectively;
- (*b*) they are relational with regard to each other, i.e. it is the x
  to y ratio that determines the type of oppositeness obtaining between the meanings of lexeme A and B;
- (*c*) they are variable, i.e. they can represent any value or range
  of values along a semantic dimension, unless either of them
  is specified with regard to the range of its value.

4.2.3   *The nature of semantic dimensions*

The following characteristics must be assumed for the semantic
dimensions that relational features operate on.

First, a distinction must be made between **scalar** dimensions
and **digital**, i.e. non-scalar, ones. Whether a pair of opposites
constitutes a scalar or a digital dimension can be inferred from
the behaviour of opposite A and opposite B with regard to
gradability. This distinction is responsible for the traditional
antonymy/complementarity distinction.

When scalar semantic dimensions are involved, a distinction
must be made between **"type of scale"** and **"kind of scale"**.

"Type of scale" refers to the distinction between **unidirectionally open scales**, i.e. scales that have a zero- or starting-
point and extend infinitely in one direction, and **bidirectionally
open scales**, i.e. scales characterized by a turning-point T
(which is not to be understood as a zero-value) from which the
scale extends infinitely in opposite directions. These two basic

types of scale are responsible for various subtypes of antonymy (including gradable complementarity).

"**Kind of scale**" refers to the distinction between "**degree scales**" and "**quality scales**".

Along **degree scales**, the features x and y express various degrees or different amounts of the properties denoted by the dimension; opposites operating over degree scales are thus ultimately reducible to adversativity in terms of MORE/LESS. Which member of a pair of opposites is referentially adequate for describing something usually involves an object-related norm.

Along **quality scales**, on the other hand, one feature expresses an evaluatively "positive"[7] specification of a dimension rather than a degree; the other feature expresses the appropriate evaluatively "negative" counterpart (cf. *good—bad* along the dimension QUALITY). Quality scales thus represent adversativity of the POSITIVE/NEGATIVE or GOOD/BAD type; which member of a pair of opposites is referentially adequate for describing something usually involves both an object-related norm and a speaker-related norm or attitude.

Degree scales exist on their own, whereas quality scales, as a consequence of their scalarity, are inherently also degree scales.

The distinction between degree scales proper and quality scales can account for the differences between 'Grad- oder Quantitäts-antonymie' (Gsell 1979, 120 ff.) and 'Wertungsantonymie' (Gsell 1979, 138 ff.).

4.2.4 *The interaction of dimensions and features*

4.2.4.1 *Digital oppositeness*

Pairs like *male—female, absolute—relative, right—wrong* constitute digital semantic dimensions. In this case the semantic features x and y have absolute values and exhaust the dimension completely; one feature can be represented as the negation of the other:

right—wrong

Dimension	CORRECTNESS
Type of dimension	digital
Features and relation	x vs. $y = (\text{NEG } x)$

Examples

> 'I was taught that everyone knew the difference between **right** and
> **wrong**. But somehow—I don't always think that is so . . .' (*TAT*,
> 105)

> 'The story is **very nearly right**,' he said slowly; 'but **not quite**. It
> was not I who . . .' (*LM*, 172)

Constructions such as *nearly right, not quite right, almost right*,
etc., though seemingly contradicting the alleged ungradability of
digital opposites (cf. Lyons 1977, 272 f.), indicate that "right"
(as well as "wrong") represent digits, and not parts or segments
of a scale, with the consequence that intensifiers indicate approximation towards the respective point (cf. Bolinger 1972, 94).

4.2.4.2   *Scalar oppositeness*

strong—weak

Dimension	STRENGTH
Type of dimension	scalar
Type of scale	S 1
Kind of scale	degree
Features and relation	$x > y > 0$

Examples

> A **weak** man in a corner is more dangerous than a **strong** man.
> (*ACP*, 136)

> But there was one factor on which Bridget had not reckoned. *Honoria
> Waynflete was mad.* Her **strength** [archilexeme?] was the **strength of
> the insane**. She fought like a devil and her insane **strength** was
> **stronger** than the sane muscled **strength** [archilexeme?] of Bridget.
> (*MIE*, 178)

The pair *strong—weak* operates over the scalar dimension
STRENGTH. Both members are gradable, but whereas the x-value
(characterizing *strong*) moves towards infinity when intensified,
the y-value (characterizing *weak*) moves towards zero, which is
characteristic of unidirectionally open degree scales. The question
arises, however, whether y can be interpreted as ever equalling
zero. Cruse points out with regard to the pair *fast—slow*:

> The value of *slow*, although it 'tends towards' zero speed, never actually
> reaches it . . . This is not a physical fact, but a linguistic one: we cannot
> say *completely slow* when we mean 'stationary'. (Cruse 1986, 206)

The same applies to pairs like *strong—weak, heavy—light, deep—shallow,* etc.

We can thus single out one type of oppositeness of meaning as being characterized by a scalar semantic dimension of the type "unidirectionally open scale with non-attainable zero-value" (symbolized as "S 1") and the feature-relation $x > y > 0$.

The situation is different for pairs like *important—unimportant*:

important—unimportant

Dimension	IMPORTANCE
Type of dimension	scalar
Type of scale	S 1 → 0
Kind of scale	degree
Features and relation	$x > y \geq 0$

Examples

'And the reason?'
  'Equally obvious, I should have thought. Gordon doesn't like losing.'
  'And what about me? Supposing I like to win?'
  'I'm afraid, my dear Luke, that that **isn't equally important**.' (*MIE*, 95)

'Sir James,' said Tuppence, plunging boldly, 'I dare say you will think it is most awful cheek of me coming here like this. Because, of course, it's nothing whatever to do with you, and then you're a **very important** person, and of course Tommy and I are **very unimportant**.' (*TSA*, 85)

'Raymond or Blunt must have pushed it back,' I suggested. 'Surely it isn't important?'
  'It is **completely unimportant**,' said Poirot. (*MRA*, 70)

In a Party member, on the other hand, not even the smallest deviation of opinion on the most **unimportant** subject can be tolerated. (*1984*, 181)

The semantic dimension IMPORTANCE is scalar; moreover, it is a unidirectionally open degree scale. In contradistinction to the *strong—weak* type, however, *completely unimportant* is perfectly possible, which goes to show that the feature y (characterizing *unimportant*) may reach the zero-value of the dimension involved. This type of oppositeness of meaning is characterized by semantic dimensions representing "unidirectionally open scales with attainable zero-value" (symbolized as "S 1 → 0") and the feature-relation $x > y \geq 0$.

It might be noted that from the point of view of word-structure the two types just discussed are almost complementary in distribution: the *weak—strong* type is represented by primary lexemes only, whereas the *important—unimportant* type consists mostly of pairs with one prefixed member.

Yet another type, made up of pairs like *certain—uncertain, clean—dirty, safe—dangerous,* is characterized by the fact that the semantic dimensions constituting them must be regarded as "uni-directionally open scales with obligatory zero-value" (symbolized as "S 1/0"), i.e. one feature represents the zero-value of the scale involved:

certain—uncertain

Dimension	DOUBT/UNCERTAINTY
Type of dimension	scalar
Type of scale	S 1/0
Kind of scale	degree
Features and relation	$0 = x < y$

Examples

'What about the colonies?' she suggested.

Tommy shook his head.

'I shouldn't like the colonies—and I'm **perfectly certain** they wouldn't like me!' (*TSA*, 10)

'Here's to our joint venture, and may it prosper!'

'The Young Adventurers, Ltd.!' responded Tommy.

They put down the cups and laughed **rather uncertainly**. (*TSA*, 14)

' . . . I noticed that there was a long branch running out from the tree in the right direction . . . But it was **mighty uncertain** whether it would bear my weight . . .' (*TSA*, 78)

There was a pause. The silence lay heavy between them. Bridget broke it at last. She said, but with a **slight uncertainty** in her tone: ' . . .' (*MIE*, 96)

Thus we can say *perfectly/completely/totally certain/clean/safe,* as well as *almost certain/clean/safe,* which indicates that approximation towards a zero-digit is possible.

Finally, the pair *pleasure—pain* can be singled out as an instance of a pair operating over a "bidirectionally open quality scale" (symbolized as "S 2"), where the dimension is measured

in terms of POSITIVE/NEGATIVE evaluation rather than in terms of
MORE/LESS. Nevertheless, both x and y do, of course, also represent degrees along the scalar dimension:

pleasure—pain

Dimension	(BODILY/MENTAL) SENSATION
Type of dimension	scalar
Type of scale	S 2
Kind of scale	degree + quality
Features and relation	x = pos. > T > y = neg.

Example

> Philip lay face down on the floor while Melanie walked up and down
> his back in her bare feet. The experience was an exquisite mixture of
> **pleasure** and **pain**. (*CP*, 100)

In this chapter the basic assumptions concerning the treatment of
central oppositeness of meaning in terms of semantic dimensions,
semantic features, and their relations have been given. The next
chapter will provide a large amount of empirical evidence, and in
Chapter 6 I will discuss the advantages that this approach has
over other treatments of systemic semantic opposition.

Notes to Chapter 4

1. This chapter is based on the typology of systemic semantic opposition as summarized in Kastovsky (1982*b*, 131–8), which, in turn, is
   based primarily on Lyons (1977) and Cruse (1976; 1980). It seems
   unnecessary, therefore, to repeat the basic properties and delimitation
   criteria of antonyms, complementaries, and gradable complementaries
   once again in this study.
2. The majority of lexical items in the *Thesaurus* corpus are deadjectival
   or deverbal nouns whose semantic properties relevant for the characterization of binary meaning-relations do not differ from their respective adjectival or verbal bases. A treatment of systemic semantic
   opposition differentiating between word-classes has therefore not
   seemed feasible, especially in view of the fact that gradability phenomena are relevant for adjectives, verbs, and nouns alike, as claimed
   by Bolinger (1972, 16 ff.).
3. Appendix B contains a list of peripheral opposites as found in the
   Thesaurus corpus. Directional opposition has been investigated in
   greater detail in connection with "verbal antonymy", e.g. by Kotschi
   (1974), Nellessen (1982); see also Cruse (1986, 223 ff.).

Converseness is discussed by e.g. Lyons (1968, 467 ff.; 1977, 279 f.; 1981, 96), Leech (1974, 110 ff.), Viehweger *et al.* (1977, 339 f.), Kastovsky (1982*b*, 136), and Cruse (1986, 231 ff.). See also Lipka (1990, 147 f.).

It is questionable whether cases of "privativity" should also be treated in the context of oppositeness of meaning. Leisi (1975, 39 f.) gives the following definition: 'Unter dem Begriff "Privativa" fassen wir diejenigen Wörter (hier Substantiva) zusammen, welche weder ein Individuum, noch eine Gruppe, noch einen Teil bezeichnen, sondern eine Abwesenheit von Substanz, z.B. Wörter wir *Loch*. . . . Der Terminus "Privativa" (zu lat.: privare = berauben) scheint uns aus zwei Gründen der Sache entsprechender als "Negativa", erstens, weil bei "Negativa" eher an die bekannten Negationen wie *nein, nicht, nie,* etc. gedacht wird, ferner darum, weil mit diesen Wörtern meist nicht nur die Abwesenheit einer Substanz an einem bestimmten Orte bezeichnet wird, sondern . . . eine vom Normalen, Erwarteten abweichende Abwesenheit, d.h. ein Fehlen' ['Under the term "privativa" we subsume those words (substantives in our case) which denote neither an individual, nor a group, nor a part, but the absence of substance, e.g. words like *hole*. . . . There are two reasons why we find the term "privativa" (from Latin *privare* = to rob of sth.) more appropriate than "negativa"; first, because "negativa" tends to evoke the well-known negators like *no, not, never,* etc., and second, because "privativa" in most cases do not just denote the absence of a substance in a specific place but rather . . . an absence that deviates from a normal, expected situation, i.e. the lack of something']. Leisi's examples of privatives are, for example, *Lücke, gap, Leere, hollow, void, blank.*

Marchand (1969, 135 f., 156, 206) as well as Hansen *et al.* (1982, 86) discuss morphologically complex privative verbs; Heinemann (1983) regards privative verbs as verbs implying a specific NEGATOR. In view of the fact that privative lexical items very often do not form pairs and that establishing a semantic dimension along which they could be opposed is, in many cases, impossible, it seems inadvisable to treat them as instances of central oppositeness of meaning.

The *Thesaurus* corpus contains the following cases that could be regarded as cases of privativity in Leisi's sense (paraphrasable as "X"—"absence of X"): *discrimination—indiscrimination, hearing—deafness, intention—chance, meaning—unmeaningness, melody—discord, motion—quiescence, odour—inodorousness, ornament—plainness, predetermination—impulse, vision—blindness, voice—aphony.* A controversial case is *life—death* (?"absence of life").

4. See also Givón (1970), Gnutzmann (1974), Mittermann (1976), Fries

(1977), Kaiser (1979), and Klein (1980), who all deal with different aspects of comparison and grading.

5. "Scalarity" is thus a property characterizing semantic dimensions, whereas "gradability" characterizes each member of a pair of opposites. Kato (1986) suggests that gradability should be regarded not as an "either/or" category but rather as a "squishy" one, pointing out that 'among the supposedly non-gradable adjectives, *dead, married, pregnant,* and *impossible* do behave as gradables given appropriate contexts even though their gradability may not be quite on a par with a typical gradable adjective, *nice,* for example' (Kato 1986, 178). It must be pointed out, however, that there is no one-to-one correlation between (various degrees of) gradability and scalarity, as will be shown in 4.2.4.

6. It is impossible to discuss the scales used by all these authors in greater detail. Suffice it to say that the scales I will postulate presently differ from the ones established so far in that they are not based on extralinguistic, psychological criteria, but are established solely on functional criteria.

7. The terms "positive" and "negative" will be used in this study exclusively with reference to evaluation, not in the philosophical sense as in Sanford (1967), or Downing (1969) and not in the mathematical sense either.

5

Central Oppositeness of Meaning: Analyses

5.1 INTRODUCTION

This chapter is dedicated to the presentation of analyses performed on lexical items presented in the 1972 edition of *Roget's Thesaurus of English words and phrases*. The choice of *Roget's Thesaurus* was motivated by the assumption that investigating part of the lexical material contained in a 'conceptual dictionary' (Lyons 1977, 300; see also Lipka 1990, 38 f.) would provide the investigator with a greater variety of phenomena demanding an explanation than any alphabetically arranged dictionary of antonyms would have done—an assumption that has, I hope, turned out to be correct. It must be admitted, of course, that *Roget's Thesaurus* contains a number of lexical items that are hardly used in contemporary English; in view of the sememic basis of analysis as outlined in the previous chapters, however, this is not really a major problem.

The reason for preferring the 1972 edition over later ones is founded on the fact that it has retained the original arrangement of words and expressions (i.e. the one devised by Peter Roget himself):

For the purpose of exhibiting with greater distinctness the relations between words expressing opposite and correlative ideas, I have, whenever the subject admitted of such an arrangement, placed them in two parallel columns in the same page, so that each group of expressions may be readily contrasted with those which occupy the adjacent column, and constitute their antitheses. (Roget 1972, 563 f.)

For this study the headwords of each such column have been selected and treated as lexical items of the English language; their meanings were checked against the respective definitions given in Hornby 1974 (and, in some more problematic cases, against Sykes 1976 as well).

This chapter contains explicit analyses (including, if possible, textual evidence) of all those pairs of opposites that could be regarded as instances of "central oppositeness of meaning" on the basis of the criteria established in the previous chapters. All the pairs listed here have been investigated against the background of the semantic and syntactico-semantic properties described in Chapters 3 and 4, which has resulted in the classification presented in the present chapter. Within each subtype the items are alphabetically ordered, and each pair of opposites has been given a separate entry.

As an example of the format used and the parameters involved consider the entries for the pair *strength—weakness*:

strength—weakness

Basis of analysis	strong (adj.)	weak (adj.)
Dimension	STRENGTH	
Type of dimension	scalar	
Type of scale	S 1	
Kind of scale	degree	
Features and relation	$x > y > 0$	

Examples

A **weak** man in a corner is more dangerous than a **strong** man. (*ACP*, 136)

'. . . You don't want equality in the world, you want the **strong** to help the **weak** . . .' (*POF*, 139)

'. . . You were right this afternoon when you asked me if I was running away from myself. That is what I have been doing for years. Because I never knew whether it was **strength** or **weakness** that took me away from Veronica, I have been afraid of myself, afraid of life, afraid of you . . .' (*TH*, 71 f.)

But there was one factor on which Bridget had not reckoned. *Honoria Waynflete was mad.* Her **strength** was the **strength of the insane**. She fought like a devil and her insane **strength** was **stronger** than the sane muscled **strength** of Bridget. (*MIE*, 178)

Cf. also:

'You fool! You crazy old fool! Do you think you are ever going to get away to tell this story?'

'I think so,' said Miss Marple. 'I'm not quite sure of it. You are a **strong** woman, a great deal **stronger** than I am.'

'I'm glad you appreciate that.' . . .

'Yes,' said Miss Marple, 'I'm old and I have **very little strength** in my arms or my legs. **Very little strength** anywhere. But I am in my own way an emissary of justice.' (*NEM*, 206 f.)

The following principles have been observed in the presentation of the investigated material:

(*a*) Linear order of opposites

The order as given in *Roget's Thesaurus* has not been changed. This means that in some cases the prefixed member precedes the unprefixed member of a given pair of opposites (e.g. *unselfishness—selfishness* as opposed to *importance—unimportance*); apart from this, the arrangement facilitates the recoverability of the lexical items investigated in the corpus. The first member of each pair is to be understood as "opposite A" and the second as "opposite B".

(*b*) Basis of analysis

As only substantives appear as headwords in the *Thesaurus* I have thought it necessary to introduce this parameter in order to emphasize the adjectival or verbal nature of many opposites. I have opted for the term "basis of analysis" rather than "derivational basis" because I do not want to enter into the discussion of derivational relationships proper, which would require a more thorough theoretical discussion of this topic and go beyond the scope of this study. Thus, in the *strength—weakness* example given above, it is clear that both nouns are deadjectival derivatives from *strong* and *weak* (cf. Marchand 1969, 349, 344 f.). In this case the basis of analysis is identical with the derivational basis. *Health—sickness*, on the other hand, is a more complicated case: *sickness* can also be regarded as deadjectival (cf. Marchand 1969, 334 f.), whereas *health* cannot be regarded as derived from *healthy* (cf. Marchand 1969, 352); we would thus have two different derivational bases. For the description of semantic relations obtaining between the members of a given pair of opposites, this type of word-formational consideration seems immaterial, and the introduction of the "basis of analysis" parameter serves the purpose of neutralizing asymmetric derivational properties.

(*c*) Semantic "dimension"

For each pair of opposites the criterial semantic dimension is given in accordance with the principles established in Chapters 3 and 4. The reader will find some dimensions more convincing than others, but I must emphasize once again that the semantic dimensions listed in this chapter are metalinguistic constructs, or labels, that must not be equated with the corresponding object-linguistic lexical items. They have been established on intralinguistic, functional grounds, and do not claim any psychological validity.

(*d*) Type of dimension

"Type of dimension" distinguishes between scalar and non-scalar (digital) semantic dimensions.

(*e*) Type of scale

"Type of scale" specifies whether the scalar semantic dimension along which opposites A and B are operative belongs to the S 1, S 1 → 0, S 1/0, or S 2 type of semantic scale (according to Chapter 4).

(*f*) Kind of scale

"Kind of scale" differentiates between degree scales (measuring in terms of "more/less") and quality scales (attributing "good/bad" to the semantic dimension).

(*g*) semantic features and relations between them

The linear order of features correlates with the linear order of opposites A and B, i.e. feature x always characterizes opposite A, whereas feature y always characterizes opposite B. The relationship of A and B in terms of semantic features (or, rather, their values along the constitutive semantic dimension) is represented in accordance with the specifications given in (*d*) to (*f*).

(*h*) Contextualized examples

This part of each entry contains appropriate evidence from the "Opposites in context" corpus, thus illustrating and supporting the analyses suggested for a given pair of opposites. As the "Opposites in context" corpus was selected independently of, and even complementarily to, the *Thesaurus* corpus there is only a partial match between items. This explains why in some cases there are "no contextualized examples", whereas in other cases there are quite a number of them. This collapsing of independent corpuses has certainly widened the investigator's horizon and has drawn his attention to a number of phenomena that would otherwise have remained undetected.

The "contextualized examples" part attached to many entries shows the contiguous occurrence of opposites A and B in a number of contexts. In addition to that, contextualized examples have turned out to be indispensable for the description of gradability phenomena. I have, of course, tried to find examples where both members of a given pair of opposites occur; sometimes, however, I have thought it wise to include passages containing only one member of such a pair, especially where prefixed lexical items are concerned, and often in cases where a piece of textual evidence has seemed appropriate for elucidating matters of gradability.

5.2   DIGITAL OPPOSITES

5.2.1   *Digital opposites proper*

absolute—relative

Dimension	DEPENDENCE
Type of dimension	digital
Features and relation	$x = (\text{NEG } y)$ vs. y

There was no contextualized example.

acquittal—condemnation

Basis of analysis	acquit (vb.) condemn (vb.)
Dimension	GUILT
Type of dimension	digital
Features and relation	$x = (\text{NEG } y)$ vs. y

The two verbs must be seen in connection with *innocent* vs. *guilty*; *condemn* could be paraphrased as "pronounce guilty", *acquit*, according to the following example, must be paraphrased as "pronounce not guilty", not "pronounce innocent", cf.:

'If Mrs Merrowdene at one time of her life was unfortunate enough to be tried and **acquitted** for murder—'
  'It's not usually considered unfortunate to be **acquitted**,' put in Evans. (*LM*, 96)

'Come now, Evans. The lady was **innocent**—you've just said so.'
  'I didn't say she was **innocent**. I said she was **acquitted**.'
  'It's the same thing.'
  'Not always.' (*LM*, 96)

affirmation—negation

Basis of analysis affirm (vb.) negate (vb.)
Dimension DECLARATION (with regard to sth.)
Type of dimension digital
Features and relation x vs. $y =$ (NEG x)

There was no contextualized example for the verbal pair, but cf.:

> Mr. Schuster looked at his partner, raising an eyebrow for an **affirmative** or a **negative**. Mr. Broadribb nodded. (*NEM*, 15)

> Hannibal, as was his habit, immediately replied in the **affirmative**. His **affirmatives** and his **negatives** were always quite impossible to miss. He wriggled his body, wagged his tail, . . . (*POF*, 27)

approbation—disapprobation

Basis of analysis approve (vb.) disapprove (vb.)
Dimension APPROVAL
Type of dimension digital
Features and relation x vs. $y =$ (NEG x)

There was no contextualized example.

assent—dissent

Basis of analysis assent (vb.) dissent (vb.)
Dimension AGREEMENT
Type of dimension digital
Features and relation x vs. $y =$ (NEG x)

There was no contextualized example.

cessation—continuance

Basis of analysis cease (vb.) continue (vb.)
Dimension KEEPING UP
Type of dimension digital
Features and relation $x =$ (NEG y) vs. y

There was no contextualized example.

continuity—discontinuity

Basis of analysis continuous (adj.) discontinuous (adj.)
Dimension CONTINUITY

Type of dimension   digital
Features and relation x vs. $y = (\text{NEG } x)$

There was no contextualized example.

convexity—concavity

Basis of analysis   convex (adj.)   concave (adj.)
Dimension   SHAPE (of outline/surface)
Type of dimension   digital
Features and relation x vs. y

There was no contextualized example.

This pair of digital opposites could also be regarded as an instance of terminological taxonomy, as there are exact extralinguistic definitions of x and y.

Linguistically speaking, it might be a case of a ternary opposition *convex—plane—concave*, which admits of an analysis of *plane* as either $(\text{NEG } x)$ or $(\text{NEG } y)$

dueness—undueness

Basis of analysis   due (adj.)   undue (adj.)
Dimension   PROPERNESS
Type of dimension   digital
Features and relation x vs. $y = (\text{NEG } x)$

Examples

'Was the will made just before her death?'
     Miss Peabody directed a sharp glance at him.
     'Thinking of **undue** influence? No, I'm afraid that's no use. And I shouldn't think poor Lawson had the brains or the nerve to attempt anything of the sort . . .' (*DW*, 75)

'For a man,' said Tuppence kindly, 'you don't really make an **undue** fuss when you are ill.' (*NOM*, 55)

Surely, even if Mrs. Perenna did notice anything amiss she would be more likely to suspect one of the servants than she would 'Mrs. Blenkensop'. And if she did suspect the latter, wouldn't it be a mere case of **undue** curiosity? (*NOM*, 88 f.)

equality—inequality

Basis of analysis   equal (adj.)   unequal (adj.)
Dimension   SAMENESS
Type of dimension   digital
Features and relation x vs. $y = (\text{NEG } x)$

There was no example for *equal—unequal*; but cf.:

From the moment when the machine first made its appearance it was clear to all thinking people that the need for human drudgery, and therefore to a great extent for human **inequality**, had disappeared. (*1984*, 166)

In a world in which everyone . . . possessed a motor-car or even an aeroplane, the most obvious and perhaps the most important form of **inequality** would already have disappeared. (*1984*, 167)

There then rose schools of thinkers who interpreted history as a cyclical process and claimed to show that **inequality** was the unalterable law of human life. (*1984*, 175)

The new movements which appeared in the middle years of the century, Ingsoc in Oceania, Neo-Bolshevism in Eurasia, Death-Worship, as it is commonly called, in Eastasia, had the conscious aim of perpetuating ***un*freedom** and ***in*equality**. (*1984*, 176)

Inequality was the price of civilization. (*1984*, 176)

existence—inexistence

Dimension	EXISTENCE (= BEING)
Type of dimension	digital
Features and relation	x vs. $y = (\text{NEG } x)$

There were no examples for *existence—inexistence*; the common digital opposite to *existence/existent* seems to be a *non*-prefixation: cf.:

It was not that, having produced the three children, he and Barbara would now . . . actually will them back into **non-existence**, but . . . (*TBMIFD*, 8)

'Quite so,' I interrupted hastily. 'Little grey cells **practically non-existent**.' (*DW*, 33)

He was also exceedingly interested in the diet administered to the ill woman, comparing it with that administered to some dead relative (**non-existent**) of his own. (*DW*, 147)

expectation—inexpectation

Dimension	AWAITING
Type of dimension	digital
Features and relation	x vs. $y = (\text{NEG } x)$

There were no examples found for nominal opposites; the usual form is the past participle of *expect* and NEG *expect*, cf.:

Marigold was off now, as all her hearers had been waiting for her to be: off, that is, not in any **expected** or **unexpected** direction, just somewhere. (*EU*, 36)

By the expression on the dead man's face, I should say that the blow was quite **unexpected**. (*MRA*, 56)

He felt dazed. Julius's words were **totally unexpected**. For the moment they benumbed his brain. (*TSA*, 144)

exteriority—interiority

Basis of analysis	exterior (adj.) interior (adj.)
Dimension	SITUATION (with regard to bounded entity)
Type of dimension	digital
Features and relation	x = (NEG y) vs. y

There was no contextualized example.

form—amorphism

Dimension	SHAPE
Type of dimension	digital
Features and relation	x vs. y = (NEG x)

There was no contextualized example.

The analysis of *form* vs. *amorphism* as a pair of digital opposites is, however, questionable. *Amorphism* "absence of form" should rather be regarded as a privative opposite to *form*.

legality—illegality

Basis of analysis	legal (adj.) illegal (adj.)
Dimension	ACCORDANCE (with law)
Type of dimension	digital
Features and relation	x vs. y = (NEG x)
Examples	

The thing that he was about to do was to open a diary. This was **not illegal** (nothing was **illegal**, since there were no longer any laws), but if detected it was reasonably certain that it would be punished by death, or at least by twenty-five years in a forced-labour camp. (*1984*, 11)

There she had remained for a year, helping to produce booklets in sealed packets with titles like *Spanking Stories* or *One Night in a Girls' School*, to be bought furtively by proletarian youths who were under the impression that they were buying something **illegal**. (*1984*, 116)

inclusion—exclusion

Basis of analysis	include (vb.) exclude (vb.)
Dimension	PART OF (regard as . . .)
Type of dimension	digital

Features and relation x vs. y = (NEG x)

There was no contextualized example.

intrinsicality—extrinsicality

Basis of analysis   intrinsic (adj.)   extrinsic (adj.)
Dimension   BELONGING TO/INHERENCE
Type of dimension   digital
Features and relation x vs. y = (NEG x)

There was no contextualized example.

On the other hand, it may be that this pair pertains rather to the field of terminological vocabulary (cf. *intrinsic* vs. *extrinsic motivation* etc.).

man—woman

Dimension   GENDER
Type of dimension   digital
Features and relation x vs. y = (NEG x)

This analysis is possible only if one assumes that the dimension GENDER is completely exhausted by the feature x = "male" and the feature y = "female" in such a way that "female" can be (functionally) defined as "NEG male". As soon as "neuter" is included, the opposition becomes ternary; the analysis proposed above seems, however, applicable to quite a number of cases (cf. Kastovsky 1981*a*, 436 f., 1982*b*, 97 f., 1982*c*, 30, 33 f.).

Male/female is a pair of digital opposites too; cf.:

> The two of us dance as one person; the tango is not **male** and **female**, but their union as a couple. (*Time*, 4 Nov. 1985, 56)

> Accuracy is more a **male** quality than a **female** one. (*NEM*, 125)

> '**Men** are more often colour-blind than **women**,' said Joanna . . . 'You know, it passes through the **female** and comes out in the **male**.' (*NEM*, 150)

Masculine/feminine, however, are gradable:

> '. . . You are more like the Snow Queen though . . . You are **very, very feminine**, Gina dear.' (*TDIWM*, 158)

manifestation—latency

Basis of analysis   manifest (adj.)   latent (adj.)
Dimension   PERCEPTIBILITY
Type of dimension   digital
Features and relation x vs. y = (NEG x)

There was no contextualized example.

This pair seems related to *actual/potential* in the following example (note the slight terminological tinge!):

'. . . To begin with, she had no illusions about Charles . . . That is, she knew him to be not only a *potential* but an *actual* criminal! He had already forged her name to a cheque . . .' (*DW*, 207)

materiality—immateriality

Basis of analysis   material (adj.)   immaterial (adj.)
Dimension   SUBSTANCE
Type of dimension   digital
Features and relation x vs. y = (NEG x)

There was no contextualized example.

permission—prohibition

Basis of analysis   permit (vb.)   prohibit (vb.)
Dimension   CONSENT
Type of dimension   digital
Features and relation x vs. y = (NEG x)

There was no contextualized example.

presence—absence

Basis of analysis   present (adj.)   absent (adj.)
Dimension   PRESENCE
Type of dimension   digital
Features and relation x vs. y = (NEG x)

Example

Its title—'Sanitation in Victorian Fiction'—seemed modest enough; but . . . the **absence** of references to sanitation was as significant as the **presence** of the same, and his work thus embraced the entire corpus of Victorian fiction. (*TBMIFD*, 40)

right—wrong

Basis of analysis   right (adj.)   wrong (adj.)
Dimension   GOODNESS/CORRECTNESS
Type of dimension   digital
Features and relation x vs. y = (NEG x)

Examples

'I was taught that everyone knew the difference between **right** and **wrong**. But somehow—I don't always think that is so . . .' (*TAT*, 105)

'We should never have let Sandra marry that fellow, Vicky.'

'That's what I said.'

'Yes—yes . . . You were **right**—and I was **wrong** . . .' (*SC*, 126, 127)

'The story is **very nearly right**,' he said slowly; 'but **not quite**. It was not I who . . .' (*LM*, 172)

'You know, Hastings, you are **not so far wrong** as you think.' (*DW*, 189)

success—failure

Basis of analysis	succeed (vb.) fail (vb.)
Dimension	ACCOMPLISHING OF PURPOSE
Type of dimension	digital
Features and relation	x vs. $y = (NEG\ x)$

Example

'If you'll excuse my saying so, you're a curious young couple. I don't know—you might **succeed** where others have **failed** . . .' (*TSA*, 30 f.)

veracity—falseness

Basis of analysis	veracious (adj.) false (adj.)
Dimension	INCLINATION TOWARDS TRUTH
Type of dimension	digital
Features and relation	x vs. $y = (NEG\ x)$

There was no contextualized example.

5.2.2 *Non-prefixation*

For reasons why this group has been singled out see 6.1.

addition—non-addition (= "NEG addition")
assemblage—non-assemblage (= "NEG assemblage")
combatant—non-combatant (= "NEG combatant")
completion—non-completion (= "NEG completion")
observance—non-observance (= "NEG observance")
payment—non-payment (= "NEG payment")
preparation—non-preparation (= "NEG preparation")
uniformity—non-uniformity (= "NEG uniformity")

5.3   SCALAR OPPOSITES

5.3.1   *Unidirectionally open scales with non-attainable zero-value*

breadth—narrowness

Basis of analysis	broad (adj.) narrow (adj.)
Dimension	LATERAL EXTENSION
Type of dimension	scalar
Type of scale	S 1
Kind of scale	degree
Features and relation	$x > y > 0$

There was no contextualized example.

dearness—cheapness

Basis of analysis	dear (adj.) cheap (adj.)
Dimension	PRICE
Type of dimension	scalar
Type of scale	S 1
Kind of scale	degree
Features and relation	$x > y > 0$

There was no contextualized example.

density—rarity

Basis of analysis	dense (adj.) rare (adj.)
Dimension	COMPACTNESS (of substance)
Type of dimension	scalar
Type of scale	S 1
Kind of scale	degree
Features and relation	$x > y > 0$

There was no contextualized example. The use of *rare* as the opposite of *dense* seems to be heavily restricted (*dense/rare atmosphere*); more often we find *dense* contrasting with *sparse*, cf.: *dense/sparse hair, population,* etc.

depth—shallowness

Basis of analysis	deep (adj.) shallow (adj.)
Dimension	VERTICAL EXTENSION BELOW SURFACE
Type of dimension	scalar
Type of scale	S 1
Kind of scale	degree
Features and relation	$x > y > 0$

There was no contextualized example.

distance—nearness

Basis of analysis	distant (adj.)	near (adj.)
Dimension	DISTANCE	
Type of dimension	scalar	
Type of scale	S 1	
Kind of scale	degree	
Features and relation	$x > y > 0$	

There was no contextualized example. In a purely local sense the pair *far/near* is found more often; *distant/near* is also used in connection with time (*distant/near future*) and—as probably non-scalar opposites—in connection with relationships (*distant/near relatives*).

frequency—infrequency

Basis of analysis	frequent (adj.)	infrequent (adj.)
Dimension	RATE OF OCCURRENCE	
Type of dimension	scalar	
Type of scale	S 1	
Kind of scale	degree	
Features and relation	$x > y > 0$	

There was no contextualized example.

greatness—smallness

Basis of analysis	great (adj.)	small (adj.)
Dimension	SIZE	
Type of dimension	scalar	
Type of scale	S 1	
Kind of scale	degree	
Features and relation	$x > y > 0$	

It is questionable, however, whether *great* and *small* really differ along a scalar dimension SIZE. Unfortunately, no contextualized example could be found. According to Hornby 1974 *great* in one of its senses means "well above the average in size, quantity or degree", which sense is relatable to *small* "not large in degree, size, etc."; Sykes 1976 gives this sense of *great* as "occupying much space, extending far, large, big, (usu. with implied surprise, admiration, contempt, indignation, etc. . . .", and the corresponding sense of *small* as "not large, of deficient or comparatively little size or strength or power or number . . ." The comparative vagueness of such dictionary definitions would make an investigation of collocations with both *great* and *small* necessary. It seems to me that the relevant dimension is rather QUANTITY (as in *a great number of/a small number of*; *a great amount/a small amount*; also: *a great/small eater*).

Small, on the other hand, differs from *big* along the dimension SIZE (physically three-dimensional), as in

> Katherine looked carefully round both compartments. 'Yes,' she said, 'there is something missing—a scarlet morocco case . . . It might have been a **small** dressing-case or a **big** jewel-case . . .' (*MBT*, 74)

as well as from *large*:

> Near to it were placed a number of suitcases, ranged neatly in order of size from **large** to **small**. (*TBF*, 7)

hardness—softness

Basis of analysis	hard (adj.) soft (adj.)
Dimension	HARDNESS
Type of dimension	scalar
Type of scale	S 1
Kind of scale	degree
Features and relation	$x > y > 0$

Examples

> Mrs. Milray turned out to be almost ludicrously unlike her daughter. Where Miss Milray was **hard**, she was **soft**, where Miss Milray was angular, she was round. (*TAT*, 161)

> . . . her lips were dry, and **hard** rather than **soft**; . . . (*LJ*, 148)

heat—coldness

Basis of analysis	hot (adj.) cold (adj.)
Dimension	TEMPERATURE
Type of dimension	scalar
Type of scale	S 1
Kind of scale	degree
Features and relation	$x > y > 0$

Examples

> Mrs. Neele had never discovered the pleasures of electric irons, slow combustion stoves, airing cupboards, **hot and cold** water from taps, and the switching on of light by a mere flick of a finger. (*PFR*, 21)

> **Hot and cold** shivers chased themselves up and down his spine. He had the sense of being caught in a terrible dilemma. (*LM*, 167)

> In the dining-room the child Terry made another scientific statement. 'Lead salts are more soluble in **cold** water than in **hot**.' (*TH*, 37)

Cf. also:

> 'You're a **cold-blooded** little devil!'
> 'That's better than being a **hot-blooded** little fool!' (*MIE*, 96)

heaviness—lightness

Basis of analysis	heavy (adj.) light (adj.)
Dimension	WEIGHT
Type of dimension	scalar
Type of scale	S 1
Kind of scale	degree
Features and relation	$x > y > 0$

Example

'Was the pile of underclothes under which the things were hidden **heavy or light**?'
  '**Heavyish.**' (*MAAS*, 159)

height—lowness

Basis of analysis	high (adj.) low (adj.)
Dimension	VERTICAL EXTENSION ABOVE SURFACE
Type of dimension	scalar
Type of scale	S 1
Kind of scale	degree
Features and relation	$x > y > 0$

Example

'. . . and I happened to notice that the Grand Duchess went into that room with **low-heeled** shoes and came out with **high-heeled** ones. It struck me as rather odd . . .' (*LM*, 121)

length—shortness

Basis of analysis	long (adj.) short (adj.)
Dimension	EXTENSION (longitudinal)
Type of dimension	scalar
Type of scale	S 1
Kind of scale	degree
Features and relation	$x > y > 0$

Example

'. . . Your left hand little finger is **short** but your right hand one is much **longer** . . .' (*TZ*, 66)

Short and *tall* are scalar opposites (S 1) along the dimension HEIGHT (usually referring to humans only), cf.

'. . . Anyway, I do, don't I, **Shorty**? . . .'
  The man Bernard Bastable had spoken to was **not short**. Nor was he **tall** enough for the name to be appropriate as an irony. (*EU*, 5)

They could be distinguished now—a **tall** figure and a **short** one—nearer still, a woman holding a child by the hand—still nearer, yes, a child in a green gingham frock. (*NOM*, 107)

loquacity—taciturnity

Basis of analysis	loquacious (adj.) taciturn (adj.)
Dimension	FONDNESS OF SPEAKING
Type of dimension	scalar
Type of scale	S 1
Kind of scale	degree
Features and relation	$x > y > 0$

There was no contextualized example; but cf.:

Poirot was alternately silent [≠ taciturn] and **loquacious**. (*TBF*, 12)

This analysis seems—intuitively—not quite satisfactory. Maybe the features x and y represent limiting values on a scalar dimension (AMOUNT OF) SPEAKING DONE (HABITUALLY) and the pair *loquacious—taciturn* should go into the extreme-value group.

Cf. also:

Sheila Perenna alone took no part in the conversation, but that might be put down to her habitual **taciturnity**. (*NOM*, 40)

The woman seemed not at all grateful for anything done for her, and was suspicious and **taciturn**. (*NOM*, 110)

loudness—faintness

Basis of analysis	loud (adj.) faint (adj.)
Dimension	VOLUME (of sound)
Type of dimension	scalar
Type of scale	S 1
Kind of scale	degree
Features and relation	$x > y > 0$

There was no contextualized example.

multitude—fewness

Basis of analysis	many (pron.) few (pron.)
Dimension	NUMBER
Type of dimension	scalar
Type of scale	S 1
Kind of scale	degree
Features and relation	$x > y > 0$

There was no contextualized example; cf. also the scalar opposites *much*/*little*, differing along the dimension AMOUNT (i.e. [-count]):

Whether there had been **much** or **little** money in the house at the time of her death was a debatable point. None had been found. (*LM*, 70)

'**How much** [archilexeme!] do you know?' he shot out.
  '**Very little** indeed,' answered Tuppence. (*TSA*, 19)

newness—oldness

Basis of analysis	new (adj.)	old (adj.)
Dimension	TIME OF EXISTENCE	
Type of dimension	scalar	
Type of scale	S 1	
Kind of scale	degree	
Features and relation	$0 < x < y$	

Example

The **new** wife and the **old** wife making friends is quite disgusting in my mind. (*TZ*, 34)

For *young/old* see s.v. "youth"—"age" later in this section.

strength—weakness

Basis of analysis	strong (adj.)	weak (adj.)
Dimension	STRENGTH	
Type of dimension	scalar	
Type of scale	S 1	
Kind of scale	degree	
Features and relation	$x > y > 0$	

Examples

A **weak** man in a corner is more dangerous than a **strong** man. (*ACP*, 136)

'. . . You don't want equality in the world, you want the **strong** to help the **weak** . . .' (*POF*, 139)

'. . . You were right this afternoon when you asked me if I was running away from myself. That is what I have been doing for years. Because I never knew whether it was **strength** or **weakness** that took me away from Veronica, I have been afraid of myself, afraid of life, afraid of you . . .' (*TH*, 71 f.)

But there was one factor on which Bridget had not reckoned. *Honoria Waynflete was mad.* Her **strength** [archilexeme?] was the **strength of the insane**. She fought like a devil and her insane **strength** was **stronger** than the sane muscled **strength** [archilexeme?] of Bridget. (*MIE*, 178)

Cf. also:

> 'You fool! You crazy old fool! Do you think you are ever going to get away to tell this story?'
>   'I think so,' said Miss Marple. 'I'm not quite sure of it. You are a **strong** woman, a great deal **stronger** than I am.'
>   'I'm glad you appreciate that.' . . .
>   'Yes,' said Miss Marple, 'I'm old and I have **very little strength** in my arms or my legs. **Very little strength** anywhere. But I am in my own way an emissary of justice.' (*NEM*, 206 f.)

velocity (if interpreted as "fastness")—slowness

Basis of analysis	fast (adj.) slow (adj.)
Dimension	SPEED
Type of dimension	scalar
Type of scale	S 1
Kind of scale	degree
Features and relation	$x > y > 0$

There was no contextualized example for the pair; but cf.:

> 'That will be a **slow** train, I'm afraid, sir. Better wait for the express [= a fast train].'
>   'It doesn't matter,' said George gloomily. 'No train could be **slower** than the one I came down by yesterday.' (*LM*, 61)

vigour—feebleness

Basis of analysis	vigorous (adj.) feeble (adj.)
Dimension	FORCEFULNESS
Type of dimension	scalar
Type of scale	S 1
Kind of scale	degree
Features and relation	$x > y > 0$

There was no contextualized example for the pair; but cf.:

> They surged closer. Hercule Poirot was surrounded. He disappeared in a wave of young, **vigorous** femininity. Twenty-five voices arose . . . (*TFL*, 61)

> She was desperately unhappy. She had all a **vigorous**, strong-minded old lady's dislike of inaction in any given situation. (*DW*, 28)

violence—moderation

Basis of analysis	violent (adj.) moderate (adj.)
Dimension	FORCE
Type of dimension	scalar

Type of scale	S 1
Kind of scale	degree
Features and relation	$x > y > 0$

There was no contextualized example for the pair; but cf.:

Major Bletchley said with **some violence**: '. . .' (*NOM*, 38)

youth—age

Basis of analysis	young (adj.) old (adj.)
Dimension	AGE
Type of dimension	scalar
Type of scale	S 1
Kind of scale	degree
Features and relation	$0 < x < y$

Examples

'. . . The children involved seem neither **old** enough nor **young** enough for it to fall into any special class. A psychological crime is indicated . . .' (*HP*, 67)

'Charles? Yes, I can put you on to him . . .'
'He is quite **young**?'
'He's what an **old** fogy like me calls **young**,' said the doctor, with a twinkle. 'Early thirties . . .' (*DW*, 68)

'. . . I guess he forgot American girls are **older** for their **age** than English ones, and take more interest in scientific subjects . . .' (*TSA*, 198)

Mrs. Sprot went with her meekly, murmuring in a dazed fashion:
'I can't imagine how Betty would go like that with a stranger.'
'She's **very young**,' said Tuppence. '**Not old enough** to be shy.'
(*NOM*, 99)

5.3.2   *Unidirectionally open scales with attainable zero-value*

activity—inactivity

Basis of analysis	active (adj.) inactive (adj.)
Dimension	ACTIVITY
Type of dimension	scalar
Type of scale	S 1 $\rightarrow$ 0
Kind of scale	degree
Features and relation	$x > y \geq 0$

There was no contextualized example for the pair; but cf.:

His body was completely helpless. His brain felt **singularly inactive**. (*NOM*, 156)

The pair *action/inaction*, derived from *act* vb., probably belongs to the digital group; cf.:

> She felt desperately unhappy. She had all a vigorous, strong-minded old lady's dislike of **inaction** in any given situation. But in this particular situation she could not decide on her line of action. (*DW*, 28)

> Three more days went by in dreary **inaction**. (*TSA*, 131)

attention—inattention

Basis of analysis	attentive (adj.)	inattentive (adj.)
Dimension	ATTENTION	
Type of dimension	scalar	
Type of scale	S $1 \rightarrow 0$	
Kind of scale	degree	
Features and relation	$x > y \geq 0$	

There was no contextualized example.

authority—laxity

Dimension	AUTHORITY
Type of dimension	scalar
Type of scale	S $1 \rightarrow 0$
Kind of scale	degree
Features and relation	$x > y \geq 0$

There was no contextualized example. This case is somewhat problematic and should perhaps be regarded as a case of privativity with *laxity* paraphrased as "absence of authority"; on the other hand, *laxity*, like *authority*, is gradable (e.g. *much authority, great laxity*).

belief—unbelief

Dimension	FAITH
Type of dimension	scalar
Type of scale	S $1 \rightarrow 0$
Kind of scale	degree
Features and relation	$x > y \geq 0$

Example

> 'And was Miss Arundell also a **believer**?'
> Miss Lawson's face clouded over a little.
> 'She was willing to be convinced,' she said doubtfully. 'But . . . she was sceptical and **unbelieving**—and once or twice her attitude attracted a most *undesirable* type of spirit! . . .' (*DW*, 115)

In the above example *believer* is derived from the intransitive verb *believe* "have faith in" (Sykes 1976); *unbelief, unbelieving,* and *unbeliever* lack a synchronic verbal basis, yet could be paraphrased as "have (little or no) faith in". Cf.:

'Tuppence, old girl, what has really come over you?'

'Oh, **unbelieving** one!' Tuppence wrenched open her bag. 'Look here, and here, and here!' (*TSA*, 23)

'You can hardly expect me to **believe** that.'

'I am afraid you are of an **unbelieving** nature, sir.' (*LM*, 57)

In the above passage the transitive verb *believe* "put trust in truth of (sth)" (Sykes 1976) is used, which has the digital opposite *disbelieve* "NEG put trust in truth of (sth)":

'You won't **believe** that, I suppose?'

'Yes,' said Poirot, 'I do **believe** it. Too many people have told me so, for me to continue **disbelieving** it.' (*HP*, 131)

And as for Catchpole's theory . . . he couldn't **believe** it. Could he **believe** it? It didn't seem the kind of theory to which **belief** or **disbelief** could be attached. (*LJ*, 237)

'You are being careful. You are quite right to be careful.'

'I have made it a habit,' said Miss Marple.

'To be careful?'

'I should not put it exactly like that, but I have made a point of being always ready to **disbelieve as well as believe** everything that is told to me.' (*NEM*, 102)

Believe in and *disbelieve in*, on the other hand, seem to operate on the dimension FAITH too:

You see, when I was very young, I had democratic ideas. **Believed in** the purity of ideals, and the equality of all men. I especially **disbelieved in** kings and princes. (*SOC*, 214)

But in her own mind she was far from feeling the confidence displayed in her words. Not that she **disbelieved in** Tommy, but occasionally she was shaken with doubts as to whether anyone so simple and honest as he was could ever be a match for the fiendish subtlety of the arch-criminal. (*TSA*, 193)

curiosity—incuriosity

Basis of analysis	curious (adj.) incurious (adj.)
Dimension	DESIRE TO KNOW
Type of dimension	scalar
Type of scale	S $1 \rightarrow 0$
Kind of scale	degree
Features and relation	$x > y \geq 0$

Examples

> Their sad, Mongolian faces gazed out over the sides of the trucks **utterly incurious**. (*1984*, 103)

> 'What's the other thing?' said Miss Marple. 'I have some natural **curiosity**, you know . . .' (*NEM*, 114)

> After the dramatic scene on the cliffs, Mrs. Sprot and Betty . . . had been driven back to Sans Souci, where hot bottles, nice cups of tea, **ample curiosity**, and finally a stiff dollop of brandy had been administered to the half-fainting heroine of the night. (*NOM*, 109)

desire—indifference

Dimension	LONGING FOR/INTEREST IN
Type of dimension	scalar
Type of scale	S 1 → 0
Kind of scale	degree
Features and relation	$x > y \geq 0$

There was no contextualized example.

difficulty—facility

Basis of analysis	difficult (adj.) easy (adj.)
Dimension	LABOUR/EFFORT (necessary to do sth.)
Type of dimension	scalar
Type of scale	S 1 → 0
Kind of scale	degree
Features and relation	$x > y \geq 0$

Examples

> His own papers were works of art on which he laboured with loving care for many hours, tinkering and polishing, weighing every word, deftly manipulating eithers and ors, judiciously balancing **difficult** questions on popular authors with **easy** questions on obscure ones, . . . (*CP*, 17 f.)

> 'Was she happy in her place with Miss Waynflete?'
>   'She found it a bit dull, sir, and the pay wasn't high. But of course after she'd been dismissed the way she was from Ashe Manor, **it wasn't so easy** to get another good place.' (*MIE*, 115)

> '. . . Really, this killing business is **almost too easy** . . ' (*MIE*, 121)

> It appeared that one of the stalls had been selling tin saucepans. They were wretched, flimsy things, but cooking-pots of any kind were always **difficult** to get. Now the supply had unexpectedly given out. (*1984*, 64)

It was **not easy** to preserve inscrutability when you did not know what your face looked like. (*1984*, 242)

elasticity—inelasticity

Basis of analysis	elastic (adj.) inelastic (adj.)
Dimension	FLEXIBILITY
Type of dimension	scalar
Type of scale	S 1 → 0
Kind of scale	degree
Features and relation	$x > y \geq 0$

There was no contextualized example.

excitability—inexcitability

Basis of analysis	excitable (adj.) unexcitable (adj.)
Dimension	ABILITY/READINESS (to be/get excited)
Type of dimension	scalar
Type of scale	S 1 → 0
Kind of scale	degree
Features and relation	$x > y \geq 0$

There was no contextualized example.

haste—leisure

Dimension	HURRIEDNESS
Type of dimension	scalar
Type of scale	S 1 → 0
Kind of scale	degree
Features and relation	$x > y \geq 0$

There was no contextualized example.

importance—unimportance

Basis of analysis	important (adj.) unimportant (adj.)
Dimension	IMPORTANCE
Type of dimension	scalar
Type of scale	S 1 → 0
Kind of scale	degree
Features and relation	$x > y \geq 0$

Examples

'And the reason?'

'Equally obvious, I should have thought. Gordon doesn't like losing.'

'And what about me? Supposing I like to win?'

'I'm afraid, my dear Luke, that that **isn't equally important**.' (*MIE*, 95)

'Sir James,' said Tuppence, plunging boldly, 'I dare say you will think it is most awful cheek of me coming here like this. Because, of course, it's nothing whatever to do with you, and then you're a **very important** person, and of course Tommy and I are **very unimportant**.' (*TSA*, 85)

'Raymond or Blunt must have pushed it back,' I suggested. 'Surely it isn't important?'

'It is **completely unimportant**,' said Poirot. (*MRA*, 70)

In a Party member, on the other hand, not even the smallest deviation of opinion on the most **unimportant** subject can be tolerated. (*1984*, 181)

intelligibility—unintelligibility

Basis of analysis	intelligible (adj.) unintelligible (adj.)
Dimension	ABILITY (to be understood)
Type of dimension	scalar
Type of scale	S $1 \rightarrow 0$
Kind of scale	degree
Features and relation	$x > y \geq 0$

Examples

But it was no use, he could not remember: nothing remained of his childhood except a series of bright-lit tableaux occurring against no background and mostly **unintelligible**. (*1984*, 9)

He remembered better the rackety, uneasy circumstances of the time: the periodical panics about air-raids and the sheltering in Tube stations, the piles of rubble everywhere, the **unintelligible** proclamations posted at street corners, . . . (*1984*, 142 f.)

Unfortunately, no example with a degree adverb could be found.

knowledge—ignorance

Dimension	THINGS KNOWN
Type of dimension	scalar
Type of scale	S $1 \rightarrow 0$
Kind of scale	degree
Features and relation	$x > y \geq 0$

There was no contextualized example for the pair; but cf.:

'. . . By Jove, I wouldn't have risked firing when she did.' . . .

'No more would she, probably, if she'd **known** more about it. It was sheer **ignorance** of the difficulty of the shot that made her bring it off.' (*NOM*, 114 f.)

light—darkness

Basis of analysis	light (adj.) dark (adj.)
Dimension	LIGHT
Type of dimension	scalar
Type of scale	S $1 \rightarrow 0$
Kind of scale	degree
Features and relation	$x > y \geq 0$

Examples

The sitting-room at Tuppeny-hapenny Cottage was the **least dark** room in the house, with a couple of fair-sized leaded windows looking onto the back garden. (*EU*, 19)

When referring to hair, *dark* contrasts with *fair*:

The girls were there, three of them—just the usual sort of girls, two with **dark** shingled heads and one with a **fair** shingled head. (*SDM*, 11)

Jane amused herself by taking stock of her immediate neighbours. In each case she managed to find something wrong—**fair** eyelashes instead of **dark**, eyes more grey than blue, **fair** hair that owed its fairness to art and not to Nature, . . . (*LM*, 106)

mutability—immutability

Basis of analysis	mutable (adj.) immutable (adj.)
Dimension	ABILITY (to change/be changed)
Type of dimension	scalar
Type of scale	S $1 \rightarrow 0$
Kind of scale	degree
Features and relation	$x > y \geq 0$

There was no contextualized example.

penitence—impenitence

Basis of analysis	penitent (adj.) impenitent (adj.)
Dimension	FEELING OF REGRET
Type of dimension	scalar
Type of scale	S $1 \rightarrow 0$
Kind of scale	degree
Features and relation	$x > y \geq 0$

There was no contextualized example.

piety—impiety

Basis of analysis	pious (adj.)　impious (adj.)
Dimension	FEELING OF PIETY
Type of dimension	scalar
Type of scale	S $1 \to 0$
Kind of scale	degree
Features and relation	$x > y \geq 0$

Example

Elizabeth . . . also disliked the drawn out and ostentatious ceremonies of the Church. This was not to say that she was **in any way impious,** but she regarded religion as an entirely personal and private matter. (*EEA*, 82)

possibility—impossibility

Basis of analysis	possible (adj.)　impossible (adj.)
Dimension	POSSIBILITY
Type of dimension	scalar
Type of scale	S $1 \to 0$
Kind of scale	degree
Features and relation	$x > y \geq 0$

Examples

'We must step very carefully. If not—the murderer will strike again.'
　'If he did you might get him.'
　'**Quite possibly,** but I prefer the life of the innocent to the conviction of the guilty . . .' (*DW*, 177)

He thought of a man whom he had passed in the street a few weeks back; . . . They were a few metres apart when the left side of the man's face was suddenly contorted by a sort of spasm . . . He remembered thinking at the time: That poor devil is done for. And what was frightening was that the action was **quite possibly** unconscious. The most deadly danger of all was talking in your sleep. There was no way of guarding against that, so far as he could see. (*1984*, 59)

The man's face, already very pale, turned a colour Winston would not have believed **possible.** It was definitely, unmistakably, a shade of green. (*1984*, 204)

It was **practically impossible** when looking at Mrs. Van Rydock to imagine what she would be like in a natural state. (*TDIWM*, 7)

It seemed **utterly impossible** that he and Mr. Brown could be one and the same. (*TSA*, 203)

'. . . The first thing I did when I arrived, of course, was to size them all up and assess, as it were, **possibilities**. Some of them seem **quite impossible**.' (*NOM*, 54)

power—impotence

Dimension	POWER
Type of dimension	scalar
Type of scale	S 1 → 0
Kind of scale	degree
Features and relation	$x > y \geq 0$

There was no contextualized example.

probability—improbability

Basis of analysis	probable (adj.)	improbable (adj.)
Dimension	PROBABILITY	
Type of dimension	scalar	
Type of scale	S 1 → 0	
Kind of scale	degree	
Features and relation	$x > y \geq 0$	

Examples

. . . and girls, girls of every shape and size and description, girls with long straight hair to their waists, girls in plaits, girls in curls, girls in short skirts, girls in long skirts, girls in jeans, girls in flared trousers, girls in Bermuda shorts, girls without bras, girls **very probably** without panties, girls white, brown, yellow, black, girls in kaftans, saris, skinny sweaters, . . . (*CP*, 194)

One Christmas, she felt sure, Peverell would fall down dead. Having either to take the risk of letting him fall down dead or of hurting his feelings to such an extent that he would **probably** prefer to be dead than alive, she had so far chosen the former alternative. (*ACP*, 31)

' . . . I was told a story—an **improbable**, but not an impossible story . . .' (*MIE*, 19)

productiveness—unproductiveness

Basis of analysis	productive (adj.)	unproductive (adj.)
Dimension	PRODUCTIVITY	
Type of dimension	scalar	
Type of scale	S 1 → 0	
Kind of scale	degree	
Features and relation	$x > y \geq 0$	

There was no contextualized example; but cf. *non-productive*:

She had made one attempt to inquire into the possibilities of a link by her visit to Esther Walters. That had been **definitely nonproductive,** Miss Marple decided. (*NEM*, 42)

In contradistinction to *unproductive, non-productive* is less gradable, cf. *slightly unproductive* vs. **slightly non-productive* (probably because of its higher syntactic recategorization-value, which is characteristic of deverbal *non*-formations).

resolution—irresolution

Basis of analysis	resolute (adj.) irresolute (adj.)
Dimension	FIXITY (of determination)
Type of dimension	scalar
Type of scale	S 1 → 0
Kind of scale	degree
Features and relation	$x > y \geq 0$

Example

He followed **irresolutely** for a little distance, half a pace behind her. (*1984*, 252)

salubrity—insalubrity

Basis of analysis	salubrious (adj.) insalubrious (adj.)
Dimension	HEALTHGIVING
Type of dimension	scalar
Type of scale	S 1 → 0
Kind of scale	degree
Features and relation	$x > y \geq 0$

There was no contextualized example.

sensibility—insensibility

Basis of analysis	sensible (adj.) insensible (adj.)
Dimension	POWER OF FEELING/EMOTION
Type of dimension	scalar
Type of scale	S 1 → 0
Kind of scale	degree
Features and relation	$x > y \geq 0$

There was no contextualized example.

sharpness—bluntness

Basis of analysis	sharp (adj.) blunt (adj.)
Dimension	SHARPNESS
Type of dimension	scalar

Type of scale	S 1 → 0
Kind of scale	degree
Features and relation	$x > y \geq 0$

Example

The Moorish knife with the **sharp** blade.
    Bridget felt slightly sick. (*MIE*, 173)

If *sharp*, however, refers to intellectual abilities, it contrasts with *stupid* (and belongs to the S 2 group); cf.:

'She's the one who swallowed hat paint in mistake for cough mixture?'
    'Yes.'
    'Rather a **stupid** thing to do?' Luke hazarded.
    '**Very stupid.**'
    'Was she **stupid**?'
    'No, she was **quite a sharp** girl.' (*MIE*, 41)

With reference to taste the appropriate pair of opposites is *sharp—bland*.

substantiality—unsubstantiality

Basis of analysis	substantial (adj.) unsubstantial (adj.)
Dimension	SOLIDNESS (of build/make)
Type of dimension	scalar
Type of scale	S 1 → 0
Kind of scale	degree
Features and relation	$x > y \geq 0$

There was no contextualized example.

temperance—intemperance

Basis of analysis	temperate (adj.) intemperate (adj.)
Dimension	SELF-RESTRAINT
Type of dimension	scalar
Type of scale	S 1 → 0
Kind of scale	degree
Features and relation	$x > y \geq 0$

There was no contextualized example.

transparency—opacity

Basis of analysis	transparent (adj.) opaque (adj.)
Dimension	PERMEABILITY (of light)
Type of dimension	scalar
Type of scale	S 1 → 0

Kind of scale	degree
Features and relation	$x > y \geq 0$

Example

In Morris Zapp's view, the root of all critical error was a naïve confusion of literature with life. Life was **transparent**, literature **opaque**. Life was an open, literature a closed system. Life was composed of things, literature of words. (*CP*, 47)

unselfishness—selfishness

Basis of analysis	unselfish (adj.) selfish (adj.)
Dimension	SELFISHNESS
Type of dimension	scalar
Type of scale	S $1 \rightarrow 0$
Kind of scale	degree
Features and relation	$0 \leq x < y$

Example

'. . . your left hand is what you are born with and the right hand is what you make of your life. So that means that you were born **unselfish** but have become **more selfish** as time goes on . . .' (*TZ*, 66)

utility—inutility

Dimension	ABILITY (to be of use)
Type of dimension	scalar
Type of scale	S $1 \rightarrow 0$
Kind of scale	degree
Features and relation	$x > y \geq 0$

There was no contextualized example.

wealth—poverty

Basis of analysis	wealthy (adj.) poor (adj.)
Dimension	PROPERTY
Type of dimension	scalar
Type of scale	S $1 \rightarrow 0$
Kind of scale	degree
Features and relation	$x > y \geq 0$

There was no contextualized example for *wealthy—poor*; but cf.:

'. . . You don't want equality in the world, you want the strong to help the weak. You want the **rich** to finance the **poor**. You want . . .' (*POF*, 139)

willingness—unwillingness

Basis of analysis	willing (adj.) unwilling (adj.)
Dimension	ACCORDANCE WITH SB.'S WILL
Type of dimension	scalar
Type of scale	S $1 \rightarrow 0$
Kind of scale	degree
Features and relation	$x > y \geq 0$

Examples

> The girl who entered the room with obvious **unwillingness** was an unattractive, frightened-looking girl, who managed to look sluttish in spite of being tall and smartly dressed in a claret-coloured uniform. (*PFR*, 31)

> One slip on Virginia's part and nine months from now he might be the **unwilling** father of not merely one but two new offspring. (*TBMIFD*, 132)

> At thirty-five he had just been **unwillingly** evicted from the Youth League, and before graduating into the Youth League he had managed to stay on in the Spies for a year beyond the statutory age. (*1984*, 23)

> They pretended, perhaps they even believed, that they had seized power **unwillingly** and for a limited time, and that just round the corner there lay a paradise where human beings would be free and equal. (*1984*, 227)

This is certainly a borderline case, where it is often difficult to determine whether it is a case of syntactic recategorization of NEG *will* or a member of a pair of scalar opposites.

wit—dullness

Dimension	SPEED (of mind/understanding)
Type of dimension	scalar
Type of scale	S $1 \rightarrow 0$
Kind of scale	degree
Features and relation	$x > y \geq 0$

There was no contextualized example.

5.3.3 *Unidirectionally open scales with one value equalling zero*

agreement—disagreement

Basis of analysis	agree (vb.) disagree (vb.)
Dimension	DISAGREEMENT
Type of dimension	scalar

Type of scale	S 1/0
Kind of scale	degree
Features and relation	$0 = x < y$

Examples

'Oh, rather,' said Tony Marsdon heartily. 'I **quite agree**.' (*NOM*, 145)

'I **agree** with you **entirely**. London is no place at the present. . .' (*NOM*, 46)

But there were points on which Rudolf **violently disagreed**. (*AHT*, 88)

On top of all her other shortcomings, Stephanie was a bigoted Roman Catholic, who was bound to **disagree** with Rudolf's anti-clerical attitude **at every point**. (*AHT*, 126)

certainty—uncertainty

Basis of analysis	certain (adj.) uncertain (adj.)
Dimension	DOUBT/UNCERTAINTY
Type of dimension	scalar
Type of scale	S 1/0
Kind of scale	degree
Features and relation	$0 = x < y$

Examples

'What about the colonies?' she suggested.
   Tommy shook his head.
   'I shouldn't like the colonies—and I'm **perfectly certain** they wouldn't like me!' (*TSA*, 10)

'. . . That man, Danvers, was shadowed on the way over, wasn't he? And it's more likely to have been a woman than a man ——'
   'I don't see that at all.'
   'I am **absolutely certain** that it would be a woman, and a good-looking one,' replied Tuppence calmly. (*TSA*, 43)

Being a man of many aunts, he was **fairly certain** that the nice old lady in the corner did not propose to travel in silence to London. (*MIE*, 10)

He turned things over in his mind. He could see no further questions to ask. He was **fairly certain** that he had extracted all that Mrs. Church knew. (*MIE*, 115)

'. . . You can play with Rose Humbleby. She's so good that you're **practically certain** to win.' (*MIE*, 98)

'Here's to our joint venture, and may it prosper !'

'The Young Adventurers, Ltd.!' responded Tommy.

They put down the cups and laughed **rather uncertainly**. (*TSA*, 14)

'. . . I noticed that there was a long branch running out from the tree in the right direction . . . But it was **mighty uncertain** whether it would bear my weight . . .' (*TSA*, 78)

Jimmy took a moment or two to answer. His voice was serious when he said at last **rather uncertainly**:
'I suppose it's just a damned odd coincidence.' (*MIE*, 18)

Luke shook his head.
'Racing's an **uncertain** game. Ever seen the Derby run?'
'No, sir, wish I had . . .' (*MIE*, 85)

'I was going to walk to the end of the lane and back,' she said in a voice that sounded weak and **uncertain** to her own ears. (*LM*, 38)

On the following morning a note arrived by hand. It was in a **rather weak, uncertain** handwriting, slanting very much uphill. (*DW*, 159)

There was a pause. The silence lay heavy between them. Bridget broke it at last. She said, but with a **slight uncertainty** in her tone: '. . .' (*MIE*, 96)

change—permanence

Dimension	CHANGE
Type of dimension	scalar
Type of scale	S 1/0
Kind of scale	degree
Features and relation	$x > y = 0$

There was no contextualized example.

cleanness—uncleanness

Basis of analysis	clean (adj.)	unclean (adj.)
Dimension	DIRTINESS	
Type of dimension	scalar	
Type of scale	S 1/0	
Kind of scale	degree	
Features and relation	$0 = x < y$	

Examples

Out of a weatherbeaten, **not too clean** face, shrewd eyes surveyed them appraisingly. (*ACP*, 202)

The negro was draping a heavy, **unclean-looking** sheet over it and smoothing it down to form a lining for the box. (*DAF*, 78)

coherence—incoherence

Basis of analysis	coherent (adj.) incoherent (adj.)
Dimension	INCOHERENCE/INCONSISTENCY
Type of dimension	scalar
Type of scale	S 1/0
Kind of scale	degree
Features and relation	$0 = x < y$

Examples

She knocked off her pince-nez, picked them up, fumbled with them and went on **even more incoherently**: . . .(*DW*, 111)

We were shown into the same crowded sitting room, and Miss Lawson came bustling in, her manner **even more incoherent** than usual. (*DW*, 190)

Tuppence became even more embarrassed, and her remarks became **slightly incoherent**. (*POF*, 215)

completeness—incompleteness

Basis of analysis	complete (adj.) incomplete (adj.)
Dimension	INCOMPLETENESS
Type of dimension	scalar
Type of scale	S 1/0
Kind of scale	degree
Features and relation	$0 = x < y$

Examples

But if [the human being] can make **complete**, utter submission, if he can escape from his identity, if he can merge himself in the Party so that he *is* the Party, then he is all-powerful and immortal. (*1984*, 228)

The tone of his voice implied at once a **complete** admission of his guilt and a sort of incredulous horror that such a word could be applied to himself. (*1984*, 201)

Which side is winning is a matter of **complete** indifference to them. (*1984*, 184)

'. . . I have no doubt that she and Charles think they have enlisted your aid in some questionable business. Charles is **almost completely** amoral . . .' (*DW*, 198)

It was, in fact, only the consciousness of her social position that enabled Ludovica to endure her marriage. First, because of the constant infidelities of her husband, and secondly, on account of his **almost complete** disregard for the responsibility of his position . . . (*EEA*, 9 f.)

Luke said:
'You certainly are **incomplete** without a broomstick, Bridget. That's how I saw you first.' (*MIE*, 139)

conciseness—diffuseness

Basis of analysis	concise (adj.)	diffuse (adj.)
Dimension	DIFFUSENESS	
Type of dimension	scalar	
Type of scale	S 1/0	
Kind of scale	degree	
Features and relation	$0 = x < y$	

There was no contextualized example.

conformity—unconformity

Dimension	DEVIATION (from standard)
Type of dimension	scalar
Type of scale	S 1/0
Kind of scale	degree
Features and relation	$0 = x < y$

There was no contextualized example.

content—discontent

Basis of analysis	content (adj.)	discontent(ed) (adj.)
Dimension	DISCONTENT	
Type of dimension	scalar	
Type of scale	S 1/0	
Kind of scale	degree	
Features and relation	$0 = x < y$	

Examples

It was not desirable that the proles should have strong political feelings . . . And even when they became **discontented**, as they sometimes did, their **discontent** led nowhere, because being without general ideas, they could only focus it on petty grievances. (*1984*, 66)

The recurrent economic crises of past times were totally unnecessary and are not now permitted to happen, but other and equally large dislocations can and do happen without having political results, because there is no way in which **discontent** can become articulate. (*1984*, 178 f.)

The **discontents** produced by this bare, unsatisfying life are deliberately turned outwards and dissipated by such devices as the Two Minutes Hate, . . . (*1984*, 181)

There are only four ways in which a ruling group can fall from power. Either it is conquered from without, or it governs so inefficiently that the masses are stirred to revolt, or it allows a strong and **discontented** Middle group to come into being, . . . (*1984*, 178)

Austria had lost prestige in the eyes of the world; her foreign policy was responsible for blunder upon blunder, . . . ; and now there was also **grave discontent** in the army because of Gyulai's devastating mistakes. (*AHT*, 11)

curvature—straightness

Basis of analysis	curved (adj.) straight (adj.)
Dimension	CURVEDNESS
Type of dimension	scalar
Type of scale	S 1/0
Kind of scale	degree
Features and relation	$x > y = 0$

Straight/curved seems collocationally rather restricted (cf. *straight/curved line* etc.); *straight/bent* is probably found more often and would also work with the following passages:

He broke off rather lamely, with an appealing glance at Mrs St Vincent. She stood **very straight**, and her eyes met his steadily. (*LM*, 22)

She had taken out a handkerchief now in a quiet, non-committal way. She brushed tears from her eyes and then sat upright, her back **very straight**, her eyes deep and tragic. (*NEM*, 139)

But cf.:

She had a small, **straight** sensitive nose, a soft alluringly **curved** mouth and a firm cleft chin. (*EEA*, 30)

Cf. also *straight—wavy* with regard to *hair*:

Caroline dissented. She said that if the man was a hairdresser, he would have **wavy** hair, not **straight**. All hairdressers did. (*MRA*, 19)

discord—concord

Dimension	DISAGREEMENT
Type of dimension	scalar
Type of scale	S 1/0
Kind of scale	degree
Features and relation	$x > y = 0$

There was no contextualized example.

health—disease

Dimension	SICKNESS
Type of dimension	scalar
Type of scale	S 1/0
Kind of scale	degree
Features and relation	$0 = x < y$

Unfortunately, no example for the pair *health—disease* (which must in this case be glossed as "unhealthy condition of body, mind, . . ." (Sykes 1976)) could be found.

The assumption of SICKNESS as the scalar dimension underlying this pair of opposites becomes more obvious if the adjective *healthy* is contrasted with *ill* or *sick*: *completely healthy*, *perfectly healthy*, etc. are possible, as well as *slightly ill*, *extremely sick*.

Cf. also:

Yes, I cannot help still believing in two lovers who wished to get married, who were ready to take each other on for better, for worse, for richer, for poorer, in **sickness** and in **health**. (*NEM*, 176)

She was lovelier than ever—even her enemies had to admit that. Those who believed her to be **ill** were surprised to see she had every appearance of **good health** [= archilexeme + modification]. (*EEA*, 146)

Sane/mad and *sane/insane* also belong to this type of scalar opposite :

'My dear fellow! **Sanity** is the one unbelievable bore. One must be **mad**—**deliciously mad**—perverted—slightly twisted—then one sees life from a new and entrancing angle.' (*MIE*, 80)

The millstone around the necks of all the members of the House of Wittelsbach was the fear of **madness** . . . Those members who were tainted were in no position to care. The **completely sane**, of whom Elizabeth was one, worried perpetually about their awful inheritance . . . (*EEA*, 90)

'Was she a mental case?'
    'She was **perfectly sane**, if that is what you mean . . .' (*TSA*, 109)

'. . . A **sane** person shut up in a lunatic asylum often ends by becoming **insane**, they say . . .' (*TSA*, 201)

'. . . How would that strike you if you read it?'
    'It would strike me as either being a hoax, or else written by a lunatic.'
    'It's **not half so insane as** a thing I read this morning beginning "Petunia" and signed "best boy".' (*TSA*, 13)

If *healthy* means "conducive to good health" (Sykes 1976) its opposite is *unhealthy*, and the pair must be regarded as belonging to the S 1 → 0 group (parallel to *salubrious/insalubrious*):

'Oh, I'm not busy. Wychwood is a **pretty healthy** place.' (*MIE*, 67)

'One can only assume that Amy, Tommy, and the publican all knew something about Dr. Thomas that it was **unhealthy** to know . . .' (*MIE*, 120)

innocence—guilt

Basis of analysis	innocent (adj.) guilty (adj.)
Dimension	GUILT
Type of dimension	scalar
Type of scale	S 1/0
Kind of scale	degree
Features and relation	$0 = x < y$

Most people would probably classify this pair as digital opposites. On the other hand, it seems to me that *innocence* is best paraphrased as "complete absence of guilt", which would account for *completely innocent*, whereas *guilty* shows as least partial gradability and goes towards infinity, cf. *I felt even guiltier than my father*, **completely guilty*, *totally guilty.

Examples

'. . . You're used to questioning people. And with all your experience you must *know*.'
    'Know what?'
    'Whether they're **innocent or guilty**.' (*LM*, 68 f.)

'Come now, Evans. The lady was **innocent**—you've just said so.'
    'I didn't say she was **innocent**. I said she was acquitted.'
    'It's the same thing.'
    'Not always.' (*LM*, 96)

'. . . You've no reason to think that Mrs Merrowdene is anything but a **perfectly innocent** woman.' (*LM*, 97)

But cf. also other senses of *innocent* not contrasting with *guilty*:

The lady-in-waiting murmured something unintelligible. Outside [the bedroom] she and the other ladies agreed miserably that 'the child was too young and obviously **completely innocent**.' (*EEA*, 63)

There was about her a kind of medieval simplicity—a strange **innocence** that could be, Poirot thought, more devastating than any voluptuous **sophistication**. (*ACP*, 65)

moisture—dryness

Basis of analysis	moist (adj.) dry (adj.)
Dimension	WETNESS
Type of dimension	scalar

Type of scale	S 1/0
Kind of scale	degree
Features and relation	$x > y = 0$

There was no contextualized example.

order—disorder

Dimension	IRREGULARITY OF ARRAY
Type of dimension	scalar
Type of scale	S 1/0
Kind of scale	degree
Features and relation	$0 = x < y$

Example

The room was in a state of **wild disorder**, clothes were flung about right and left, a suitcase and a hat box, half-packed, stood in the middle of the floor. (*TSA*, 92)

Organization and *inorganization* probably work along the same lines. Unfortunately, no contextualized examples could be found.

perfection—imperfection

Basis of analysis	perfect (adj.) imperfect (adj.)
Dimension	IMPERFECTION
Type of dimension	scalar
Type of scale	S 1/0
Kind of scale	degree
Features and relation	$0 = x < y$

Example

'I really think our kitchen is **almost perfect** by now,' she said. 'Only I can't find the proper kind of flour bin yet.' (*POF*, 36)

purity—impurity

Basis of analysis	pure (adj.) impure (adj.)
Dimension	CONTAINING ADDITIONAL MATERIAL
Type of dimension	scalar
Type of scale	S 1/0
Kind of scale	degree
Features and relation	$0 = x < y$

In this sense probably limited to referring to substances; cf.:

Mrs. Sprot was very much what Tuppence thought of as 'the hygienic mother.' Always terrified of germs, of **impure** food, or of the child sucking a soiled toy. (*NOM*, 90)

reasoning—intuition

Dimension	RECOURSE TO REASON
Type of dimension	scalar
Type of scale	S 1/0
Kind of scale	degree
Features and relation	$x > y = 0$

There was no contextualized example.

regularity—irregularity

Basis of analysis	regular (adj.) irregular (adj.)
Dimension	INCONSISTENCY (of shape/recurrence)
Type of dimension	scalar
Type of scale	S 1/0
Kind of scale	degree
Features and relation	$0 = x < y$

Examples

A heavy black volume, amateurishly bound, with no name or title on the cover. The print also looked **slightly irregular**. (*1984*, 162)

At **irregular** intervals they presented him with a dirty slip of paper which they said was the bill, but he had the impression that they always undercharged him. (*1984*, 249)

safety—danger

Basis of analysis	safe (adj.) dangerous (adj.)
Dimension	DANGER
Type of dimension	scalar
Type of scale	S 1/0
Kind of scale	degree
Features and relation	$0 = x < y$

Examples

'If ever I'm not here, look after yourself, Rosaleen. Life isn't **safe**, remember—it's **dangerous, damned dangerous**. And I've an idea it's **specially dangerous** for you.' (*TATF*, 55)

'. . . When Amy was discharged from the Manor I engaged her at once. I think the hat paint idea was *quite* clever—and the door being locked on the *inside* made *me* **quite safe**. But of course I was always **safe** because I never had any *motive*, and you can't expect [*sic*] any one of murder if there isn't a motive . . .' (*MIE*, 176)

'. . . You would have said, wouldn't you, that any one would be **quite safe** in the middle of a crowded city.'

'You mean,' said Miss Waynflete, 'that any one's **safety** depends principally on the fact that nobody wishes to kill them?' (*MIE*, 165)

'New, isn't she?'

'She came in to-day. The other was a fiend. This girl seems all right. She waits well.'

Tuppence lingered a moment longer by the door which she had carefully neglected to close, and heard him say:

'**Quite safe**, I suppose?'

'Really, Boris, you are absurdly suspicious . . .' (*TSA*, 70)

'But I do suggest that Miss Finn should remain here. She will be **perfectly safe**, and I am afraid she is absolutely worn out with all she has been through.' (*TSA*, 206)

Miss Waynflete said:

'But don't you see—that's **horribly dangerous**. *Horribly!*' (*MIE*, 128)

similarity—dissimilarity

Basis of analysis	similar (adj.) dissimilar (adj.)
Dimension	DISSIMILARITY
Type of dimension	scalar
Type of scale	S 1/0
Kind of scale	degree
Features and relation	$0 = x < y$

This analysis might seem slightly problematic, especially in view of the *totally dissimilar* in the following examples, which might be taken as evidence suggesting the classification of the pair as belonging to the S 1 $\rightarrow$ 0 type along a dimension SIMILARITY. Still, it seems to me that, parallel to *identical/different*, DISSIMILARITY is the open-ended dimension. On the other hand, whereas *identical* can be paraphrased as "complete absence of difference" and is modifiable by *completely* and *almost*, *completely similar* sounds odd (*almost similar* seems possible, however). Even if *totally dissimilar* is interpreted as "showing a high degree of dissimilarity", thus establishing DISSIMILARITY as going towards infinity, we are still left with the problem of determining the x-value pertaining to *similar*.

Examples

He was reminded of Mr. Carter. The two men, totally unlike so far as physical resemblance went, produced a **similar** effect. (*TSA*, 153)

Approaching them from the house was a figure that, seen side by side with Miss Greenshaw, seemed ludicrously **dissimilar**. (*ACP*, 203)

'Then we have four deaths—all **totally dissimilar**, one heart failure, one blood poisoning, one suicide and one tetanus.' (*PI*, 101)

His friendship with Ackroyd has always puzzled me a little. The two men are so **totally dissimilar**. (*MRA*, 32)

smoothness—roughness

Basis of analysis	smooth (adj.)	rough (adj.)
Dimension	ROUGHNESS	
Type of dimension	scalar	
Type of scale	S 1/0	
Kind of scale	degree	
Features and relation	$0 = x < y$	

There was no contextualized example (cf. *take the rough with the smooth* in Chapter 3).

sobriety—drunkenness

Basis of analysis	sober (adj.)	drunk(en) (adj.)
Dimension	INTOXICATION	
Type of dimension	scalar	
Type of scale	S 1/0	
Kind of scale	degree	
Features and relation	$0 = x < y$	

Example

But though **slightly drunk** he was also suffering under some grief that was genuine and unbearable. (*1984*, 33)

sound—silence

Dimension	SOUND
Type of dimension	scalar
Type of scale	S 1/0
Kind of scale	degree
Features and relation	$x > y = 0$

Examples

There was **complete silence** for a moment. Everyone realised what this seemingly innocent remark really meant. (*EEA*, 32)

He appeared to stumble and fall against her. While doing so he raised his arm and plunged his stiletto into her breast. **Silently**, without uttering a **sound**, Elizabeth fell backwards on to the ground. (*EEA*, 272)

sufficiency—insufficiency

Basis of analysis	sufficient (adj.)	insufficient (adj.)
Dimension	INSUFFICIENCY	

Type of dimension	scalar
Type of scale	S 1/0
Kind of scale	degree
Features and relation	$0 = x < y$

There was no contextualized example.

5.3.4 *Bidirectionally open scales*

beauty—ugliness

Basis of analysis	beautiful (adj.) ugly (adj.)
Dimension	BEAUTY
Type of dimension	scalar
Type of scale	S 2
Kind of scale	degree + quality
Features and relation	$x > T > y$

Example

' . . It's awfully difficult at first, you know because people look rather alike and wear the same sort of clothes and you don't know at first which is which. I mean, unless somebody is **very beautiful** or **very ugly**.' (*POF*, 34)

Cf. also:

I was always a one for seeing things in extremes, and because I wasn't as **beautiful** as Louise I assumed I was as **plain** as Daphne . . . (*SBC*, 21)

benefactor—evildoer

Dimension	ACTIVITY (towards others)
Type of dimension	scalar
Type of scale	S 2
Kind of scale	degree + quality
Features and relation	$x = \text{pos.} > T > y = \text{neg.}$

There was no contextualized example.

benevolence—malevolence

Dimension	ATTITUDE (towards others)
Type of dimension	scalar
Type of scale	S 2
Kind of scale	degree + quality
Features and relation	$x = \text{pos.} > T > y = \text{neg.}$

There was no contextualized example.

care—neglect

Basis of analysis	care (vb.) neglect (vb.)
Dimension	ATTENTIVENESS (to sb.'s needs etc.)
Type of dimension	scalar
Type of scale	S 2
Kind of scale	degree + quality
Features and relation	$x > T > y$

There was no contextualized example.

cheerfulness—dejection

Basis of analysis	cheerful (adj.) deject(ed) (adj.)
Dimension	STATE OF SPIRIT
Type of dimension	scalar
Type of scale	S 2
Kind of scale	degree + quality
Features and relation	$x = \text{pos.} > T > y = \text{neg.}$

There was no contextualized example.

courage—cowardice

Dimension	BRAVENESS
Type of dimension	scalar
Type of scale	S 2
Kind of scale	degree + quality
Features and relation	$x > T > y$

There was no contextualized example for the pair; but cf.:

He was shrewd and hard, arrogant and **very courageous**. (*AHT*, 83)

courtesy—discourtesy

Dimension	POLITENESS
Type of dimension	scalar
Type of scale	S 2
Kind of scale	degree + quality
Features and relation	$x > T > y$

Examples

Elizabeth accepted the challenge.

'You forget, Aunt,' she began, deliberately omitting all titles of **courtesy** and treating her enemy simply as a relative in her own family, . . . (*EEA*, 77)

The Crown Prince received them with **great courtesy**. (*AHT*, 203)

'Who are you?' demanded Franz Joseph, startled into an apparent **discourtesy** in his curiosity. (*EEA*, 30)

credulity—incredulity

Basis of analysis	credulous (adj.) incredulous (adj.)
Dimension	READINESS TO BELIEVE
Type of dimension	scalar
Type of scale	S 2
Kind of scale	degree (+ quality?)
Features and relation	$x > T > y$

Examples

'What about Lord Whitfield?'

'He'll be all right. He's quite uneducated and **completely credulous**—actually believes things he reads in his own papers . . .' (*MIE*, 22)

The Commander was clearly surprised this time.

'Mystery man? Old Bletchley?' He sounded **frankly incredulous**. (*NOM*, 124)

Adela felt not only despair, but **some incredulity**; she did not see the import of her brother's behaviour as clearly as Marigold did. (*EU*, 66)

The tone of his voice implied at once a complete admission of his guilt and a sort of **incredulous** horror that such a word could be applied to himself. (*1984*, 201)

disobedience—obedience

Basis of analysis	disobedient (adj.) obedient (adj.)
Dimension	OBEDIENCE
Type of dimension	scalar
Type of scale	S 2
Kind of scale	degree/(quality)
Features and relation	$x < T < y$

Example

The whole matter of Shorty, Adela and the bottles could be taken as, among other things, illustrating in him that strange, inseparable mixture of real, almost instinctive **obedience** and covert, largely futile **disobedience** which long Army service in the ranks so often creates. (*EU*, 12)

elegance—inelegance

Basis of analysis	elegant (adj.) inelegant (adj.)
Dimension	ELEGANCE
Type of dimension	scalar
Type of scale	S 2

Kind of scale	degree + quality
Features and relation	$x > T > y$

There was no contextualized example.

expedience—inexpedience

Basis of analysis	expedient (adj.) inexpedient (adj.)
Dimension	SUITABILITY
Type of dimension	scalar
Type of scale	S 2
Kind of scale	degree/(quality)
Features and relation	$x > T > y$

There was no contextualized example.

flatterer—detractor

Basis of analysis	flatter (vb.) detract (vb.)
Dimension	UNJUST/UNTRUE ASSESSMENT
Type of dimension	scalar
Type of scale	S 2
Kind of scale	degree + quality
Features and relation	$x = \text{pos.} > T > y = \text{neg.}$

There was no contextualized example.

flattery—detraction

Basis of analysis	flatter (vb.) detract (vb.)

See the analysis of *flatterer/detractor*. There was no contextualized example.

fragrance—fetor

Dimension	QUALITY OF SMELL
Type of dimension	scalar
Type of scale	S 2
Kind of scale	degree + quality
Features and relation	$x = \text{pos.} > T > y = \text{neg.}$

There was no contextualized example.

friend—enemy

Dimension	ATTITUDE (characterizing sb. with regard to sb.)
Type of dimension	scalar
Type of scale	S 2
Kind of scale	(degree)/quality
Features and relation	$x = \text{pos.} > T > y = \text{neg}$

Examples

'. . . I told him it might be possible to bring down a lawyer, a Queen's Counsel, to see what points there might be in his favour, and other things. I approached him as **a friend but also as an enemy** so that I could see how he responded to different approaches, . . .' (*NEM*, 110 f.)

'. . . We want to turn some of our **enemies** into **friends**—those that are worth while . . .' (*NOM*, 176)

Cf. also:

'. . . But there was also a second personality, someone who was forced . . . to kill **not an enemy,** but **the person he loved,** and so he killed Verity . . .' (*NEM*, 174)

Cf. *enemy—ally*, which looks more like a digital pair:

'. . . But things are slightly altered now. You must make up your mind if I am your **enemy** or your **ally.**' (*NEM*, 103)

A main point had to be decided. Were the three sisters to be her **allies** or were the three sisters **enemies?** They might fall into either category. She must think about that carefully. (*NEM*, 72 f.)

friendship—enmity

Basis of analysis   friend   enemy

See the analysis of *friend/enemy*. There was no contextualized example.

good—evil

Dimension	MORAL QUALITY
Type of dimension	scalar
Type of scale	S 2
Kind of scale	degree + quality
Features and relation	$x = $ pos. $> T > y = $ neg.

Examples

She would hear, she was sure, all about the house by the bridge, who had lived there, who had been of **evil** or **good** repute in the neighbourhood, . . .(*POMT*, 76)

Morris Zapp experiences a rush of missionary zeal to the head. He will do a good deed, instruct this innocent in the difference between **good** and **evil**, talk her out of her wicked intent. (*CP*, 33)

'I'm a religious man. I believe in **good and evil** and eternal justice. There *is* such a thing as divine justice, Fitzwilliam, not a doubt of it.' (*MIE*, 145)

Cf. *good—bad* differing along the dimension QUALITY only:

'. . . But I do think things come in—in waves.'
'Waves?'
'Waves of **bad** luck and **good** luck . . .' (*MIE*, 76)

She shook her head. 'He's a **bad** loser.'
'But you, Mademoiselle, are a **good** loser.' (*DON*, 214)

gratitude—ingratitude

Dimension	THANKFULNESS
Type of dimension	scalar
Type of scale	S 2
Kind of scale	degree + quality
Features and relation	$x > T > y$

There was no contextualized example for the pair; but cf.:

But in his view the Balkan people had only one aim: their own independence; they showed **little gratitude** for help for anything else. (*AHT*, 152)

She did not feel **in the least grateful** to Elizabeth, thanks to whose influence she did not have to appear after her wedding night at a Court breakfast to be stared at by everyone. (*AHT*, 74)

'Lord Whitfield has been a great benefactor to Wychwood,' said Miss Waynflete. 'It grieves me that there are people who are **sadly ungrateful**.' (*MIE*, 48)

hindrance—aid

Basis of analysis	hinder (vb.) aid (vb.)
Dimension	HELP
Type of dimension	scalar
Type of scale	S 2
Kind of scale	degree + quality
Features and relation	$x = \text{neg.} < T < y = \text{pos.}$

There was no contextualized example for *hinder—aid*; but cf.:

'. . . I am of a very susceptible nature—I wish to **assist** a love affair—not to **hinder** it.' (*TAT*, 121)

The pair *opponent/auxiliary* works along the same dimension and thus probably belongs to the S 2 group too.

intelligence—imbecility

Basis of analysis	intelligent (adj.) imbecile (adj.)
Dimension	ABILITY OF MIND

Type of dimension	scalar
Type of scale	S 2
Kind of scale	degree + quality
Features and relation	x = pos. > T > y = neg.

The pair as given here can probably be used for characterizing natural, i.e. physiologically determined, qualities of the mind only; ABILITY OF INTELLECT is represented by e.g. *intelligent—unintelligent.* Cf.:

> Battle was a stolid-looking man with a wooden face. He looked **supremely unintelligent** and more like a commissionaire than a detective. (*SDM*, 58)

love—hate

Basis of analysis	love (vb.) hate (vb.)
Dimension	EMOTION TOWARDS OTHERS
Type of dimension	scalar
Type of scale	S 2
Kind of scale	degree + quality
Features and relation	x = pos. > T > y = neg.

Example

> '. . . **Love** turns to **hate** more easily than you think, Mr. Strange . . .' (*TZ*, 172)

philanthropy—misanthropy

Dimension	ATTITUDE TOWARDS MANKIND
Type of dimension	scalar
Type of scale	S 2
Kind of scale	degree + quality
Features and relation	x = pos. > T > y = neg.

There was no contextualized example.

pleasurableness—painfulness

Basis of analysis	pleasurable (adj.) painful (adj.)

See the analysis of *pleasure/pain.* There was no contextualized example.

pleasure—pain

Dimension	(BODILY/MENTAL) SENSATION
Type of dimension	scalar
Type of scale	S 2
Kind of scale	degree + quality
Features and relation	x = pos. > T > y = neg.

Example

> Philip lay face down on the floor while Melanie walked up and down his back in her bare feet. The experience was an exquisite mixture of **pleasure** and **pain**. (*CP*, 100)

probity—improbity

Dimension	HONESTY
Type of dimension	scalar
Type of scale	S 2
Kind of scale	degree + quality
Features and relation	$x > T > y$

There was no contextualized example.

prosperity—adversity

Basis of analysis	prosperous (adj.) adverse (adj.)
Dimension	FORTUNE
Type of dimension	scalar
Type of scale	S 2
Kind of scale	(degree +) quality
Features and relation	$x = $ pos. $> T > y = $ neg.

There was no contextualized example.

rashness—caution

Basis of analysis	rash (adj.) cautious (adj.)
Dimension	CAUTION
Type of dimension	scalar
Type of scale	S 2
Kind of scale	degree + quality
Features and relation	$x < T < y$

Examples

> This article is revealing of Rudolf's understanding of the political situation, and also of the fact that in matters requiring judgement, he could be **rash** and unsound. (*AHT*, 133)

> Both the granddaughter of . . . and his great-niece . . . have told me that Tisza was an **exceedingly cautious** politician . . . (*AHT*, 84)

rejoicing—lamentation

Basis of analysis	rejoice (vb.) lament (vb.)
Dimension	FEELING
Type of dimension	scalar
Type of scale	S 2

Kind of scale	(degree +) quality
Features and relation	$x = \text{pos.} > T > y = \text{neg.}$

There was no contextualized example.

repute—disrepute

Dimension	ASSESSMENT (by others)
Type of dimension	scalar
Type of scale	S 2
Kind of scale	(degree +) quality
Features and relation	$x = \text{pos.} > T > y = \text{neg.}$

There was no contextualized example.

respect—disrespect

Dimension	ESTEEM/COURTESY
Type of dimension	scalar
Type of scale	S 2
Kind of scale	degree + quality
Features and relation	$x = \text{pos.} > T > y = \text{neg.}$

Examples

We listened to Parker for some time with the **respect** of the novice for the expert. (*PI*, 48)

'. . . Was any act committed by those four men which might seem to denote **disrespect** to the spirit of Menher-Ra?' (*PI*, 101)

Cf. also:

'I'm going to see the old man' (thus **disrespectfully** did Leach speak of his Chief Constable) . . . (*TZ*, 110)

reward—penalty

Dimension	RETURN (for sth. done)
Type of dimension	scalar
Type of scale	S 2
Kind of scale	(degree +) quality
Features and relation	$x = \text{pos.} > T > y = \text{neg.}$

There was no contextualized example.

sage—fool

Dimension	WISDOM
Type of dimension	scalar
Type of scale	S 2
Kind of scale	degree + quality
Features and relation	$x > T > y$

There was no contextualized example for the pair *sage—fool*, which is not surprising in view of the fact that *sage*, according to Sykes 1976, means something like "profoundly wise man, esp. any of the ancients traditionally reputed wisest of their time" and thus is much more restricted in sense than *fool*. There seems to be no appropriate nominal opposite to *fool*: cf.:

> She drew out from her handbag the letter she had received that morning from Lady Tamplin. Katherine was **no fool**. She understood the *nuances* of that letter as well as anybody and the reason of Lady Tamplin's show of affection towards a long-forgotten cousin was not lost upon her. It was for profit and not for pleasure that Lady Tamplin was so anxious for the company of her dear cousin. (*MBT*, 51 f.)

> 'Now that you remind me of the fact, it is true that there is one thing more. It would be **most unwise** on your part to attempt to silence me as you silenced M. Ackroyd. That kind of business does not succeed against Hercule Poirot, you understand.'
>   'My dear Poirot,' I said, smiling a little, 'whatever else I may be, I am **not a fool**.' (*MRA*, 218)

> 'You are a **clever** woman, Rita; but you are also a **fool**! Be guided by me, and give up Peel Edgerton.' (*TSA*, 71)

Usually, the adjective *foolish* contrasts with *wise* or *clever* along the dimension WISDOM:

> She had had so many of these **foolish** middle-aged women to minister to her—all much the same, kind, fussy, subservient and almost entirely mindless. (*DW*, 22)

savouriness—unsavouriness

Basis of analysis	savoury (adj.) unsavoury (adj.)
Dimension	QUALITY OF TASTE/SMELL
Type of dimension	scalar
Type of scale	S 2
Kind of scale	(degree +) quality
Features and relation	x = pos. > T > y = neg.

There was no contextualized example.

skill—unskilfulness

Dimension	EXPERTNESS
Type of dimension	scalar
Type of scale	S 2
Kind of scale	degree/(quality)

Features and relation $\quad x > T > y$

There was no contextualized example.

virtue—vice

Dimension	MORAL QUALITY
Type of dimension	scalar
Type of scale	S 2
Kind of scale	(degree +) quality
Features and relation	$x = \text{pos.} > T > y = \text{neg.}$

Examples

> I mean there are occasions when, coward that one is, one prefers to let people think the worst. It is the homage **virtue** pays to **vice**. (*TBMIFD*, 106)

> In that reticence could be found the keynote of Emily Arundell's character. She was, in every respect, the typical product of her generation. She had both its **virtues** and its **vices**. (*DW*, 6)

Virtue also contrasts with *fault*, apparently along the same dimension, but with the feature [+count] obligatorily present:

> '. . . I do, sometimes, know what people are like. I mean, I know what people are like, because they remind me of certain other people I have known. So I know some of their **faults** and some of their **virtues** . . .' (*NEM*, 42)

> Her qualities were all excellent qualities, but sometimes Edward wished she had **more faults** and **less virtues**. (*LM*, 82)

6

Central Oppositeness of Meaning: Some Further Issues

6.1 OPPOSITENESS OF MEANING VS. NEGATION

6.1.1 *"Negative" prefixes*[1]

Lyons (1977) points out that morphologically unrelated pairs of opposites in English

> are outnumbered in the vocabulary by such morphologically related pairs as 'married' : 'unmarried', 'friendly' : 'unfriendly', 'formal' : 'informal', 'legitimate' : 'illegitimate', etc. In each case the base-form of one member of the pair is derived from the base-form of the other by the addition of the **negative** prefixes *un-* or *in-*. (Lyons 1977, 275 [my emphasis])

Thus the English prefixes *un-*, *dis-*, and *non-* have often been referred to as "negative prefixes" (e.g. by Funk (1971, 1986), Stein (1971), Kastovsky (1982*b*)); they have been described in connection with 'affixal and non-affixal negation' (Tottie 1980, 101) or as instances of 'präfixale[r] (morphematisch gebundene[r]) Negation im Englischen' (Welte 1978, 186). H. Schmidt (1985, 58) regards cases such as *anständig : unanständig, artig : unartig, gerecht : ungerecht, sportlich : unsportlich, Ruhe : Unruhe, Schuld : Unschuld*, etc. as 'Gegensatzwörter mit gesonderter lexikalisierter Anzeige der Polarität bei nur einem Partner' and points out:

> Gerade für diese Gruppe bestehen z.T. Zweifel an der Auffassung der Partnerwörter als Antonyme [im weiteren Sinn (A.M.)]. Es ist zuzugeben, dass das Präfix *un-* in einigen Fällen nur negativierend wirkt, in anderen scheint es aber in der Tat zur Benennung des Gegensatzes zu dienen. Wir kennen kein Verfahren, das beide Funktionen eindeutig trennt, sehen darin aber kein ausreichendes Gegenargument gegen die Annahme einer bereits paradigmatisch angelegten Antonymiebedeutung des *un-*.[2] (H. Schmidt 1985, 58 f.)

Klima (1964, 312) assumes an underlying constituent *neg* for *in-*, *un-*, and *dis-*prefixation; Chapin (1970) uses syntactic criteria to distinguish between *un-1*, which 'attaches to verb stems with the characteristic result that the meaning of the derivative is an action which reverses the action designated by the stem (*unlock*, *untie*, *undress*)' (Chapin 1970, 57),[3] and *un-2*, which 'attaches to adjective stems with the semantic effect of simple negation: *unhappy*, *unwise*, *unfaithful*' (Chapin 1970, 58). From a semantic point of view Chapin's account of *un-2*-prefixation seems grossly oversimplified. As early as 1917[4] Jespersen pointed out:

The modification in sense brought about by the addition of the prefix [*un-*] is generally that of a simple negative: *unworthy* = 'not worthy', etc. The two terms are thus contradictory terms. But very often the prefix produces a 'contrary' term or at any rate what approaches one: *unjust* (and *injustice*) generally imply the opposite of *just* (*justice*); *unwise* means more than *not wise* and approaches *foolish*, *unhappy* is not far from *miserable*, etc. (Jespersen 1966, 144)

Any description of the semantic relations obtaining between the members of such pairs of lexemes must involve a consideration of two fundamental issues, viz. the status of the prefixed lexeme with regard to the word-formational system of English, and the function which is performed by the prefix with regard to the unprefixed member of the pair. Prefixes are defined as

bound morphemes which are preposed to free morphemes. In a syntagma AB they fill the position A, i.e. they normally function as determinants of the word B to which they are prefixed. Prefixal combinations are expansions which must meet the condition of analysability after the formula AB=B. (Marchand 1969, 129)

Unequal, *unimportant*, *unhappy*, and *dishonest*, to cite a few examples, could thus be regarded as expansions of their respective bases, where '[s]emantically speaking, the determinatum represents the element whose range of applicability is limited by the determinant' (Marchand 1969, 11). In what way, then, does the prefix limit the range of applicability of the unprefixed basis?

This question can be answered satisfactorily only if the two basic functions of word-formation are taken into account, viz. the naming (or labelling) function and the syntactic recategorization function. The former is defined in the following way:

word-formation is . . . regarded primarily as a means of systematically enlarging the vocabulary. This lexical aspect of word-formation is of course connected with the central linguistic category of this linguistic level, the word, or lexical item, or lexeme. It is the basic function of this category to serve as a label, as a designation for some segment of extralinguistic reality **which for some reason requires a name as a constant, and conventionalized means of referring to it, and not only some kind of *ad hoc* description.** Words are listed in the dictionary or lexicon, which thus is the repository of all the designations the language in question possesses to refer to extralinguistic reality. (Kastovsky 1986*b*, 64 f. [my emphasis])

The syntactic recategorization function, on the other hand, is to be understood as consisting of

replacing a complex syntactic construction, e.g. a VP or a whole sentence, by a more or less synonymous nominal, adjectival, or verbal complex lexical item . . . This phenomenon has a text-linguistic basis and is related to pronominalization in the broadest sense of the term, in so far as the word-formation syntagma in question refers anaphorically or cataphorically to some explicit part of the context, either taking it up again in condensed, 'lexicalized' form, with or without additional stylistic implications, or itself being explained further by the following context. (Kastovsky 1982*a*, 182 f.)

'More or less synonymous' in the above quotation should be understood as "without additional semantic charge" as stated in Motsch's definition of the syntactic function of word-formation:

[Die syntaktische Funktion] tritt in reinster Form bei der Umkategorisierung auf, d.h. bei der Bildung von Wörtern einer bestimmten Wortart aus solchen einer anderen ohne semantische Zusätze . . . Von syntaktischer Funktion wollen wir aber auch in solchen Fällen sprechen, wo WBR [= Wortbildungsregeln] die systematische Möglichkeit bieten, syntaktische Ausdrücke durch Ausdrücke mit Wortbildungen zu ersetzen.[5] (Motsch 1982, 66)

The following examples are cases in point:

(1) Iris . . . sat there white and ghostlike pushing **uneaten** food about her plate. (*SC*, 91)

(2) You may be right, you may not, but you have no business to condemn a man **unheard**. (*MRA*, 160)

(3) He threw away his **unlighted** cigarette, and put the match carefully into his pocket. (*SOC*, 180)

(4) He is beginning to weary of sitting still, he fidgets in his seat in an effort to find some **untried** disposition of his limbs . . . (*CP*, 34)

(5) 'I can swear to it, and besides, if they had had the key or a duplicate, why should they waste time to **force** an obviously **unforceable** lock?' (*PI*, 84)

Marsh-Stefanovska (1982, 69 ff.) regards pairs like *curable—incurable, used—disused, damaged—undamaged, objectionable—unobjectionable,* etc. as complementaries and points out:

In the lists above, some adjectives are included which are derived from the past participles of verbs. Among the complementaries, there is an almost infinite list of such forms (*broken : unbroken, eaten : uneaten, roasted : unroasted, spoken : unspoken, swept : unswept* . . .). (Marsh-Stefanovska 1982, 69 f.)

It seems doubtful, however, whether these cases can be regarded as pairs of systemic opposites as defined in Chapter 4 of this study, i.e. as pairs of lexemes that constitute semantic micro-fields, share the same archisememe, and differ along one semantic dimension. Rather, they should be interpreted as instances of syntactically recategorized negation.[6] The prefixed lexical items systematically replace complex syntactic constructions, and their occurrence is syntactically predictable (cf. Tottie 1980):

Most participial adjectives of the type *unread* and *unreadable* are nothing but transformed negative sentences, derived from *X has not been read, X cannot be read.* It is completely immaterial whether unprefixed adjectives, say *abbreviated, identified, read, spoken, caused* actually exist. The *un-*adjectives are not derived from unprefixed adjectives, but are adjectivalizations of sentences such as *X has not been abbreviated, identified, read, spoken, caused.* Negation is concerned with the predication, meaning simply that the predication is not applied to the subject of the underlying sentence . . . The predication is either made or not made, as a yes-or-no decision, but in the event of 'no', negation cannot be further qualified in degree. Something either is or is not. (Marchand 1966, 139)

*Non-*prefixations[7] have been singled out in 5.2 above for the same reason. Cf.:

(6) 'No, darling, you shan't. I absolutely agree about Dr Jore—he's a **bore**.'

'There you are, with your scale of false values! You divide human souls into **bores** and **non-bores**, don't you? I'm a **bore** and **Basil isn't**, that I've always known. You ought to be considering where everybody stands in the universal scheme instead of laughing at them and saying they are **bores**.' (*DTA*, 141)

(7) '. . . What should we have to drink there, I wonder?'
'Well-water, I should think,' I replied with a shudder.
'Or **non-alcoholic** cider. It was that kind of place . . .'
(*DW*, 86)

(8) Straightening up, he gave another smile, this time at Dixon, paused, as if to emphasize his **non-intention** of setting out any of the tea things, and moved off counterfeiting a heavy limp. (*LJ*, 198)

(9) Dinner was a solitary meal. Tuppence was rather surprised at Tommy's **non-return**, Julius, too, was absent . . . (*TSA*, 64)

(10) . . . a very funny parody of the worst kind of American AM radio, based on the simple but effective formula of having **non-commercial commercials**. (*CP*, 71)

With regard to *non*-prefixation Marchand points out that

non-words are the only ones that in all formative patterns are perfectly explained as transforms of sentences: just as *non-American* is derived from *X/is not/American*, the recent *nonstudent* is explained from *X/is not/a student*. The prefixed words contain no denotative addition to the content of the respective underlying sentences. (Marchand 1966, 140)

The situation is different with regard to pairs like *equal—unequal*, *legal—illegal*, *material—immaterial*, analysed as digital opposites in 5.2.1 of this study, and pairs like *conscious—unconscious*, *married—unmarried*, and *animate—inanimate* (treated as complementaries by Marsh-Stefanovska (1982, 69)). These pairs constitute digital semantic dimensions, and the feature y that characterizes the prefixed lexeme can be represented as (NEG x), i.e. as the negation of the feature x which characterizes the unprefixed member of the pair with regard to the semantic dimension.[8] Digital opposites of this type show quite clearly that the labelling function and the syntactic recategorization function of word-formation 'are . . . not mutually exclusive; rather, they represent opposite poles on a functional scale, on which each single word-formation syntagma can be located' (Kastovsky 1986*b*, 66). On the one hand the prefixed member of a pair of digital opposites is fully paraphrasable as the negation of its unprefixed counterpart (and can thus be regarded as a case of lexicalized negation), on the other hand the meaning-relation between the prefixed and the unprefixed members of such a pair of lexical items is one of oppositeness of meaning, i.e. along the semantic dimension ACCORDANCE WITH LAW, *legal* and *illegal* behave exactly like *male* and *female* along the semantic dimension GENDER.

When scalar semantic dimensions are involved, the prefixed member of a pair of opposites cannot simply be paraphrased by "not + unprefixed member", i.e. *unimportant* cannot be represented as "not important". The analyses in Chapter 5 have shown that the prefix names, or labels, a specific value or range of values along the scalar semantic dimension depending on the nature of the scale involved:

(*a*) unidirectionally open scales with attainable zero-value: in pairs like *important—unimportant, curious—incurious, possible—impossible, envious—unenvious, selfish—unselfish*, etc. the prefix always represents a feature-value that stands in a "<" relationship to the feature-value characterizing the unprefixed member of the pair along the scalar dimension. Moreover, the feature-value represented by the prefix can also include zero; cf.:

(11) 'Sir James,' said Tuppence, plunging boldly, 'I dare say you will think it most awful cheek of me coming here like this. Because, of course, it's nothing whatever to do with you, and then you're a **very important** person, and of course Tommy and I are **very unimportant**.' (*TSA*, 85)

'Raymond or Blunt must have pushed it back,' I suggested. 'Surely it isn't **important**?'

'It is **completely unimportant**,' said Poirot. (*MRA*, 70)

(12) I ended up **totally unenvious** of Louise's new ménage, and somehow strangely sympathetic towards her. (*SBC*, 126 f.)

(13) . . . your left hand is what you are born with and your right hand is what you make of your life. So that means that you were born **unselfish** but have become **more selfish** as time goes on. (*TZ*, 66)

(*b*) bidirectionally open scales: in pairs like *repute—disrepute, respect—disrespect, savoury—unsavoury, attractive—unattractive, honest—dishonest, honourable—dishonourable* the prefix represents the "negative evaluation" part of the scalar dimension (see 4.2.4.2). The bidirectionality of the scalar dimension allows intensification towards infinity in opposite directions: along the "positive evaluation" part of the scale (*much respect, more respect,* etc.) and along the "negative evaluation" part (*much disrespect, more disrespect,* etc.); cf.:

(14) . . . it is one of the great consolations in nature that a man, **however unattractive**, will find that he is **attractive**—even what appears to be **madly attractive**—to some woman. (*HP*, 31)

(15) Three weeks ago I wrote you that everything was all right and I had made up my mind and felt **happy** but I am still **unhappy, unhappier** in a way than I was before. (*TLO*, 101)

(16) Lady Kidderminster was silent, unperturbed by the thrust. Sandra was the least dear to her of her children— nevertheless she was at this moment a mother, and a mother only—willing to defend her young by any means, **honourable** or **dishonourable**. (*SC*, 128)

'. . . Timid and easily frightened people like Miss Lawson often acquire a number of **mildly dishonourable** habits which are a great solace and recreation to them.' (*DW*, 144)

(17) It disappeared from her dressing-room at the theatre, and there was a lingering suspicion in the minds of the authorities that she herself might have engineered its disappearance. Such things have been known as a publicity stunt, or indeed from **more dishonest** motives. (*MMFC*, 29 f.)

'. . . I admit that I gained Miss Theresa's confidence by a trick. I let her think that I would be—shall we say, **reasonably dishonest**—for money. She believed that without the least difficulty.' (*DW*, 198 f.)

(*c*) unidirectionally open scales with one value equalling zero: with pairs like *agree—disagree, certain—uncertain, clean—unclean, order—disorder, perfect—imperfect, pure—impure, regular—irregular* the situation is fundamentally different: in these cases the feature-value of the unprefixed member represents the zero-value of the scalar dimension, while that of the prefixed member represents the rest of the scale. This explains the fact that the unprefixed lexemes can be modified by degree adverbs like *completely, perfectly, absolutely*, or, like digital opposites proper, by degree adverbs expressing approximation towards a digit (like *almost*), whereas the prefixed lexemes are fully gradable. Cf.:

(18) 'Oh, rather,' said Tony Marsden heartily. 'I **quite agree**.' (*NOM*, 145)

'I **agree** with you **entirely**. London is no place at the present . . .' (*NOM*, 46)

But there were points on which Rudolf **violently disagreed**. (*AHT*, 88)

(19) 'What about the colonies?' she suggested.
Tommy shook his head.
'I shouldn't like the colonies—and I'm **perfectly certain** they wouldn't like me!' (*TSA*, 10)

Jimmy took a moment or two to answer. His voice was serious when he said at last **rather uncertainly**: 'I suppose it's just a damned odd coincidence.' (*MIE*, 18)

There was a pause. The silence lay heavy between them. Bridget broke it at last. She said, but with a **slight uncertainty** in her tone: '. . .' (*MIE*, 96)

(20) 'I really think our kitchen is **almost perfect** by now.' (*POF*, 36)

(21) A heavy black volume, amateurishly bound, with no name or title on the cover. The print also looked **slightly irregular**. (*1984*, 162)

With many pairs of opposites that operate along unidirectionally open scales with one value equalling zero, the unprefixed lexeme (representing the zero-value) is evaluatively positive, and the prefixed lexeme denotes 'degrees of some undesirable property' (Cruse 1980, 21) such that the "negative" prefix is evaluatively negative too.

6.1.2 *"Positive" and "negative"*

In connection with "negative" prefixes a few remarks on the notions "positive" and "negative" would not go amiss. Lyons (1977, 275) describes lexemes such as *unfriendly* and *informal* as 'morphologically negative' in opposition to their 'morphologically positive' unprefixed counterparts. This labelling is misleading in view of the well-established distinction between "morphologically marked" and "morphologically unmarked", and therefore has not been adopted in this study.[9]

The terms "positive" and "negative" have frequently been used in connection with the notion of polarity:

> Many opposite pairs are formally asymmetrical, in that one member bears a negative affix, while the other has no formal mark: *happy* : *unhappy*, *like* : *dislike*, etc. For a very few, in English, both members have a formal mark: *increase* : *decrease, accelerate* : *decelerate* . . . In the case of the formally asymmetrical pairs, we may confidently speak of the 'positive' and 'negative' terms of the opposition. Even with the doubly marked pairs there is a strong intuition of polarity: *accelerate* and *increase*, for instance, are felt to be positive, and *decelerate* and *decrease* are felt to be negative. (Cruse 1986, 246)

Apparently Cruse's use of "positive" and "negative" in the above quotation is founded on the belief that a term that denotes more of a certain property should be assigned "positive polarity", a term that denotes less of the same property should be regarded as exhibiting "negative polarity" (cf. Lyons 1968, 467; 1977, 275 f.). In fact, Lyons (1977, 276, in combination with 1968, 467) equates "semantically positive" with "unmarked" (e.g. *big*) and "semantically negative" with "marked" (e.g. *small*).[10] Concurring with such an interpretation of positive and negative polarity Lehrer (1974) points out that

> it can be noticed that it is the negative case which approaches some limit or zero point, while this is not true of the positive cases. A thing can be so narrow or so short or so small that it approaches zero in extension, but there is no limit to how large, wide, or tall something can be. (Lehrer 1974, 27)

In view of the bidirectionally open scales established in this study, Lehrer's statement must be regarded as having limited validity only.

Cruse (1980) defines "positive" and "negative" with regard to quantity as well:

A distinction can . . . be introduced between the members of a pair of gradable opposites: the term which denotes less of the scaled property will be labelled 'Q-negative'; its partner, which indicates a greater quantity of the scaled property, will be termed 'Q-positive'. In the case of the pair *heavy* : *light*, it is *heavy* which is Q-positive, since it denotes 'more weight'. (Cruse 1980, 15)

Since, in the present study, I have represented "more/less" relations in terms of relations obtaining between variable relational features, the application of "positive" and "negative" to characterize DEGREE has become superfluous,[11] and the terms have become free to be used with reference to "evaluation" only.

6.2 THE PROBLEM OF MARKEDNESS

In this study the concept of "markedness" has not yet been introduced, although it figures rather prominently in a number of descriptions of oppositeness of meaning (e.g. Coseriu (1975), Van Overbeke (1975), Lyons (1977), Geckeler (1980), Palmer (1981), Marsh-Stefanovska (1982), Lehrer (1985)). The matter is usually discussed in connection with gradable adjectives, and it is stated

that in each pair one of the terms is the MARKED term and the other UNMARKED in that only one is used simply to ask about or describe the degree of the gradable quality. We say *How high is it? How wide is it? It is three feet high, It is four yards wide*, with no implication that it is either high or wide. But the other term of the pair is not so used—it is the marked term. Thus *How low is it? How narrow is it?* imply that the object in question actually is low or narrow . . . Notice also that the same member of the pair is used to form the nouns, *height* and *width*, which are equally neutral as compared with *lowness* and *narrowness*. In the English examples it is the 'larger' term that appears to be unmarked . . . (Palmer 1981, 95 f.)

Whereas British semanticists like John Lyons correlate semantic marking with distribution, cf.:

A semantically marked lexeme is one that is more specific in sense than the corresponding semantically unmarked lexeme [. . . A]ll semantically

marked lexemes are (by virtue of their more specific sense) distribution-
ally marked . . . (Lyons 1977, 307)

continental structuralists like Eugenio Coseriu have adopted the
concept of markedness from phonology together with the notion
of "privative opposition", which

in phonology is generally described as a contrastive relation between two
phonemes one of which (the marked member) contains a distinctive feature lacking in the other (the unmarked member) . . . One particular
characteristic of this type of opposition is that under certain conditions it
can be neutralized, in which case the unmarked member is substituted
for the marked member. (Kastovsky 1982*c*, 36)

It has turned out, however, that it is impossible to draw exact
parallels between privative opposition in phonology and oppositeness of meaning (cf. Kastovsky (1982*b*, 95 f.; 1982*c*). Ljung
(1974) has suggested an alternative approach. He assumes that in
neutral *how*-questions (with the stress on the adjective) of the
type

(22) How old is your brother?
     How long is the ship?
     How wide is the passage?

the adjectives are unmarked and have archilexemic function
(HAVING AGE, HAVING LENGTH, HAVING WIDTH), whereas the corresponding negative members (*young, short, narrow*) cannot be
unmarked and, therefore, cannot appear in neutral *how*-
questions. Ljung would suggest analysing a pair like *long—short*
as 'a semantically related trio of adjectives' (Ljung 1974, 84) with
long split up into two homonymous lexemes LONG-1 (unmarked)
and *long*-2 (marked) vs. *short* (marked):

One [of the adjectives forming the trio]—the UNMARKED one—refers
to the entire dimension, while the other two—the MARKED ones—refer
to the POSITIVE and NEGATIVE parts of the dimension; i.e. the positive form indicates a great amount of the dimension, the negative one
denotes a small amount of it. (Ljung 1974, 84)

All the analyses in this study have been carried out on the basis
of Ljung's theory, as his assumptions allow the treatment of central systemic opposites as sememes that share the same theoretical status with regard to the semantic dimensions involved, and it

is this equality of status that has made the analyses in terms of dimensions and feature-relations possible. The following examples and schema illustrate the relations obtaining between the pair *much—little*:

(23) 'How much [1] do you know?' he shot out.
'Very little [3] indeed,' answered Tuppence, . . . (*TSA*, 19)

Whether there had been much [2] or little [3] money in the house at the time of her death was a debatable point. None had been found. (*LM*, 70)

Archisememe	HAVING QUANTITY *much* [1]
Dimension	QUANTITY (S 1)
Features	x (QUANTITY) $<$ y (QUANTITY)
	little [3] *much* [2]

The same principle of analysis is also valid for pairs of opposites with one prefixed member, and thus, from the point of view of word-structure (i.e. from an analytical point of view), it is not really appropriate to speak of "negative" prefixes; cf.:

(24) Archisememe	HAVING IMPORTANCE *important* [1]
Dimension	IMPORTANCE (S 1 $\to$ 0)
Features	$0 \leq x$ (IMPORTANCE) $<$ y (IMPORTANCE)
	unimportant [3] *important* [2]

In some cases, however, it is not quite clear when an opposite should be interpreted as the archilexeme [=1] or as one member of the respective pair of opposites [=2]. Cf.:

(25) But there was one factor on which Bridget had not reckoned. *Honoria Waynflete was mad.* Her strength [1] was the strength [2] of the insane. She fought like a devil and her insane strength [2?] was stronger than the sane muscled strength [2?] of Bridget. (*MIE*, 178)

6.3 SOME REMAINING PROBLEMS

6.3.1 *Remarks on the scope of the investigation*

This study represents an attempt to describe semantic relations of various kinds, traditionally known as "antonymy", in a systematic way. What I have tried to show is the interrelation of semantic dimensions and semantic features in one rather limited field of linguistic structure. Apart from this, I have tried to demonstrate how concepts and notions introduced and developed by a number of European structuralist semanticists can be successfully applied to one specific task and to show what results they can produce. There are, of course, some questions that have to remain unanswered at present. First of all, only semantic microstructures have been investigated (from an analytical point of view). More textual evidence would be necessary for an analysis from an onomasiological point of view in order to complement this study and allow generalizations as to how the vocabulary of the investigated language is organized in terms of semantic macrostructures.

6.3.2 *Reflections on the cognitive perspective*

In Chapter 3 of this work I drew a rather sharp line dividing non-systemic opposites from systemic ones, and the remainder of the book was dedicated entirely to the analysis of systemic opposites and to a discussion of their semantic properties, based on the assumption that within the language-system meaning is something (at least for a certain period of time) constant and systematic. Consequently, meaning-relations can also be regarded as constant, systematic, and thus structurally analysable. In actual language-use, however, both groups of opposites behave in a similar way (as has been shown in Chapter 2), and it would, therefore, be desirable to assume a common underlying principle. The assumption of such a principle can be based on the "positive" definition of linguistic signs as denoting objects, properties, and relations of extralinguistic reality, which might lead to transcending the structuralist paradigm and to assuming "adversativity" (as introduced in Chapter 1) as a higher-level, cognitive entity. "Adversativity" could be defined as a conceptual category that is operative in our perception of the world and seems to be an important structuring principle for a number of cognitive domains (cf. Taylor 1989, 83 ff.).

Adversativity would have to be characterized by the simultaneous implementation of two functors: a "conceptual integrator" and a "conceptual differentiator", the conceptual integrator accounting for the sameness of two entities with regard to certain properties, the conceptual differentiator stating with regard to which properties two entities are different. Thus, the conceptual integrator covers one important prerequisite for opposites, viz. the fact that there must be a basis of comparison; the conceptual differentiator states 'ce qui est commun aux différences entre ces termes' (Coseriu 1975, 36), i.e. the common basis against which the opposition as such is established.

Our intuitive feeling that some pairs of opposites are "better", "more typical", or "more systematic" than others could then be explained by observing the way in which 'cognitive structures happen to be lexicalized in a particular language' (Taylor 1989, 83).

Pairs like *boy—girl, high—low, dark—light*, etc. are characterized by a very stable, more or less context-independent relationship between the meanings of the pair members. Adversativity has been completely lexicalized ("versprachlicht"), i.e. found its place in the language-system. The task of the conceptual integrator is performed by the archisememe, that of the conceptual differentiator by the semantic dimension. These "systemic opposites" seem to be part of the linguistic system a speaker has acquired and do not—either for their use in actual speech or for their interpretation—depend on extralinguistic, encyclopaedic knowledge.

"Non-systemic opposites" have been characterized in this work as not admitting of an analysis in terms of archisememes, semantic dimensions, and semantic features. In cases like (26) and (27), which could be labelled "terminological opposites", the task of the conceptual integrator is performed by a "frame", i.e. a (static) configuration of knowledge (Taylor 1989, 87):

(26) 'How lovely. You are kind. I do love money! I'll keep beautiful accounts of our expenses—all **debit** and **credit**, and the balance on the right side . . .' (*TSA*, 37)
Frame: ACCOUNTING

(27) Unable to decide on the relative accuracy of the **oral** and **rectal** methods of taking her temperature, Barbara had decided to employ both. (*TBMIFD*, 10)
Frame: TEMPERATURE-TAKING

"Encyclopaedic opposites" proper as instanced by (28) to (31) show that adversativity can be implemented by a great variety of conceptual integrators:

(28) Lucy, Henry, Edward . . . they were all divided from her by an impassable gulf—the gulf that separates the **leisured** from the **working**. (*TH*, 110)

(29) So all he did was pass the time . . . No brain-work of any kind before luncheon: nothing but a long sojourn—from **necessity**, not **choice**—on the lavatory . . . (*EU*, 50)

(30) 'It's a special form of scholarly neurosis', said Camel. 'He's no longer able to distinguish between **life** and **literature**.' (*TBMIFD*, 56)

(31) Edward wondered whether the Marchesa Bianca would have made an excellent wife. Somehow, he doubted it . . . No, Bianca was **Romance**, and this was **real life**. He and Maud would be very happy together. She had so much common sense . . . (*LM*, 82)

These pairs of opposites rely for their interpretation on knowledge of the world, which must, however, be common knowledge, i.e. either the speaker assumes that the hearer can establish the conceptual integrator from the knowledge he has (as in (28) and (29)) or by inferring from the context (as in (30) and (31)).

A treatment of opposites from the cognitive point of view would probably have to assume a scale of increasing amount of encyclopaedic knowledge that is necessary for establishing conceptual integrators and differentiators, starting from a zero-value (characteristic of systemic opposites), becoming more with terminological opposites, and reaching a maximum with encyclopaedic opposites. These assumptions are, however, still highly speculative at the moment.

6.3.3 *Reflections on semantic dimensions*

It would, of course, be interesting to discover more about the psychological and/or conceptual status of the semantic dimensions that have been established in this study. Digital opposites seem to involve well-defined concepts that can be kept apart easily, either because they have acquired a slightly terminological tinge (*absolute—relative, convex—concave, equal—unequal, exterior—interior, legal—illegal, intrinsic—extrinsic, manifest—latent, material—immaterial, present—absent*) or because they express two possibilities of reaction to a given stimulus (*affirm—negate, approve—disapprove, acquit—condemn, permit—prohibit, succeed—fail*).

Scalar opposites, on the other hand, involve concepts that admit of degrees, either in terms of "more/less" or in terms of "good/bad". Semantic dimensions that constitute unidirectionally open scales with non-attainable zero-value comprise (in most cases) measurable properties like EXTENSION (lateral as in *broad—narrow*, longitudinal as in *long—short*, vertical below surface as in *deep—shallow*, above surface as in *high—low*), DISTANCE (*far—near*), SIZE (*great—small*), TEMPERATURE (*hot—cold*), WEIGHT (*heavy—light*), VOLUME (*loud—faint*), SPEED (*fast—slow*), AGE (*young—old*), and many others. They could be regarded as having high cultural saliency. It should also be pointed out that this group consists of underived lexemes only.

Almost complementary to the S 1 group mentioned above, the group made up of opposites constituting unidirectionally open scales with attainable zero-value contains an exceedingly large number of pairs with one prefixed member: *active—inactive, curious—incurious, elastic—inelastic, important—unimportant, intelligible—unintelligible, penitent—impenitent, possible—impossible, probable—improbable, salubrious—insalubrious, sensible—insensible, selfish—unselfish*, and many others. Apparently in all these cases word-formational devices have been exploited systematically to "name" that part of the scale that is close to (and includes) the zero-value.

Bidirectionally open scales are constituted by lexemes from the fields of emotion or what might be called "inner qualities" (*cheerfulness—dejection, courage—cowardice, intelligence—imbecility, love—hate, pleasure—pain, rashness—caution, sage—fool, virtue—vice*), and they all involve a strong evaluative component dependent on social norms (*beauty—ugliness, benefactor—evildoer, courtesy—discourtesy, elegance—inelegance, fragrance—fetor, friend—enemy, good—evil, repute—disrepute, respect—disrespect*, etc.).

From a conceptual point of view, opposites operating along unidirectionally open scales with one value equalling zero are probably the most interesting ones. In cases like *certain—uncertain, clean—unclean, coherent—incoherent, complete—incomplete, order—disorder, perfect—imperfect, regular—irregular* (where the unprefixed member always represents the zero-value of the scalar dimension) as well as in cases like *straight—curved, health—*

sickness, innocent—guilty, dry—moist, safety—danger, smooth—rough, silence—sound (where the first member represents the zero-value) the zero-value of the scale very often represents a norm that seems to be conceptualized as an attainable digit; however, as with digital opposites, the relation between the members of the above pairs is one of "either/or", in many cases also because the scaled property is an undesirable one. Cf.:

In the case of an UNDESIRABLE property . . . the most important question for the language user is whether the property is present or absent. The desirable state is zero value of the property, and this is signalled by one of the terms of the opposition; any positive value represents an unsatisfactory state, and this is signalled by the other term of the opposition. This explains simultaneously why the use of gradable complementaries is governed by a norm, rather than an average, and why they are contradictories. (Cruse 1980, 23)

One last question remains: could the scales established for central oppositeness of meaning in English be regarded as non-language-specific? In view of the material from other languages that I have briefly looked at (e.g. Novikov (1973*a*, *b*) for Russian, Gsell (1979) for Romance languages, Zimmer (1964) for "negative" prefixation in a variety of Indo-European and non-Indo-European languages) and from my own knowledge of Russian and Chinese I think this question can—with due caution—be answered in the affirmative. Any positive proof would, however, presuppose the analysis of a large amount of lexical material along the lines suggested in this study—a task that will have to be left for the future.

Notes to Chapter 6

1. This subsection is not intended to be a description of "negative prefixes" in English; rather, I wish to point out the considerations which have led to the treatment of pairs of opposites with one prefixed member along the same principles that have been adopted for the treatment of morphologically unrelated pairs.

    For a description and discussion of negative prefixes from an analytical point of view see Funk (1971), Stein (1971), Staib (1981), Marsh-Stefanovska (1982), Mettinger (1986; 1988*a*); see also s.vv. *un-, dis-, non-*, etc. in Marchand (1969), Hansen *et al.* (1982), Bauer (1983); one of the most comprehensive studies of negative prefixation from the point of view of productivity is Zimmer (1964); in this context see also Funk (1986).

It should be mentioned here that suffixes, too, can be used to form opposites. They can, however, be disregarded in the discussion of oppositeness of meaning, as their 'basic function . . . is to express privation, or the lack of the quality expressed in the base form. Thus in English we have -*less* and -*free* . . . Again, and more commonly, these affixes do not always indicate opposition in the derived form to the concept in the base (which may itself have an affix indicating possession of a quality, such as -*ful* in English). So we find such "false" opposites as *helpful* : *helpless*, *mindful* : *mindless*, *shameful* : *shameless*' (Marsh-Stefanovska 1982, 12 f.).

Such "false pairs" can, of course, be found among those including one prefixed member too, cf.: *flammable—inflammable*, *graceful—disgraceful*, *passive—impassive*, *possessed—dispossessed*, *valuable—invaluable* (all mentioned by Marsh-Stefanovska (1982, 20)). The *Thesaurus* corpus contains the following "false pairs": *evidence—counter-evidence*, *interpretation—misinterpretation*, *judgement—misjudgement*, *relation—irrelation*, *representation—misrepresentation*.

2. 'Especially with regard to this group doubts have been raised as to the classification of the partner words as antonyms [in the broad sense (A.M.)]. It must be admitted that the prefix *un-* has a purely negating function in some cases, while in others it really seems to serve the purpose of denoting opposition. We do not know of any method that is able to differentiate between the two functions, but we do not regard this as a valid counterargument against the assumption of a paradigmatically established antonymous meaning of *un-*.'

3. In this study "reversativity" is not regarded as belonging to oppositeness of meaning proper. Though reversives have repeatedly been treated as one subgroup of lexical opposites (e.g. by Nida (1975, 18, 109), Cruse (1979; 1986, 226 ff.), Geckeler (1980, 52), Staib (1981, 84 ff.), Nellessen (1982, 95 ff.), Marsh-Stefanovska (1982, 77 ff.)) it seems to me that such a treatment is not fully justified. On the one hand, it is often not clear along which semantic dimension a pair of reversives operates: pairs like *rise—fall*, *advance—retreat*, *enter—leave* are closely related to directional opposition (cf. Cruse 1986, 226); others, like *lengthen—shorten*, *accelerate—decelerate*, *increase—decrease*, go back to adjectival opposites (constituting S 1 scalar dimensions: LENGTH, VELOCITY, AMOUNT) in the comparative form (cf. Cruse 1986, 230). On the other hand, 'it is not the action which has to be reversed with a pair of reversives: it is rather the change of states. With all reversive pairs two states of the affected object are defined: an initial and a final state; and it is these which are reversed by the action of the members of the pair of verbs' (Marsh-Stefanovska

1982, 77). Cruse (1986, 226) thus glosses *appear* as "change from being invisible to being visible" and *disappear* as "change from being visible to being invisible". Although one might assume that the pair *appear—disappear* is in some way operative along the digital dimension VISIBILITY one would still need some specification as to the direction of the change of states involved. Despite Cruse's subdivision of reversives into "independent reversives" and "restitutives" (Cruse 1986, 228 ff.) on the basis of whether one of the members of a pair of reversives necessarily denotes the restitution of a former state, no satisfactory solution to this problem has yet been offered. It seems that Marchand's (1969, 205) paraphrase of *untie* "cause the object of the verb to be no longer V-ed" is the most appropriate one; it seems to me that pairs like *tie—untie, dress—undress,* and *lock—unlock* exhibit a ternary structure of the type "cause to be V-ed"—("be V-ed")—"cause to be no longer V-ed".

The following (deverbal) lexical items from the *Thesaurus* corpus could be analysed in this way: *acquisition—loss, arrangement— disarrangement, ?combination—decomposition, junction—disjunction, location—displacement, production—destruction (producer—destroyer), record—obliteration, retention—relinquishment*; without "cause": *appearance—disappearance, conversion—reversion, ?expansion— contraction.*

For the treatment of *improvement—deterioration* and *increase— decrease* see Cruse (1986, 227, 230).
4. Zimmer (1964, 10 ff.) mentions some interesting early works concerned with negative affixation, such as Rudolf v. Jhering's *Der Zweck im Recht* (appearing in 1883), Wilhelm Wundt's 'Das Sittliche in der Sprache' (1886) and J. v. Ginneken's *Principes de linguistique psychologique* (1907), which seem to have influenced Otto Jespersen.
5. '[The syntactic function] in its purest form can be found in cases of recategorization, i.e. in the process of forming words of a particular part of speech from those of another part of speech without additional semantic charge . . . We will speak of the syntactic function also in those cases where word-formation rules offer the systematic possibility of replacing syntactic expressions by expressions resulting from word-formation processes.'
6. For negation see also Jespersen (1924, 322 ff.), Kürschner (1983), Bîtea (1984*a, b*). Cf. in this context also Marchand's (1966, 138) differentiation of "transpositional derivatives" (which are mere transforms of sentences) and "semantic derivatives" (which contain an additional element of content). Funk (1971, 365 f.) distinguishes "syntactic derivatives" (which, with regard to affixal negation, are mere equivalents of negated relative clauses) and "semantic derivatives" (along the same lines as Marchand (1966)).

7. One of the most interesting comparisons of various negative affixes is Funk (1971), especially with regard to their similarities and differences. In this chapter I do not wish to discuss differences between *un-* and *non-* in greater detail. Suffice it to say that *un-* produces both gradable and ungradable lexical items, whereas *non-* produces only ungradable ones. Cf.:

> 'Iris, dear, don't. What a terrible thought—so **un-Christian**.'
> 'Why **un-Christian**? It's the Day of the Dead. In Paris people used to go and put flowers on the graves.'
> 'Oh, I know, dear, but then they are **Catholics**, aren't they?' (*SC*, 142)

versus

> How different it must be, he thought, the life of an ordinary, **non-Catholic** parent, free to decide . . . whether to have or not to have a child. (*TBMIFD*, 8)

Bauer (1983, 279) points out that 'the prefixation of *non-* divides the world up into two classes: those things denoted by the non-prefixed lexeme, and those denoted by the prefixed lexeme'. Cf. in this context the following German example:

> Man kann die Menschen sehr beliebig **in zwei Sorten teilen**. In Dicke und Dünne, in Gescheite und Dumme, in ÖVP- und SPÖ-Wähler, in Lustige und Traurige, in Junge und Alte, in Glückliche und Unglückliche, in Erfolgreiche und Versager, in Schöne und Hässliche. Oder: in **Patience-Leger** und **Nicht-Patience-Leger**. [One can freely **divide** people **into two groups**: fat ones and thin ones, wise ones and stupid ones, those who vote Conservative and those who vote Socialist, merry ones and sad ones, young ones and old ones, happy ones and unhappy ones, successful ones and unsuccessful ones, beautiful ones and ugly ones. Or **those who play patience** and **those who do not**.] (*Die ganze Woche* 1987/23, 5)

For further information on *non-* see Marsh-Stefanovska (1982, 72) and, especially, Bauer (1983, 279 ff.).

8. Cf. Kastovsky (1982*b*, 97): 'Die beiden Merkmale erschöpfen die Dimension vollständig, und das eine Merkmal stellt die logische Negation des anderen Merkmals dar, z.B. *MALE : FEMALE = MALE : NOT MALE . . .*' ['The two features fully exhaust the dimension, and the one feature represents the logical negation of the other, e.g. *MALE : FEMALE = MALE : NOT MALE . . .*']. See also Kastovsky (1982*b*, 134) as to the choice of the feature to be negated.

9. A passage from Steinthal's *Geschichte der Sprachwissenschaft bei den Griechen und Römern mit besonderer Rücksicht auf die Logik* (2nd edn. 1890) is quite interesting in this context. Discussing the category

"opposition" as conceived of by the Stoics Steinthal points out 'dass die negativen Wörter und die negativen Vorstellungen sich keineswegs decken, sondern vielfach in Widerstreit mit einander liegen. Bald drücken positive Wörter eine Beraubtheit oder ein Entblösstsein aus wie *Armut* die Entblösstheit von Vermögen, *blind* die Beraubtheit des Gesichts: bald drückt umgekehrt ein negatives Wort einen positiven Begriff aus . . . Privation . . . , Negation . . . und Gegensatz . . . sind nicht dasselbe; **denn das Gegenteil ist ja eben so wol [*sic*] etwas Positives, wie das, dessen Gegenteil es ist**, die Sprache aber vermischt häufig in ihren privativen Bildungen jene ersteren mit den beiden letzteren. So bezeichnet sie zwar ganz richtig den Gegensatz von *Tapferkeit* und *Feigheit* durch zwei positive Wörter; aber wenn man *Gerechtigkeit* und *Ungerechtigkeit* sagt, so drückt man einen Gegensatz, dessen beide Glieder eben so positiv sind, dennoch durch ein positives und ein negatives Wort aus' ['that negative words and negative concepts are by no means identical but are very often in conflict with one another. There are positive words expressing the lack of something, such as *poverty* (lack of fortune/means), *blindness* (lack of eyesight/vision); and negative words expressing a positive concept . . . Privation . . . , negation . . . and opposition are not the same thing: **an opposite is as positive as the thing whose opposite it is**, yet language in its privative coinages often confuses positive and negative words with negation and opposition. Thus language correctly denotes the opposition between *braveness* and *cowardice* by two positive words; if one, however, uses *justice* and *injustice* one expresses an opposition with two equally positive terms by one positive and one negative word'] (Steinthal 1890, 361 f. [my emphasis]).

10. I will show presently (in 6.2) that this marked–unmarked distinction must be given up.

11. Kastovsky (1982c) has investigated the transferability of the +/- notation derived from privative opposition in phonology to semantic opposition, arriving at the conclusion that in fact it is appropriate only for gradable complementaries and, if Ljung's (1974) analysis is adopted, for antonyms.

Opposites in Context: Index of Sources

1   adventurous—peaceful   *TH*, 10
2   alive—dead (cf. 33)   *PEC*, 197
3   amateur—professional   *SC*, 91
4   angular—round (cf. 20)   *TAT*, 161
5   anything—something   *POMT*, 125
6   arrival—departure   *SOC*, 72
7   artistic—inartistic   *TAT*, 149
8   ask—answer   *TBF*, 18
9   assist—hinder   *TAT*, 121
10   attractive—unattractive   *HP*, 31
11   bad—good (cf. 43, 61)   *DON*, 214
12   bad-tempered—sweet-tempered   *TZ*, 24
13   before—afterwards   *SC*, 141
14   belief—disbelief   *LJ*, 237
15   believe—disbelieve   *SOC*, 214
16   black—white   *HP*, 30
17*a* black and white   *SC*, 10
17*b* black-and-white   *SC*, 25
18   body—soul   *TH*, 25
19   break down—build up   *DON*, 78
20   broad—angular (cf. 4)   *HP*, 51
21   businesslike—unbusinesslike   *DON*, 75
22   buyer—seller   *POMT*, 127
23   cat—mouse   *TZ*, 138
24   cause—effect   *SC*, 182
25   chance—design   *DON*, 212
26   clench—unclench   *LJ*, 183f.
27   cold—hot (cf. 72)   *TH*, 37
28   command—appeal   *TH*, 64
29   constructive—destructive   *NOM*, 79
30   convenience—inconvenience   *TAT*, 129
31   correct—incorrect   *EU*, 106
32   crazy about—tired of   *TZ*, 105
33   dead—alive (cf. 2)   *SC*, 75
34   death—life (cf. 86)   *SC*, 41

35 delicate—indelicate   *SOC*, 29
36 dependent—independent   *TATF*, 129f.
37 disappear—reappear   *TBF*, 114
38 early—late   *TZ*, 112
39 embarrassed—thrilled   *DON*, 97
40 enemy—friend   *NOM*, 176
41 entangle—disentangle   *MMFC*, 72
42 everything—nothing   *TAT*, 153
43 evil—good (cf. 11)   *POMT*, 76
44 excitement—apathy   *SC*, 26
45 exciting—dull   *TAT*, 16
46 exercise—restrain   *DON*, 45
47 expected—unexpected   *EU*, 36
48 expression—non-expression   *HP*, 171
49 face—avoid   *SC*, 72
50 fact—idea   *TZ*, 146
51 false—true   *EU*, 106
52 fat—thin   *HP*, 38
53 flush—pale   *DON*, 144
54 former—present (cf. 118)   *TZ*, 102
55 fortunate—unfortunate   *TZ*, 71
56 forward—back   *TZ*, 95
57 friendly—rude (cf. 115, 131)   *DON*, 79
58 general—particular   *SC*, 135
59 glad—sorry   *LJ*, 19
60 going up—going down (cf. 158)   *TZ*, 18
61 good—bad (cf. 11)   *TDIWM*, 186
62 guilt—innocence   *TAT*, 72
63 guilty—innocent   *TZ*, 12
64 hang—drown   *HP*, 87
65 happiness—unhappiness   *EU*, 118
66 happy—unhappy   *SC*, 21
67 hard—soft   *TAT*, 161
68 head—heel   *SOC*, 55
69 heavy—light   *MAAS*, 159
70 high—low   *TBF*, 75
71 honourable—dishonourable   *SC*, 128
72 hot—cold (cf. 27)   *PFR*, 21
73 human—inhuman   *HP*, 173
74 imaginative—unimaginative   *PFR*, 5
75 impulse—habit   *SOC*, 30
76 in—out   *TZ*, 151
77 infant—grown-up   *HP*, 120
78 insult—compliment   *TAT*, 138

123 qualifications—disqualifications *LJ*, 234
124 real—artificial (cf. 101) *POMT*, 100
125 real—supposed *LJ*, 66
126 reality—illusion *TDIWM*, 171
127 reap—sow *TZ*, 62
128 remembrance—oblivion *SC*, 29
129 right—wrong *TAT*, 105
130 rough—smooth *NOM*, 28
131 rude—friendly (cf. 57, 115) *SC*, 69
132 sad—gay *POMT*, 24
133 safe—dangerous *TATF*, 55
134 sanity—insanity (cf. 97) *PFR*, 161
135 satisfied—dissatisfied *HP*, 98
136 say—do *EU*, 83
137 selfish—unselfish *TZ*, 66
138 senior—junior *PFR*, 127
139 severe—lenient *TDIWM*, 49
140 short—long *TZ*, 66
141 short—tall *EU*, 5
142 silent—loquacious *TBF*, 12
143 simple—complex *TH*, 185
144 simplicity—complexity *TH*, 212
145 sleepy—awake *DON*, 94
146 small—big (cf. 82) *PFR*, 173
147 smile—sigh *SC*, 51
148 social—anti-social *HP*, 39
149 soon(er)—late(r) *TATF*, 27
150 soothe—enrage *TDIWM*, 67
151 statement—question *PFR*, 35
152 steady—unsteady *TAT*, 68
153 strength—weakness *TH*, 71f.
154 stupid—intellectual *HP*, 68
155 supply—demand *POMT*, 9
156 tomorrow—yesterday *TZ*, 95
157 ugly—pretty *HP*, 157
158 up—down (cf. 60) *HP*, 63
159 usual—unusual *POMT*, 34
160 win—lose (cf. 94) *NOM*, 11
161 wits—looks *TZ*, 36

APPENDIX B

The *Roget's Thesaurus* Corpus

1 LIST OF ITEMS IN ALPHABETICAL ORDER

absolute—relative
acquisition—loss
acquittal—condemnation
action—inaction
activity—inactivity
addition—non-addition
affirmation—negation
agreement—disagreement
amusement—weariness
angel—Satan
animal—plant
animality—vegetability
appearance—disappearance
approach—recession
approbation—disapprobation
arrangement—derangement
arrival—departure
ascent—descent
assemblage—non-assemblage
assent—dissent
attack—defence
attention—inattention
attraction—repulsion
attribution—chance
authority—laxity

beauty—ugliness
beginning—end
belief—unbelief
benefactor—evildoer
benevolence—malevolence
breadth—narrowness

calefaction—refrigeration
care—neglect
cause—effect
certainty—uncertainty
cessation—continuance
change—permanence
cheerfulness—dejection
chronometry—anachronism
circularity—convolution
cleanness—uncleanness
clergy—laity
coherence—incoherence
colour—achromatism
combatant—non-combatant
combination—decomposition
commission—abrogation
completeness—incompleteness
completion—non-completion
component—extraneousness
conciseness—diffuseness
concurrence—counteraction
conformity—unconformity
content—discontent
contention—peace
continuity—discontinuity
convergence—divergence
conversion—reversion
convexity—concavity
copy—prototype
courage—cowardice
courtesy—discourtesy
covering—centrality
credit—debt

credulity—incredulity
cry—ululation
cunning—artlessness
curiosity—incuriosity
curvature—straightness

dearness—cheapness
demonstration—confutation
density—rarity
depth—shallowness
desire—indifference
difficulty—facility
direction—deviation
disclosure—ambush
discord—concord
discrimination—indiscrimination
disobedience—obedience
distance—nearness
diuturnity—transientness
dueness—undueness
dupe—deceiver
duration—timelessness

earliness—lateness
elasticity—inelasticity
elegance—inelegance
elevation—depression
equality—inequality
eventuality—destiny
evidence—counterevidence
excitability—inexcitability
exertion—repose
existence—inexistence
expansion—contraction
expectation—inexpectation
expedience—inexpedience
expenditure—receipt
exteriority—interiority

fasting—gluttony
fatigue—refreshment
flatterer—detractor
flattery—detraction
food—excretion

forgiveness—revenge
form—amorphism
fragrance—fetor
freedom—subjection
frequency—infrequency
friction—lubrication
friend—enemy
friendship—enmity
front—rear
futurity—preterition

generality—speciality
giving—receiving
good—evil
grammar—solecism
gratitude—ingratitude
greatness—smallness
gulf—plain

habit—desuetude
hardness—softness
haste—leisure
health—disease
hearing—deafness
heat—cold
heaven—hell
heaviness—lightness
height—lowness
hindrance—aid
hope—hopelessness

identity—contrariety
importance—unimportance
improvement—deterioration
impulse—recoil
inclusion—exclusion
increase—decrease
information—concealment
ingress—egress
innocence—guilt
inquiry—answer
insertion—extraction
insolence—servility
intelligence—imbecility

intelligibility—unintelligibility
intention—chance
interlocution—soliloquy
interpretation—misinterpretation
interval—contiguity
intrinsicality—extrinsicality
inversion—crossing
investment—divestment

journey—navigation
judgement—misjudgement
junction—disjunction

keeper—prisoner
knowledge—ignorance

laterality—antiposition
layer—filament
leap—plunge
legality—illegality
lending—borrowing
length—shortness
liberality—economy
liberation—restraint
life—death
light—darkness
liquefaction—vaporization
location—displacement
loquacity—taciturnity
loudness—faintness
love—hate
luminary—shade

man—woman
manifestation—latency
marriage—celibacy
master—servant
materiality—immateriality
maxim—absurdity
meaning—unmeaningness
melody—discord
memory—oblivion
mid-course—circuit
mixture—simpleness

moisture—dryness
morning—evening
motion—quiescence
motive—absence of motive
multitude—fewness
mutability—immutability

newness—oldness
news—secret
nobility—commonalty
nomenclature—misnomer

observance—non-observance
obstinacy—tergiversation
occasion—intempestivity
ocean—land
odour—inodorousness
offer—refusal
opening—closure
opponent—auxiliary
opposition—co-operation
order—disorder
organization—inorganization
ornament—blemish
overestimation—underestimation

parallelism—obliquity
payment—non-payment
pendency—support
penitence—impenitence
perfection—imperfection
perforator—stopper
period—course
permission—prohibition
perpetuity—instantaneity
perspecuity—obscurity
philanthropy—misanthropy
piety—impiety
plainness—ornament
pleasurableness—painfulness
pleasure—pain
plurality—zero
poetry—prose
possession—participation

possibility—impossibility
power—impotence
precedence—sequence
precession—sequence
precursor—sequel
predetermination—impulse
preparation—non-preparation
presence—absence
price—discount
pride—humility
priority—posteriority
probability—improbability
probity—improbity
prodigality—parsimony
producer—destroyer
production—destruction
productiveness—unproductiveness
proficient—bungler
progression—regression
propulsion—traction
prosperity—adversity
provision—waste
pulpiness—unctuousness
purchase—sale
purity—impurity
pursuit—avoidance

quantity—degree

rashness—caution
reasoning—intuition
reception—ejection
record—obliteration
refuge—pitfall
regret—relief
regularity—irregularity
rejoicing—lamentation
relation—irrelation
remedy—bane
representation—misrepresentation
repute—disrepute
request—deprecation
resolution—irresolution
respect—disrespect

restoration—relapse
retaliation—resistance
retention—relinquishment
reward—penalty
right—wrong
river—wind
rotation—evolution
rule—multiformity

safety—danger
sage—fool
salubrity—insalubrity
sanity—insanity
savouriness—unsavouriness
scholar—ignoramus
sensations of touch—numbness
sensibility—insensibility
severity—lenity
sharpness—bluntness
similarity—dissimilarity
size—littleness
skill—unskilfulness
smoothness—roughness
snap—roll
sobriety—drunkenness
sociality—seclusion
sound—silence
space—region
speech—stammering
strength—weakness
substantiality—unsubstantiality
substitution—interchange
success—failure
sufficiency—insufficiency
summit—base
superiority—inferiority
sweetness—sourness
symmetry—distortion

taking—restitution
taming—agriculture
taste—insipidity
taste—vulgarity
teacher—learner

temperance—intemperance
toughness—brittleness
transparency—opacity
traveller—mariner
truth—error

uniformity—non-uniformity
unity—accompaniment
unselfishness—selfishness
utility—inutility

vanity—modesty
velocity—slowness
veracity—falseness
verticality—horizontality
vigour—feebleness
vindication—accusation
violence—moderation
virtue—vice

visibility—invisibility
vision—blindness
voice—aphony

warfare—pacification
water—air
wealth—poverty
whole—part
whiteness—blackness
will—necessity
willingness—unwillingness
wit—dullness
wonder—expectance
word—neology
writing—printing

youth—age

zoology—botany

2. LIST OF PERIPHERAL OPPOSITES

2.1. *Directional opposites* (according to Cruse 1986, 223 ff.)

approach—recession
arrival—departure
ascent—descent
attraction—repulsion
convergence—divergence
elevation—depression

ingress—egress
insertion—extraction
progression—regression
propulsion—traction
summit—base ("antipodal"; cf.
    Cruse (1986, 224 f.))

2.2 *The "antecedence—consequence" type* (according to Lyons (1977, 282); see also Nellessen (1982, 86 f.))

attack—defence
cause—effect

inquiry—answer

2.3 *Converseness* (according to Lyons (1977, 279 f.) and Cruse (1986, 231 ff.))

dupe—deceiver
front—rear
giving—receiving
keeper—prisoner
lending—borrowing

master—servant
precedence—sequel
precession—sequence
precursor—sequel
priority—posteriority

purchase—sale   teacher—learner
superiority—inferiority

3 LIST OF NON-SYSTEMIC OPPOSITES (ACCORDING TO THE CRITERIA ESTABLISHED IN CHAPTER 3)

angel—Satan
animal—plant
animality—vegetability
beginning—end
clergy—laity
credit—debt
cry—ululation
cunning—artlessness
forgiveness—revenge
freedom—subjection
futurity—preterition
generality—speciality
gulf—plain
heaven—hell
infant—veteran
information—concealment
interlocution—soliloquy
journey (on land)—navigation
liberality—economy

liquefaction—vaporization
marriage—celibacy
mid-course—circuit
morning—evening
nobility—commonality
ocean—land
opposition—co-operation
plurality—zero
poetry—prose
river—wind
scholar—ignoramus
sweetness—sourness
taming—agriculture
traveller—mariner (cf. "journey" above)
water—air
will—necessity
writing—printing
zoology—botany

4 LIST OF NON-OPPOSITES (UNANALYSABLE AND/OR STYLISTICALLY INCOMPATIBLE)

amusement—weariness
attribution—chance
chronometry—anachronism
circularity—convolution
colour—achromatism
commission—abrogation
component—extraneousness
concurrence—counteraction
contention—peace
copy—prototype
covering—centrality
demonstration—confutation
direction—deviation
disclosure—ambush

diuturnity—transientness
duration—timelessness
eventuality—destiny
exertion—repose
expenditure—receipt
fatigue—refreshment
food—excretion
friction—lubrication
grammar—solecism
habit—desuetude
impulse—recoil
interval—contiguity
inversion—crossing
laterality—antiposition

layer—filament
leap—plunge
liberation—restraint
luminary—shade
maxim—absurdity
memory—oblivion
news—secret
nomenclature—misnomer
obstinacy—tergiversation
occasion—intempestivity
offer—refusal (but: acceptance—
  refusal)
parallelism—obliquity
pendency—support
perforator—stopper
period—course
perpetuity—instantaneity
possession—participation
price—discount
proficient—bungler
provision—waste
pulpiness—unctuousness
pursuit—avoidance

quantity—degree
reception—ejection
refuge—pitfall
regret—relief
remedy—bane
request—deprecation
restoration—relapse
retaliation—resistance
rotation—evolution
rule—multiformity
snap—roll
sociality—seclusion
space—region
speech—stammering
substitution—interchange
symmetry—distortion
truth—error (but: truth—
  falseness)
unity—accompaniment
warfare—pacification
whole—part
word—neology

Bibliography

Agricola, C., and Agricola, E. (1979), *Wörter und Gegenwörter: Antonyme der deutschen Sprache*, 2nd edn. (Leipzig: VEB Bibliographisches Institut Leipzig).

Agricola, E. (1982), 'Ein Modellwörterbuch lexikalisch-semantischer Strukturen', in E. Agricola, J. Schildt, and D. Viehweger (edd.), *Wortschatzforschung heute: aktuelle Probleme der Lexikologie und Lexikographie* (Linguistische Studien; Leipzig: VEB Verlag Enzyklopädie), 9–22.

—— (1983), 'Mikro-, Medio- und Makrostrukturen als Informationen im Wörterbuch', in J. Schildt and D. Viehweger (edd.), *Die Lexikographie von heute und das Wörterbuch von morgen: Analysen — Probleme — Vorschläge* (Linguistische Studien, Reihe A, Arbeitsberichte 109; Berlin: Akademie der Wissenschaften der DDR, Zentralinstitut für Sprachwissenschaft), 1–24.

Aitchison, J. (1987), *Words in the mind: an introduction to the mental lexicon* (Oxford: Blackwell).

Allan, K. (1986), review of Rusiecki (1985), in *Language* 62/3: 716.

Atlas, J. D. (1984), 'Comparative adjectives and adverbials of degree: an introduction to radically radical pragmatics', *Linguistics and philosophy* 7: 347–77.

Bahr, J. (1974), 'Aspekte eines Lexikmodells: zur theoretischen Grundlegung der Lexikographie', *Zeitschrift für germanistische Linguistik* 2: 145–70. Reprint in L. Zgusta (ed.) (1985), *Probleme des Wörterbuchs* (Wege der Forschung 612; Darmstadt: Wissenschaftliche Buchgesellschaft), 162–98.

Baker, C. L. (1970), 'Problems of polarity in counterfactuals', in J. M. Sadock and A. L. Vanek (edd.), *Studies presented to Robert B. Lees by his students* (Current inquiry into language and linguistics 14; Edmonton: Linguistic Research Inc.), 1–15.

Bartsch, R., and Vennemann, T. (1973), *Semantic structures: a study in the relation between semantics and syntax*, 2nd edn. (Frankfurt am Main: Athenäum).

Barz, I. (1983), 'Wortbedeutung und Wortbildungsbedeutung', *Zeitschrift für Germanistik* 1983/1: 65–9.

Bauer, L. (1983), *English word-formation* (Cambridge: CUP).

Beaugrande, R. de, and Dressler, W. U. (1981), *Einführung in die Textlinguistik* (Konzepte der Sprach- und Literaturwissenschaft 28; Tübingen: Niemeyer).

Bendix, E. H. (1964), *Componential analysis of general vocabulary: the semantic structure of a set of verbs in English, Hindi, and Japanese* (Bloomington: Indiana University; The Hague: Mouton).

Bierwisch, M. (1967), 'Some semantic universals of German adjectivals', *Foundations of language* 3: 1–36.

—— (1969) 'On certain problems of semantic representations', *Foundations of language* 5: 153–84.

—— (1986), *On the nature of semantic form in natural language* (LAUDT Papers, Series A 167; Duisburg: LAUDT).

—— *et al.* (= Forschungsgruppe kognitive Linguistik des Zentralinstituts für Sprachwissenschaft der Akademie der Wissenschaften der DDR) (1984), 'Dimensionsadjektive: semantische Struktur und begriffliche Interpretation', *Zeitschrift für Phonetik, Sprachwissenschaft und Kommunikationsforschung* 37/4: 490–512; 37/6: 664–86.

Bîtea, I. N. (1984*a*), 'The Jespersen–Smith hypothesis concerning "the negation of quantitative terms"', *Revue roumaine de linguistique* 29/1: 17–31.

—— (1984*b*), 'Towards a theory of simple-statement negation, I. The scope of simple-statement negation', *Revue roumaine de linguistique* 29/6: 499–512.

Blutner, R. (1985), 'Prototyp-Theorien und strukturelle Prinzipien der mentalen Kategorisierung', in *Generische Sätze, Prototypen und Defaults* (Linguistische Studien, Reihe A, Arbeitsberichte 125; Berlin: Akademie der Wissenschaften der DDR, Zentralinstitut für Sprachwissenschaft), 86–135.

Bolinger, D. (1967), 'Adjective comparison: a semantic scale', *Journal of English linguistics* 1 : 2–10.

—— (1968), 'Entailment and the meaning of structures', *Glossa* 2/2: 119–27.

—— (1972), *Degree words* (The Hague: Mouton).

Borkin, A. (1971), 'Polarity items in questions', *Papers from the seventh regional meeting: Chicago Linguistic Society: April 16-18, 1971*: 53–62.

Burton-Roberts, N. (1984), 'Modality and implicature', *Linguistics and philosophy* 7: 181–206.

Bussmann, H. (1983), *Lexikon der Sprachwissenschaft* (Kröners Taschenausgabe 452; Stuttgart: Kröner).

Čermak, F. (1983), 'Lexikální opozice, paradigma a systém', *Slovo a slovesnost* 44/3: 207–19.

Cerutti, U. (1957), *Sinn und Gegensinn im Englischen* (Winterthur: Keller).

Chafe, W. L. (1970), *Meaning and the structure of language* (Chicago and London: The University of Chicago Press).

Chapin, P. G. (1970), 'On affixation in English', in M. Bierwisch and K. E. Heidolph (edd.), *Progress in linguistics: a collection of papers* (Janua linguarum, Series maior 43; The Hague: Mouton), 51–63.

Clark, H. H. (1970), 'Word associations and linguistic theory', in J. Lyons (ed.), *New horizons in linguistics* (Harmondsworth: Penguin), 271–86.

—— (1974), 'Semantics and comprehension', in T. A. Sebeok (ed.), *Current trends in linguistics*, 12/2 (The Hague: Mouton), 1291–1428.

—— and Clark, E. V. (1977), *Psychology and language: an introduction to psycholinguistics* (New York: Harcourt Brace Jovanovich).

Colombo, L., and Seymour, P. H. K. (1983), 'Semantic and pragmatic factors in the representation of "near" and "far"', *Journal of psycholinguistic research* 12/2: 75–92.

Cooper, N. (1967), 'Scale-words', *Analysis* 27/5: 153–9.

Coseriu, E. (1964), 'Pour une sémantique diachronique structurale', *Travaux de linguistique et de littérature* 2: 139–86.

—— (1967), 'Lexikalische Solidaritäten', *Poetica* 1: 293–303.

—— (1970*a*), *Einführung in die strukturelle Betrachtung des Wortschatzes. In Zusammenarbeit mit Erich Brauch und Gisela Köhler herausgegeben von Gunter Narr* (TBL 14; Tübingen: Narr).

—— (1970*b*), 'Die lexematischen Strukturen', in E. Coseriu, *Sprache: Strukturen und Funktionen: 12 Aufsätze zur allgemeinen und romanischen Sprachwissenschaft. In Zusammenarbeit mit Hansbert Bertsch und Gisela Köhler herausgegeben von Uwe Petersen* (TBL 2; Tübingen: Narr), 159–79.

—— (1973), *Probleme der strukturellen Semantik: Vorlesung gehalten im Wintersemester 1965/66 an der Universität Tübingen. Autorisierte und bearbeitete Nachschrift von Dieter Kastovsky* (TBL 40; Tübingen: Narr).

—— (1975), 'Vers une typologie des champs lexicaux', *Cahiers de lexicologie* 27: 30–51.

—— and Geckeler, H. (1974), 'Linguistics and semantics', in T. A. Sebeok (ed.), *Current trends in linguistics*, 12/1 (The Hague and Paris: Mouton), 103–71.

—— (1981), *Trends in structural semantics* (TBL 158; Tübingen: Narr).

Cruse, D. A. (1975), 'Hyponymy and lexical hierarchies', *Archivum linguisticum*, NS 6: 26–31.

—— (1976), 'Three classes of antonym in English', *Lingua* 38: 281–92.

—— (1979), 'Reversives', *Linguistics* 17: 957–66.

—— (1980), 'Antonyms and gradable complementaries', in D. Kastovsky (ed.), *Perspektiven der lexikalischen Semantik: Beiträge zum Wuppertaler Semantikkolloquium vom 2.-3. Dezember 1977* (Gesamthochschule Wuppertal, Schriftenreihe Linguistik 2; Bonn: Bouvier), 14–25.

—— (1986), *Lexical semantics* (Cambridge textbooks in linguistics; Cambridge: CUP).

Csapó, J. (1977), 'A contrastive study of lexical relations in English and Hungarian', *Studia Anglica Posnaniensia* 9: 105–17.

Davis, S. (1973), 'Katz on contradiction', *Synthese* 26: 113–21.

Di Cesare, D. (1981), 'Die Semantik bei Aristoteles', *Sprachwissenschaft* 6: 1–30.

Diensberg, B. (1985), 'Historical morphology and markedness', *Studia Anglica Posnaniensia* 17: 39–50.

Dinu, M. (1984), 'Une variété graduelle de neutralisation sémantique: la synonymie médiate des . . . antonymes', *Revue roumaine de linguistique* 29/6: 485–91.

Dirven, R., and Taylor, J. (1986), *The conceptualisation of vertical space in English: the case of "tall"* (LAUDT Papers, Series A 163; Duisburg: LAUDT).

Downing, P. (1969), 'Positive and negative terms', *Analysis* 29/4: 131–5.

Eco, U. (1985a), *Einführung in die Semiotik. Autorisierte deutsche Ausgabe von Jürgen Trabant*, 5th edn. (1st edn. 1968) (UTB 105; Munich: Fink).

—— (1985b), *Semiotik und Philosophie der Sprache. Übersetzt von Christiane Trabant-Rommel und Jürgen Trabant* (Supplemente 4; Munich: Fink).

Emons, R. (1986), review of Kastovsky (1982b), in *Anglia* 104/1, 2: 136–44.

Ernst, G. (1981), 'Ein Blick durch die durchsichtigen Wörter: Versuch einer Typologie der Wortdurchsichtigkeit und ihrer Einschränkungen', *Linguistica* 21: 47–72.

Evans, M. J. (1983), 'Complementarity, antonymy, and semantic development: a method and some data', in C. Johnson and C. Thew (edd.), *Proceedings of the second international congress for the study of child language*, 2 (Lanham, Md.: University Press of America) (preprint).

Fabricius-Hansen, C. (1975), *Transformative, intransformative und kursive Verben* (Linguistische Arbeiten 26; Tübingen: Niemeyer).

Fauconnier, G. (1975), 'Polarity and the scale principle', in R. E. Grossmann *et al.* (edd.), *Papers from the parasession on functionalism: 1975* (Chicago Linguistic Society, Department of Linguistics, University of Chicago), 188–99.

Fill, A. (1985), 'Zwänge in der Sprache: mandatorische Kategorien und ihre Auswirkungen im Englischen und Deutschen', *Arbeiten aus Anglistik und Amerikanistik* 10/1, 2: 241–9.

—— (1987), review of Rusiecki (1985), in *Anglia* 105: 432–4.

Fillmore, C. J. (1972), '"How to know whether you're coming or going"', in K. Hyldgaard-Jensen (ed.), *Linguistik 1971: Referate des 6. Linguistischen Kolloquiums 11.-14. August 1971 in Kopenhagen* (Athenäum-Skripten Linguistik 1; Frankfurt am Main: Athenäum), 369–79.

Fleischer, W. (1982a), *Wortbildung der deutschen Gegenwartssprache*, 5th edn. (Tübingen: Niemeyer).

Fleischer, W. (1982*b*), *Phraseologie der deutschen Gegenwartssprache* (Leipzig: VEB Bibliographisches Institut).

Fomina, M. I. (1978), *Sovremennyj russkij jazyk: leksikologija* (Moscow: Vysšaja škola).

Frenzel, M. (1984), 'Lexikalisch-semantische Gruppe von Adjektiven, die einen Wärmegrad bezeichnen: vergleichend dargestellt am Deutschen, Polnischen und Russischen', in W. Bahner *et al.* (edd.), *Untersuchungen zur slawischen Lexikologie* (Linguistische Studien, Reihe A, Arbeitsberichte 117; Berlin: Akademie der Wissenschaften der DDR, Zentralinstitut für Sprachwissenschaft), 24–51.

Fries, P. H. (1977), 'English predications of comparison', *Studia Anglica Posnaniensia* 9: 95–103.

Funk, W. P. (1971), 'Adjectives with negative affixes in Modern English and the problem of synonymy', *Zeitschrift für Anglistik und Amerikanistik* 19: 364–86.

—— (1979), '"Blind" oder "unsichtbar"? Zur Bedeutungsstruktur deverbaler negativer Adjektiva im Koptischen', in P. Nagel (ed.), *Studien zum Menschenbild in Gnosis und Manichäismus* (Martin-Luther-Universität Halle-Wittenberg, Wissenschaftliche Beiträge 1979/39 (K5); Halle an der Saale), 55–65.

—— (1986), 'Towards a definition of semantic constraints on negative prefixation in English and German', in D. Kastovsky and A. Szwedek (edd.), *Linguistics across historical and geographical boundaries: in honour of Jacek Fisiak on the occasion of his fiftieth birthday*, 2. *Descriptive, contrastive, and applied linguistics* (Trends in linguistics, Studies and monographs 32; Berlin: Mouton de Gruyter), 877–89.

Gauger, H. M. (1972), *Zum Problem der Synonyme. Avec un résumé en français: Apport au problème des synonymes* (TBL 9; Tübingen: Narr).

Geach, P. T. (1969), 'Contradictories and contraries', *Analysis* 29/6: 187–90.

Geckeler, H. (1978), 'Observations sur la structure sémantique des adjectifs', in W. U. Dressler and W. Meid (edd.), *Proceedings of the twelfth international congress of linguists: Vienna, August 28–September 2, 1977* (Innsbrucker Beiträge zur Sprachwissenschaft; Innsbruck: Institut für Sprachwissenschaft der Universität Innsbruck), 182–4.

—— (1979), 'Antonymie und Wortart', in E. Bülow and P. Schmitter (edd.), *Integrale Linguistik: Festschrift für Helmut Gipper* (Amsterdam: John Benjamins), 455–82.

—— (1980), 'Die Antonymie im Lexikon', in D. Kastovsky (ed.), *Perspektiven der lexikalischen Semantik: Beiträge zum Wuppertaler Semantikkolloquium vom 2.-3. Dezember 1977* (Gesamthochschule Wuppertal, Schriftenreihe Linguistik 2; Bonn: Bouvier), 42–69.

Geckeler, H. (1981*a*), 'Structural semantics', in H. J. Eikmeyer and H. Rieser (edd.), *Words, worlds, and contexts: new approaches in word semantics* (Berlin and New York: De Gruyter), 381–413.

—— (1981*b*), 'Lexeme ohne Antonyme', in H. Stimm and W. Raible (edd.), *Zur Semantik des Französischen: Beiträge zum Regensburger Romanistentag* (Zeitschrift für französische Sprache und Literatur, Beiheft 9; Wiesbaden: Franz Steiner Verlag), 71–9.

—— (1981*c*), review of Gsell (1979), in *Zeitschrift für romanische Philologie* 97/3, 4: 414–21.

Givón, T. (1970), 'Notes on the semantic structure of English adjectives', *Language* 46/4: 816–37.

Gläser, R. (1986), *Phraseologie der englischen Sprache* (Tübingen: Niemeyer).

Glucksberg, S., Hay, A., and Danks, J. H. (1976), 'Words in utterance contexts: young children do not confuse the meanings of *same* and *different*', *Child development* 47: 737–41.

Gnutzmann, C. (1974), 'Zur Graduierbarkeit von Adjektiven im Englischen', *Linguistische Berichte* 31: 1–12.

—— (1975), 'Some aspects of grading', *English studies* 56: 421–33.

Goverdovskij, V. I. (1985), 'Dialektika konnotacii i denotacii (Vzaimodejstvie emocional'nogo i racional'nogo v leksike)', *Voprosy jazykoznanija* 1985/2: 71–9.

Gsell, O. (1979), *Gegensatzrelationen im Wortschatz romanischer Sprachen: Untersuchungen zur lexikalischen Struktur des Französischen, Italienischen, Rumänischen und Spanischen* (Beihefte zur Zeitschrift für Romanische Philologie 172; Tübingen: Niemeyer).

Halliday, M. A. K., and Hasan, R. (1976), *Cohesion in English* (English Language Series 9; London: Longman).

Hansen, B., Hansen, K., Neubert, A., and Schentke, M. (1982), *Englische Lexikologie: Einführung in Wortbildung und lexikalische Semantik* (Leipzig: VEB Verlag Enzyklopädie).

Hansen, K. (1980), 'Probleme der Konstituentenanalyse von Wortbildungen im Englischen', in K. Hansen and A. Neubert (edd.), *Studien zur Lexik und Grammatik der englischen Sprache der Gegenwart: Martin Lehnert zum 70. Geburtstag* (Linguistische Studien, Reihe A, Arbeitsberichte 67; Berlin: Akademie der Wissenschaften der DDR, Zentralinstitut für Sprachwissenschaft), 12–26.

Heinemann, W. (1983), 'Zur Semantik der privativen Verben', in *Wissenschaftliche Konferenz 'Aspekte und Probleme semasiologischer Sprachbetrachtung in synchronischer und diachronischer Sicht': 31. August–4. September 1982 in Neubrandenburg (DDR)* (Linguistische Studien, Reihe A, Arbeitsberichte 107/II; Berlin: Akademie der Wissenschaften der DDR, Zentralinstitut für Sprachwissenschaft), 36–47.

Henrici, G. (1975), *Die Binarismus-Problematik in der neueren Linguistik* (Linguistische Arbeiten 28; Tübingen: Niemeyer).

Higgins, E. T. (1977), 'The varying presuppositional nature of comparatives', *Journal of psycholinguistic research* 6/3: 203–22.

Holenstein, E. (1982), 'On the cognitive underpinnings of language', *Semiotica* 41/1-4: 107–34.

Horn, L. R. (1978), 'Lexical incorporation, implicature, and the least effort hypothesis', in D. Farkas, W. M. Jacobsen, and K. W. Todrys (edd.), *Papers from the parasession on the lexicon: Chicago Linguistic Society: April 14–15, 1978* (Chicago: University of Chicago), 196–209.

—— and Bayer, S. (1984), 'Short-circuited implicature: a negative contribution', *Linguistics and philosophy* 7: 397–414.

Hundsnurscher, F. (1971), *Neuere Methoden der Semantik: eine Einführung anhand deutscher Beispiele*, 2nd edn. (1st edn. 1970) (Tübingen: Niemeyer).

—— and Splett, J. (1982), *Semantik der Adjektive des Deutschen: Analyse der semantischen Relationen* (Forschungsberichte des Landes Nordrhein-Westfalen 3137, Fachgruppe Geisteswissenschaften; Opladen: Westdeutscher Verlag).

Iliescu, M. (1977), 'Oppositions sémantiques: antonymie linguistique et antonymie logique', *Folia linguistica* 10/1-2: 151–68.

Isaev, A. V. (1972), 'K voprosu o sootnošenii lingvističeskogo i logičeskogo v učenii ob antonimach', *Filologičeskie nauki* 1972/1: 49–56.

Itälä, M. L. (1985), 'Denken, Sprache, Wirklichkeit als Ansatz kontrastiver Sprachbetrachtung', *Neuphilologische Mitteilungen* 86/2: 258–65.

Jespersen, O. (1924), *The philosophy of grammar* (London: Allen & Unwin).

—— (1966), *Negation in English and other languages*, 2nd edn. (1st edn. 1917) (Copenhagen: Ejnar Munksgaard).

Kaiser, G. (1979), 'Hoch und gut — Überlegungen zur Semantik polarer Adjektive', *Linguistische Berichte* 59: 1–26.

Kalverkämper, H. (1980), review of Gsell (1979), in *Romanistisches Jahrbuch* 31: 153–59.

Karl, I. (1983), 'Zur Abgrenzung von Sememen', in J. Schildt and D. Viehweger (edd.), *Die Lexikographie von heute und das Wörterbuch von morgen: Analysen — Probleme — Vorschläge* (Linguistische Studien, Reihe A, Arbeitsberichte 109; Berlin: Akademie der Wissenschaften der DDR, Zentralinstitut für Sprachwissenschaft), 25–36.

Kastovsky, D. (1974), review of K. Heger, *Monem, Wort und Satz*, (1971), in *Anglia* 92: 185–94.

—— (1976), 'Intensification and semantic analysis: some notes on Bolinger's degree words', *Foundations of language* 14: 377–98.

—— (1977), 'Word-formation, or: at the cross-roads of morphology, syntax, semantics, and the lexicon', *Folia linguistica* 10/1-2: 1–33.

—— (1981*a*), 'Lexical fields and word-formation', in *Logos semantikos: studia linguistica in honorem Eugenio Coseriu 1921–1981*, 3, *Separata* (Berlin, New York, and Madrid: DeGruyter/Gredos), 429–45.

—— (1981*b*), 'Interaction of syntax and the lexicon: lexical converses', in J. Esser and A. Hübler (edd.), *Forms and functions: papers in general, English, and applied linguistics presented to Vilém Fried on the occasion of his sixty-fifth birthday* (Tübingen: Narr), 123–36.

—— (1982*a*), 'Word-formation: a functional view', *Folia linguistica* 16/1-4: 181–98.

—— (1982*b*), *Wortbildung und Semantik* (Studienreihe Englisch 14; Düsseldorf, Berne, and Munich: Bagel und Francke).

—— (1982*c*), '"Privative opposition" and lexical semantics', *Studia Anglica Posnaniensia* 14: 29–45.

—— (1986*a*), 'The problem of productivity in word formation', *Linguistics* 24: 585–600.

—— (1986*b*), 'Word-formation and pragmatics', in O. Rauchbauer (ed.), *A yearbook of studies in English language and literature 1985/86: Festschrift für Siegfried Korninger* (Wiener Beiträge zur Englischen Philologie 80; Vienna: Braumüller), 63–78.

Kato, K. (1986), 'Gradable gradability', *English studies* 1986/2: 174–81.

Katz, J. J. (1972), *Semantic theory* (Studies in language; New York: Harper and Row).

Kempson, R. M., and Quirk, R. (1971), 'Controlled activation of latent contrast', *Language* 47/3: 548–72.

Klein, E. (1980), 'A semantics for positive and comparative adjectives', *Linguistics and philosophy* 1980/4: 1–45.

Klima, E. S. (1964), 'Negation in English', in J. A. Fodor and J. J. Katz (edd.), *The structure of language: readings in the philosophy of language* (Englewood Cliffs, NJ: Prentice-Hall), 246–323.

Klimonov, W. D. (1984), 'Semantische und formale Struktur der Dimensionsadjektive in typologisch unterschiedlichen Sprachen', in W. Bahner *et al.* (edd.), *Untersuchungen zur slawischen Philologie*, 2 (Linguistische Studien, Reihe A, Arbeitsberichte 120; Berlin: Akademie der Wissenschaften der DDR, Zentralinstitut für Sprachwissenschaft), 217–54.

Koch, M. (1984), *Wird die Linguistik der Bedeutung gerecht?* (TBL 203; Tübingen: Narr).

Kočergan, M. P. (1981), 'Sintagmatičeskij i paradigmatičeskij aspekty slova (na materiale temporal'noj leksiki)', *Russkoe jazykoznanie* 3: 33–8.

Komissarov, V. N. (1957), 'Problema opredelenija antonima (O sootnošenii logičeskogo i jazykovogo v semasiologii)', *Voprosy jazykoznanija* 1957/2: 49–58.

Kotschi, T. (1974), *Probleme der Beschreibung lexikalischer Strukturen:*

Untersuchungen am Beispiel des französischen Verbs (Linguistische Arbeiten 19; Tübingen: Niemeyer).

Krivonosov, A. T. (1986), 'Otricanie v predloženii i otricanie v umozaključenii (Opyt semantičeskogo analiza otricanij v tekste)', *Voprosy jazykoznanija* 1986/1: 35–49.

Kuczaj II, S. A., and Maratsos, M. P. (1975), 'On the acquisition of *front, back*, and *side*', *Child development* 46: 202–10.

Kürschner, W. (1983), *Studien zur Negation im Deutschen* (Studien zur deutschen Grammatik 12; Tübingen: Narr).

Ladusaw, W. A. (1979), 'Polarity sensitivity as inherent scope relations' (dissertation, The University of Texas at Austin).

Lakoff, G. (1970), 'Linguistics and natural logic', *Synthese* 22: 151–271.

Lang, E. (1984), *The semantics of coordination* (translation of *Semantik der koordinativen Verknüpfung*, Berlin, 1977) (Studies in Language Companion Series 9; Amsterdam: John Benjamins).

Langacker, R. W. (1983*a*), *Foundations of cognitive grammar I: Orientation* (LAUT Series A, Paper 99; Trier: LAUT).

—— (1983*b*), *Foundations of cognitive grammar II: Semantic structure* (LAUT Series A, Paper 100; Trier: LAUT).

—— (1987), *Transitivity, case, and grammatical relations: a cognitive grammar prospectus* (LAUD Series A, Paper 172; Duisburg: LAUD).

Langendoen, D. T., and Bever, T. G. (1973), 'Can a not unhappy person be called a not sad one?', in S. R. Anderson and P. Kiparsky (edd.), *A festschrift for Morris Halle* (New York: Holt, Rinehart and Winston), 392–409.

Lazerson, B. H. (1977), 'Antonymy and ten Modern English color-names', *Journal of psycholinguistic research* 6/1: 21–36.

Leech, G. (1974), *Semantics* (Harmondsworth: Penguin).

Lehrer, A. (1970), 'Indeterminacy in semantic description', *Glossa* 4/1: 87–110.

—— (1974), *Semantic fields and lexical structure* (North-Holland linguistic series 11; Amsterdam and London: North-Holland).

—— (1985), 'Markedness and antonymy', *Journal of linguistics* 21/2: 397–429.

—— and Lehrer, K. (1982), 'Antonymy', *Linguistics and philosophy* 5: 483–501.

Leisi, E. (1975), *Der Wortinhalt: seine Struktur im Deutschen und Englischen*, 5th edn. (1st edn. 1952) (UTB 95; Heidelberg: Quelle & Meyer).

—— (1985), *Praxis der englischen Semantik*, 2nd edn. (Sprachwissenschaftliche Studienbücher, Abt. 1; Heidelberg: Winter).

Leiss, E. (1986), 'Das Lexikon ist keine Enzyklopädie. Antwort auf J. Ziegler, LB 93 (1984)', *Linguistische Berichte* 101: 74–84.

Lerchner, G. (1983), 'Zur Beschreibbarkeit von Konnotationen', in

Wissenschaftliche Konferenz 'Aspekte und Probleme semasiologischer Sprachbetrachtung in synchronischer und diachronischer Sicht': 31. August–4. September 1982 in Neubrandenburg (DDR) (Linguistische Studien, Reihe A, Arbeitsberichte 107/II; Berlin: Akademie der Wissenschaften der DDR, Zentralinstitut für Sprachwissenschaft), 61–9.

Leuninger, H. (1986), 'Mentales Lexikon, Basiskonzepte, Wahrnehmungsalternativen: Neuro- und psycholinguistische Überlegungen', *Linguistische Berichte* 103: 224–51.

Linebarger, M. C. (1981), *The grammar of negative polarity* (Bloomington, Ind.: IULC).

Lipka, L. (1980), 'Methodology and representation in the study of lexical fields', in D. Kastovsky (ed.), *Perspektiven der lexikalischen Semantik: Beiträge zum Wuppertaler Semantikkolloquium vom 2.–3. Dezember 1977* (Gesamthochschule Wuppertal, Schriftenreihe Linguistik 2; Bonn: Bouvier), 93–114.

—— (1985), 'Inferential features in historical semantics', in J. Fisiak (ed.), *Historical semantics: historical word-formation* (Trends in linguistics, Studies and monographs 29; Berlin: Mouton), 339–54.

—— (1986a), 'Semantic features and prototype theory in English lexicology', in D. Kastovsky and A. Szwedek (edd.), *Linguistics across historical and geographical boundaries: in honour of Jacek Fisiak on the occasion of his fiftieth birthday*, 1. *Linguistic theory and historical linguistics* (Trends in linguistics, Studies and monographs 32; Berlin: Mouton de Gruyter), 85–94.

—— (1986b), 'Homonymie, Polysemie oder Ableitung im heutigen Englisch', *Zeitschrift für Anglistik und Amerikanistik* 1986/2: 128–38.

—— (1990), *An outline of English lexicology: lexical structure, word semantics, and word-formation* (Forschung und Studium Anglistik 3; Tübingen: Niemeyer).

Ljung, M. (1974), 'Some remarks on antonymy', *Language* 50/1: 74–88.

Lounsbury, F. G. (1964), 'The structural analysis of kinship semantics', in *Proceedings of the Ninth International Congress of linguists (Cambridge, Mass., 1962)* (The Hague), 1073–1090. Reprinted in (and quoted from) H. Geckeler (ed.) (1978), *Strukturelle Bedeutungslehre* (Wege der Forschung 426; Darmstadt: Wissenschaftliche Buchgesellschaft), 164–92.

Lyons, J. (1968), *Introduction to theoretical linguistics* (Cambridge: CUP).

—— (1977), *Semantics*, 2 vols. (Cambridge: CUP).

—— (1981), *Language, meaning and context* (Bungay, Suffolk: Fontana).

Magnusson, U., and Persson, G. (1986), *Facets, phases and foci: studies in lexical relations in English* (Acta Universitatis Umensis, Umeå studies in the humanities 75; Stockholm: Almqvist & Wiksell).

Makkai, A. (1972), *Idiom structure in English* (Janua linguarum, Series maior 48; The Hague and Paris: Mouton).

Marchand, H. (1966), review of Zimmer (1964), in *Language* 42/1: 134–42.

—— (1969), *The categories and types of present-day English word-formation*, 2nd edn. (Munich: Beck).

Marsh-Stefanovska, P. J. (1982), 'A contrastive study of some morphologically related opposites in English and Macedonian' (unpublished MA dissertation, University of Manchester).

Martin, R. (1973), 'Logique et mécanisme de l'antonymie', *Travaux de linguistique et de littérature publiés par le Centre de philologie et de littératures romanes de l'Université de Strasbourg* 11/1: 37–51.

Mathe, J., and Schveiger, P. (1972), 'Antonymy–conversity and synonymy–homonymy in the grammar of language', *Revue roumaine de linguistique* 17/2: 141–58.

Mettinger, A. (1986), 'Unendurable unpersons unmask unexampled untruths: remarks on the functions of negative prefixes in Orwell's *1984*', in O. Rauchbauer (ed.), *A yearbook of studies in English language and literature 1985/86: Festschrift für Siegfried Korninger* (Wiener Beiträge zur Englischen Philologie 80; Vienna: Braumüller), 109–18.

—— (1987), 'Sinn, Unsinn, Gegensinn, oder Irrsinn? *Un*-Bildungen im Englischen', *Grazer linguistische Studien* 28: 67–79.

—— (1988*a*), 'Negativpräfixe im Englischen: Opposition oder Negation?', in K. Hyldgaard-Jensen and A. Zettersten (edd.), *Symposium on lexicography III: proceedings of the Third International Symposium on Lexicography May 14–16, 1986 at the University of Copenhagen* (Lexicographica, Series maior 19; Tübingen: Niemeyer), 485–501.

—— (1988*b*), 'Pay Caesar what is due to Caesar. . .: semantic features vindicated', in W. Hüllen and R. Schulze (edd.), *Understanding the lexicon: meaning, sense and world knowledge in lexical semantics* (Linguistische Arbeiten 210; Tübingen: Niemeyer), 148–56.

Miller, E. N. (1984), 'Polisemija leksičeskich antonimov (na materiale nemeckogo jazyka)', *Filologičeskie nauki* 1984/6: 80–1.

Mills, C. (1984), 'English color terms: language, culture, and psychology', *Semiotica* 52/1-2: 95–109.

Mittermann, H. (1976), 'Zur Analyse der englischen Approximatoren', in W. Meid and K. Heller (edd.), *Textlinguistik und Semantik: Akten der 4. Arbeitstagung Österreichischer Linguisten: Innsbruck, 6. bis 8. Dezember 1975* (Innsbrucker Beiträge zur Sprachwissenschaft 17; Innsbruck: Institut für Sprachwissenschaft der Universität Innsbruck), 83–9.

Motsch, W. (1977), 'Ein Plädoyer für die Beschreibung von Wortbildungen auf der Grundlage des Lexikons', in H. E. Brekle and D. Kastovsky (edd.), *Perspektiven der Wortbildungsforschung: Beiträge zum Wuppertaler Wortbildungskolloquium vom 9.-10. Juli 1976:*

anlässlich des 70. Geburtstages von Hans Marchand am 1. Oktober 1977 (Gesamthochschule Wuppertal, Schriftenreihe Linguistik 1; Bonn: Bouvier), 180–202.

—— (1982), 'Wortbildungen im einsprachigen Wörterbuch', in E. Agricola, J. Schildt, and D. Viehweger (edd.), *Wortschatzforschung heute: aktuelle Probleme der Lexikologie und Lexikographie* (Linguistische Studien; Leipzig: VEB Verlag Enzyklopädie), 62–71.

Müller, R. (1977), *Methodisches und Empirisches zur kontrastiven Semantik* (LAUT Series B, Paper 30; Trier: LAUT).

Nellessen, H. (1982), *Die Antonymie im Bereich des neufranzösischen Verbs. Avec un résumé en français* (TBL 174; Tübingen: Narr).

Nelson, K., and Benedict, H. (1974), 'The comprehension of relative, absolute, and contrastive adjectives by young children', *Journal of psycholinguistic research* 3/4: 333–42.

Nida, E. A. (1975), *Componential analysis of meaning: an introduction to semantic structures* (The Hague and Paris: Mouton).

Novikov, L. A. (1966), 'Logičeskaja protivopoložnost' i leksičeskaja antonimija', *Russkij jazyk v škole: metodičeskij žurnal Ministerstva prosveščenija RSFSR* 1966/4: 79–87.

—— (1973*a*), *Antonimija v russkom jazyke (Semantičeskij analiz protivopoložnosti v leksike)* (Moscow: Izdatel'stvo Moskovskogo universiteta).

—— (1973*b*), 'Semantičeskij analiz protivopoložnosti v leksike: principy, aspekty, metod', *Filologičeskie nauki* 1973/3: 55–67.

Osgood, C. E., Suci, G. J., and Tannenbaum, P. H. (1957), *The measurement of meaning* (Urbana: University of Illinois Press).

Palmer, F. R. (1981), *Semantics*, 2nd edn. (Cambridge: CUP).

Persson, G. (1990), *Meanings, models and metaphors: a study in lexical semantics in English* (Acta Universitatis Umensis, Umeå studies in the humanities 92; Stockholm: Almqvist & Wiksell).

Putseys, Y. (1984), *Adjectives* (Pedagogical English grammar 3; Trier: LAUT).

Rohdenburg, G. (1985), 'Unmarked and marked terms in English', in F. Hoppenbrouwers, P. Seuren, and A. Weijters (edd.), *Meaning and the lexicon* (Dordrecht: Foris), 63–71.

Rudzka-Ostyn, B. (ed.) (1988), *Topics in cognitive linguistics* (Amsterdam studies in the theory and history of linguistic science, Series IV, Current issues in linguistic theory 50; Amsterdam and Philadelphia: John Benjamins).

Rusiecki, J. (1985), *Adjectives and comparison in English: a semantic study* (London and New York: Longman).

—— (1986), 'The semantics of antonymic pairs of adjectives: elicitation test evidence from English and Polish', in D. Kastovsky and A. Szwedek (edd.), *Linguistics across historical and geographical boundaries: in honour of Jacek Fisiak on the occasion of his fiftieth birthday*, 2. *Descriptive, contrastive, and applied linguistics* (Trends in linguistics, Studies and monographs 32; Berlin: Mouton de Gruyter), 1427–1441.

Sanford, D. (1967), 'Negative terms', *Analysis* 27/6: 201–5.

Saussure, F. de (1916 (1983)), *Course in general linguistics*, ed. C. Bally and A. Sechehaye in collaboration with A. Reidlinger, translated and annotated by R. Harris (London: Duckworth).

Schertzer, C. B. (1981), 'Semantic properties of commonly used scaling adjectives' (Phil. diss., University of Cincinnati; Michigan: University Microfilms International/Ann Arbor).

Schippan, T. (1983), 'Lexikalisch-semantische Relationen als Gegenstand einer funktional orientierten Semasiologie', in *Wissenschaftliche Konferenz 'Aspekte und Probleme semasiologischer Sprachbetrachtung in synchronischer und diachronischer Sicht': 31. August–4. September 1982 in Neubrandenburg (DDR)* (Linguistische Studien, Reihe A, Arbeitsberichte 107/II; Berlin: Akademie der Wissenschaften der DDR, Zentralinstitut für Sprachwissenschaft), 91–104.

—— (1984), 'Wilhelm Schmidts Beitrag zur Theorie der Wortbedeutung', *Zeitschrift für Phonetik, Sprachwissenschaft und Kommunikationsforschung* 37/2: 133–42.

Schmidt, G. D. (1982), 'Kann ein "elementares Sprachzeichen" polysem sein? Bemerkungen zum polysemen Sprachzeichenmodell', *Linguistische Berichte* 79: 1–11.

Schmidt, H. (1985), *Untersuchungen zu konzeptionellen Problemen der historischen Lexikographie (Bedeutungen, Definitionen, Stichwortlisten, Aussagebereich)* (Linguistische Studien, Reihe A, Arbeitsberichte 134; Berlin: Akademie der Wissenschaften der DDR, Zentralinstitut für Sprachwissenschaft).

Schmidt, W. (1963), *Lexikalische und aktuelle Bedeutung: ein Beitrag zur Theorie der Wortbedeutung* (Berlin: Akademie).

Schnelle, H. (1973), 'Meaning constraints', *Synthese* 26: 13–37.

Schreyer, R. (1976), *Synonyms in context* (Trier: LAUT).

Seuren, P. A. M. (1978), 'The structure and selection of positive and negative gradable adjectives', in D. Farkas, W. M. Jacobsen, and K. W. Todrys (edd.), *Papers from the parasession on the lexicon: Chicago Linguistic Society: April 14–15, 1978* (Chicago: University of Chicago), 336–46.

Shannon, T. F. (1985), review of Hundsnurscher and Splett (1982), in *Language* 61/3: 713–14.

Sîrbu, R. (1979), 'L'antonymie comme manifestation des relations de système dans le lexique', *Linguistica* 19/1: 157–69.

—— (1981), 'L'antonymie des séries dérivatives', *Linguistica* 21: 119–43.

Smith, S. B. (1969), *The semantics of negation* (Bloomington, Ind.: IULC).

—— (1972), 'Relations of inclusion', *Language* 48/2: 276–84.

Snell-Hornby, M. (1985), 'Verb-descriptivity in German and English: a contrastive study in "untranslatable" lexemes', *Zeitschrift für Anglistik und Amerikanistik* 33/4: 341–9.

Somers, H. L. (1982), 'The use of verb features in arriving at a "meaning representation"', *Linguistics* 20: 237–65.

Spiewok, W. (1983), 'Gibt es eine stilistische Bedeutung?', in *Wissenschaftliche Konferenz 'Aspekte und Probleme semasiologischer Sprachbetrachtung in synchronischer und diachronischer Sicht': 31. August–4. September 1982 in Neubrandenburg (DDR)* (Linguistische Studien, Reihe A, Arbeitsberichte 107/II; Berlin: Akademie der Wissenschaften der DDR, Zentralinstitut für Sprachwissenschaft), 48–60.

Sprengel, K. (1980), 'Über semantische Merkmale', in D. Kastovsky (ed.), *Perspektiven der lexikalischen Semantik: Beiträge zum Wuppertaler Semantikkolloquium vom 2.-3. Dezember 1977* (Gesamthochschule Wuppertal, Schriftenreihe Linguistik 2; Bonn: Bouvier), 145–77.

Staib, B. (1981), 'Antonymische Relationen bei sekundären Verben: zur Funktionsbestimmung des Verbalpräfixes *dé-*', in H. Stimm and W. Raible (edd.), *Zur Semantik des Französischen: Beiträge zum Regensburger Romanistentag* (Zeitschrift für französische Sprache und Literatur, Beiheft 9; Wiesbaden: Franz Steiner Verlag), 80–91.

Starosta, S. (1982), 'Lexical decomposition: features or atomic predicates?', *Linguistic analysis* 9/4: 379–93.

Stein, G. (1971), *Primäre und sekundäre Adjektive im Französischen und Englischen* (TBL 22; Tübingen: Narr).

Steinthal, H. (1890), *Geschichte der Sprachwissenschaft bei den Griechen und Römern mit besonderer Rücksicht auf die Logik*, 2nd edn. (1st edn. 1863) (Berlin: Dümmler).

Stemmer, N. (1984), 'The nature of meanings: a cognitive-empiricist approach', *Revue roumaine de linguistique* 29/4: 355–70.

Strauss, J. (1986), 'Concepts, fields, and "non-basic" lexical items', in D. Kastovsky and A. Szwedek (edd.), *Linguistics across historical and geographical boundaries: in honour of Jacek Fisiak on the occasion of his fiftieth birthday, 1. Linguistic theory and historical linguistics* (Trends in linguistics, Studies and monographs 32; Berlin: Mouton de Gruyter), 135–44.

Syrbu (=Sîrbu), R. (1975), 'Semnyj analiz antonimov (Metodičeskij aspekt)', *Russkij jazyk za rubežom* 1975/5: 86–9.

Talmy, L. (1986), *The relations of grammar to cognition* (LAUDT Papers, Series A 165; Duisburg: LAUDT).

Taylor, J. R. (1989), *Linguistic categorization: prototypes in linguistic theory* (Oxford: OUP).

Teller, P. (1969), 'Some discussion and extension of Manfred Bierwisch's work on German adjectivals', *Foundations of language* 5: 185–217.

Tottie, G. (1980), 'Affixal and non-affixal negation in English—two systems in (almost) complementary distribution', *Studia linguistica* 34/2: 101–23.

Trench, R. C. (1882), *On the study of words: five lectures*, 19th edn. (repr. 1904; 1st edn. 1851) (Everyman's Library 788; London and New York).

Trubetzkoy, N. S. (1958), *Grundzüge der Phonologie*, 4th edn. (repr. 1967; 1st edn. 1939), (Göttingen: Vandenhoeck & Ruprecht).

Ulherr, H. (1986), review of Hansen *et al.* (1982), in *Journal of English linguistics* 19/1: 137–40.

Van Fraassen, B. C. (1971), *Formal semantics and logic* (New York: Macmillan).

Van Overbeke, M. (1975), 'Antonymie et gradation', *La Linguistique* 11/1: 135–54.

Verschueren, J. (1981), 'Problems of lexical semantics', *Lingua* 53: 317–51.

Viehweger, D. (1982), 'Semantiktheorie und praktische Lexikographie', *Zeitschrift für Germanistik* 1: 143–55.

—— *et al.* (1977), *Probleme der semantischen Analyse* (Studia grammatica 15; Berlin: Akademie).

Vol'f, E. M. (1986), 'Ocenočnoe značenie i sootnošenie priznakov "chorošo/plocho"', *Voprosy jazykoznanija* 1986/5: 98–106.

Warczyk, R. (1981), 'Antonymie, négation ou opposition?', *La Linguistique* 17/1: 29–48.

Weinreich, U. (1969), 'Problems in the analysis of idioms', in J. Puhvel (ed.), *Substance and structure of language: lectures delivered before the Linguistic Institute of the Linguistic Society of America, University of California, Los Angeles, June 17–August 12, 1966* (Berkeley and Los Angeles: University of California Press), 23–81.

Weiss, W. (1969), 'Zur Stilistik der Negation', in U. Engel, P. Grebe, and H. Rupp (edd.), *Festschrift für Hugo Moser zum 60. Geburtstag am 19. Juni 1969* (Düsseldorf: Schwann), 263–81.

Welke, K. (1983), 'Sensorische und rationale semantische Merkmale', *Zeitschrift für Germanistik* 3: 271–7.

Welte, W. (1978), *Negationslinguistik: Ansätze zur Beschreibung und Erklärung von Aspekten der Negation im Englischen* (Munich: Wilhelm Fink Verlag).

Westney, P. (1986), 'Notes on scales', *Lingua* 69: 333–54.

Wheeler III, S. C. (1972), 'Attributives and their modifiers', *Nous* 6: 310–44.

Wierzbicka, A. (1972), *Semantic primitives* (Linguistische Forschungen 22; Frankfurt am Main: Athenäum).

—— (1974), review of Hundsnurscher (1970), in *Linguistics* 131: 102–10.

Wotjak, G. (1983), 'Zum Verhältnis von Bedeutung und Abbild im Lichte moderner semantischer Analysen', *Zeitschrift für Phonetik, Sprachwissenschaft und Kommunikationsforschung* 36/5: 574–85.

Žanalina, L. K. (1983), 'Vzaimodejstvie leksičeskogo i slovoobrazovatel'nogo značenij v rjadach protivopostavlenij s otricatel'nymi prilagatel'nymi', *Filologičeskie nauki* 1983/6: 77–80.

Zelinsky-Wibbelt, C. (1984), *Wie werden sprachliche Bezeichnungen motiviert? Ein Beispiel zur Analyse von Verstehensprozessen* (Trier: LAUT).

Zgusta, L. (1971), *Manual of lexicography* (Janua linguarum, Series maior 39; The Hague and Paris: Mouton).

Ziegler, J. (1984), 'Gibt es lexikalische Lücken?', *Linguistische Berichte* 93: 66–79.

—— (1986), 'Nebelfelder: Replik auf eine Antwort von E. Leiss (LB 101)', *Linguistische Berichte* 106: 484–8.

Zimmer, K. E. (1964), *Affixal negation in English and other languages: an investigation of restricted productivity*, supplement to *Word* 20/2 (Monograph 5).

Dictionaries

Browning, D. C. (ed.) (1972), *Roget's Thesaurus: the Everyman edition* (London and Sydney: Pan Books).

Busse, W., and Dubost, J. B. (1977), *Französisches Verblexikon: die Konstruktion der Verben im Französischen* (Stuttgart: Klett-Cotta).

Hornby, A. S. (1974), *Oxford advanced learner's dictionary of current English*, 3rd edn. (Berlin and Oxford: Cornelsen and Oxford University Press).

Juilland, A., Brodin, D., and Davidovitch, C. (1970), *Frequency dictionary of French words* (The Hague and Paris: Mouton).

Kolesnikov, N. P. (1972), *Slovar' antonimov russkogo jazyka. Pod redakciej člena-korrespondenta APN SSSR prof. N. M. Šanskogo* (Tbilisi: Izdatel'stvo Tbilisskogo universiteta).

Sykes, J. B. (1976), *The concise Oxford dictionary of current English: based on the Oxford English Dictionary and its supplements. First edited by H. W. Fowler and F. G. Fowler*, 6th edn. (Oxford: Clarendon Press).

Woolf, H. B., *et al.* (edd.) (1973), *Webster's new dictionary of synonyms: a dictionary of discriminated synonyms with antonyms and analogous and contrasted words*, 4th edn. (Springfield, Mass.: Merriam Company).

CORPUS OF INVESTIGATED TEXTS

1 *Texts that form the basis of the investigation in Chapter 2*

Amis, K. (1954), *Lucky Jim* (Harmondsworth: Penguin). (*LJ*)
—— (1974), *Ending up* (Frogmore, St Albans: Triad/Panther Books).
(*EU*)
Christie, A. (1920 (1978)), *The mysterious affair at Styles* (Frogmore, St
Albans: Triad/Panther Books). (*MAAS*)
—— (1925), *The secret of Chimneys* (London: Pan Books). (*SOC*)
—— (1927), *The big four* (Glasgow: Fontana/Collins). (*TBF*)
—— (1935), *Three act tragedy* (Glasgow: Fontana/Collins). (*TAT*)
—— (1937), *Death on the Nile* (Glasgow: Fontana/Collins). (*DON*)
—— (1941), *N or M?* (London and Glasgow: Fontana/Collins). (*NOM*)
—— (1944), *Towards zero* (Harmondsworth: Penguin). (*TZ*)
—— (1945), *Sparkling cyanide* (London: Pan Books). (*SC*)
—— (1946), *The hollow* (London: Pan Books). (*TH*)
—— (1948), *Taken at the flood* (Glasgow: Fontana/Collins). (*TATF*)
—— (1952), *They do it with mirrors* (Glasgow: Fontana/Collins).
(*TDIWM*)
—— (1954 (10th pr. 1976)), *A pocket full of rye* (New York: Pocket
Books). (*PFR*)
—— (1968), *By the pricking of my thumbs* (London/Glasgow:
Fontana/Collins). (*POMT*)
—— (1969), *Hallowe'en party* (London: Fontana/Collins). (*HP*)
—— (1973), *Postern of fate* (Glasgow: Fontana/Collins). (*POF*)
—— (1974), *Poirot's early cases* (London: Fontana/Collins). (*PEC*)
—— (1979), *Miss Marple's final cases* (Glasgow: Fontana/Collins).
(*MMFC*)
Marsh, N. (1941), *Surfeit of Lampreys* (Harmondsworth: Penguin).
(*SOL*)

2 *Further texts that have been investigated*

Cartland, B. (1959), *The private life of Elizabeth Empress of Austria* (New
York: Pyramid Books). (*EEA*)
Christie, A. (1922), *The secret adversary* (London: Triad/Grafton). (*TSA*)
—— (1923), *The murder on the links* (London and Sidney: Pan Books).
(*MOL*)
—— (1924), *Poirot investigates* (London: Pan Books). (*PI*)
—— (1926), *The murder of Roger Ackroyd* (Glasgow: Fontana/Collins).
(*MRA*)
—— (1928), *The mystery of the Blue Train* (Glasgow: Fontana/Collins).
(*MBT*)

—— (1929), *The seven dials mystery* (London and Glasgow: Fontana/ Collins). (*SDM*)

—— (1934 (1970)), *The Listerdale mystery* (London: Pan Books). (*LM*)

—— (1937), *Dumb witness* (London: Pan Books). (*DW*)

—— (1939), *Murder is easy* (Glasgow: Fontana/Collins). (*MIE*)

—— (1953), *After the funeral* (Glasgow: Fontana/Collins). (*AF*)

—— (1960), *The adventure of the Christmas pudding and a selection of entrées* (Glasgow: Fontana/Collins). (*ACP*)

—— (1961), *13 for luck* (New York: Dell). (*TFL*)

—— (1971), *Nemesis* (New York: Dodd/Mead). (*NEM*)

Drabble, M. (1963), *A summer bird-cage* (Harmondsworth: Penguin). (*SBC*)

Fleming, I. (1956), *Diamonds are forever* (New York: Signet). (*DAF*)

—— (1963), *On Her Majesty's secret service* (New York: Signet). (*HMSS*)

Listowel, J. (1978), *A Habsburg tragedy: Crown Prince Rudolf* (London: Ascent). (*AHT*)

Lodge, D. (1965), *The British Museum is falling down* (Harmondsworth: Penguin). (*TBMIFD*)

—— (1975), *Changing places: a tale of two campuses* (Harmondsworth: Penguin). (*CP*)

—— (1984), *Small world: an academic romance* (Harmondsworth: Penguin). (*SW*)

Mitford, N. (1960), *Don't tell Alfred* (Harmondsworth: Penguin). (*DTA*)

Orwell, G. (1948), *1984* (repr. 1984; Harmondsworth: Penguin). (*1984*)

Waugh, E. (1948), *The loved one: an Anglo-American tragedy* (Harmondsworth: Penguin). (*TLO*)

Index